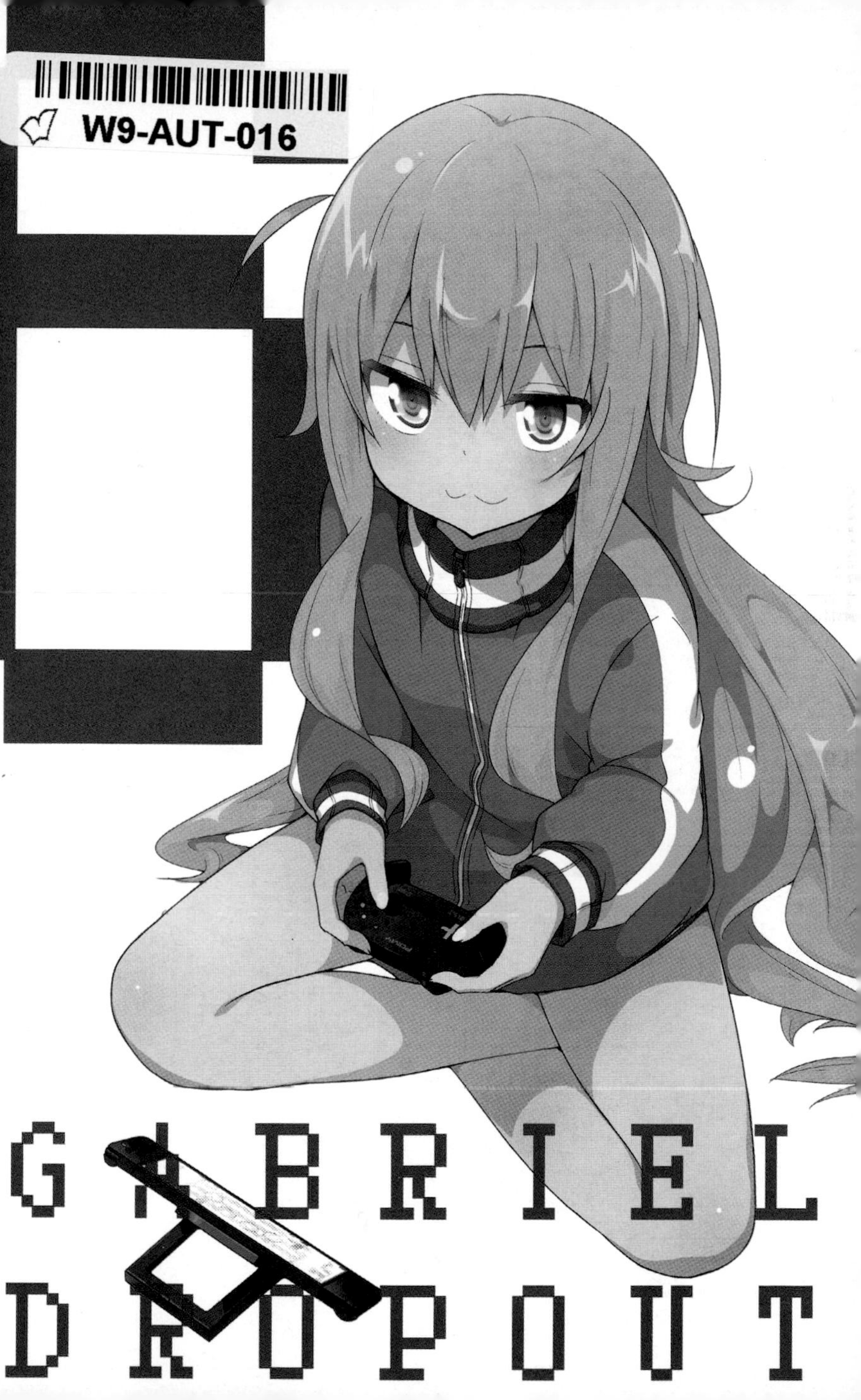
GABRIEL
DROPOUT

Contents

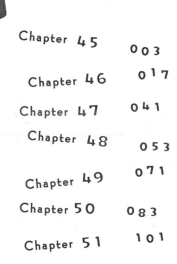

Gabriel Dropout

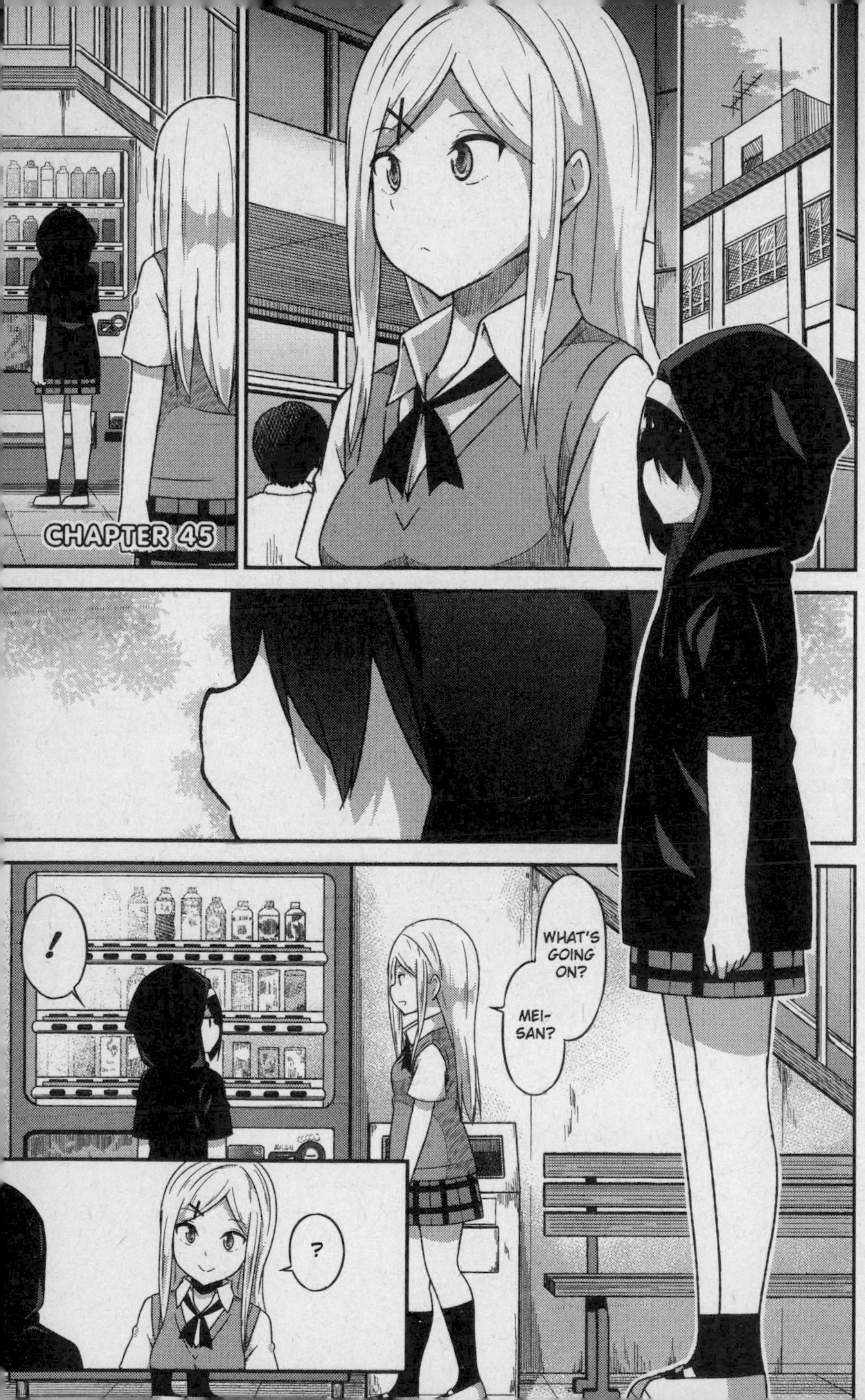
CHAPTER 45
WHAT'S GOING ON?
MEI-SAN?
!
?

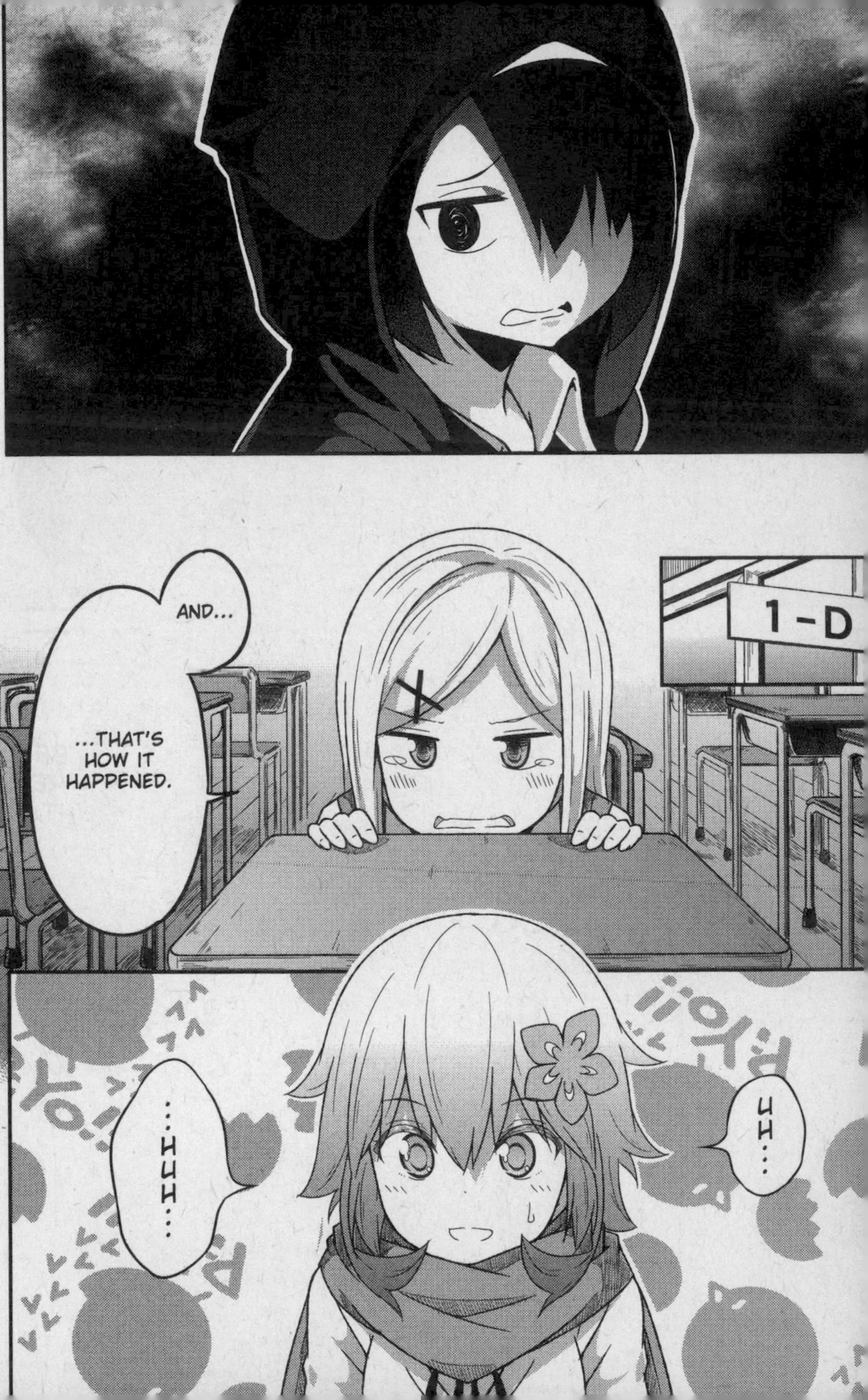
AND...
...THAT'S HOW IT HAPPENED.
UH...
...HUH...

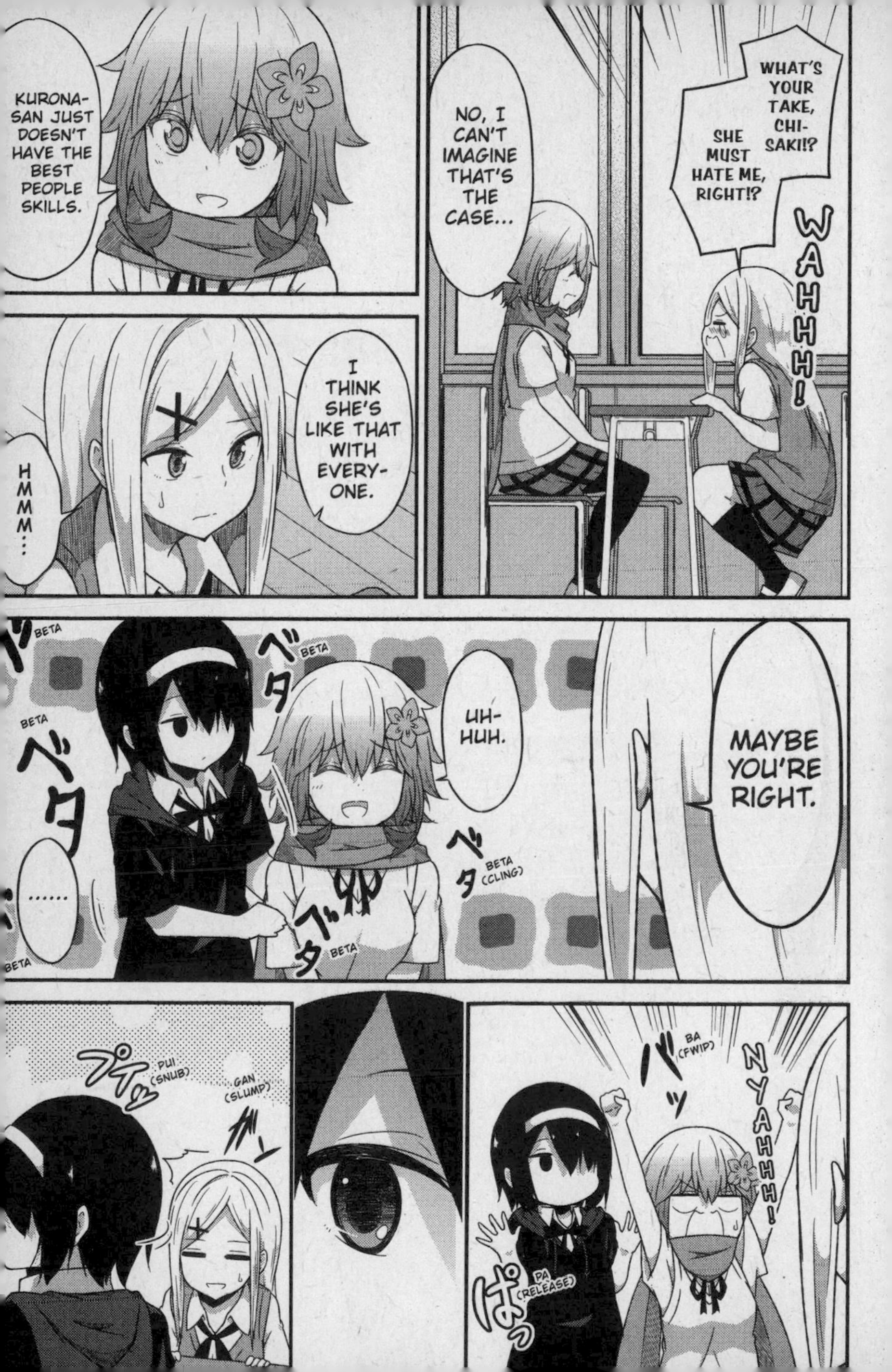
WHAT'S YOUR TAKE, CHI-SAKI!? SHE MUST HATE ME, RIGHT!?
WAHHHH!
NO, I CAN'T IMAGINE THAT'S THE CASE...
KURONA-SAN JUST DOESN'T HAVE THE BEST PEOPLE SKILLS.
I THINK SHE'S LIKE THAT WITH EVERYONE.
HMMM...
MAYBE YOU'RE RIGHT.
UH-HUH.
ベタ BETA (CLING)
ベタ BETA
ベタ BETA
ベタ BETA
BETA
......
BETA
バッ BA (FWIP)
NYAHHHH!
ぱっ PA (RELEASE)
ガーン GAN (SLUMP)
プイッ PUI (SNUB)

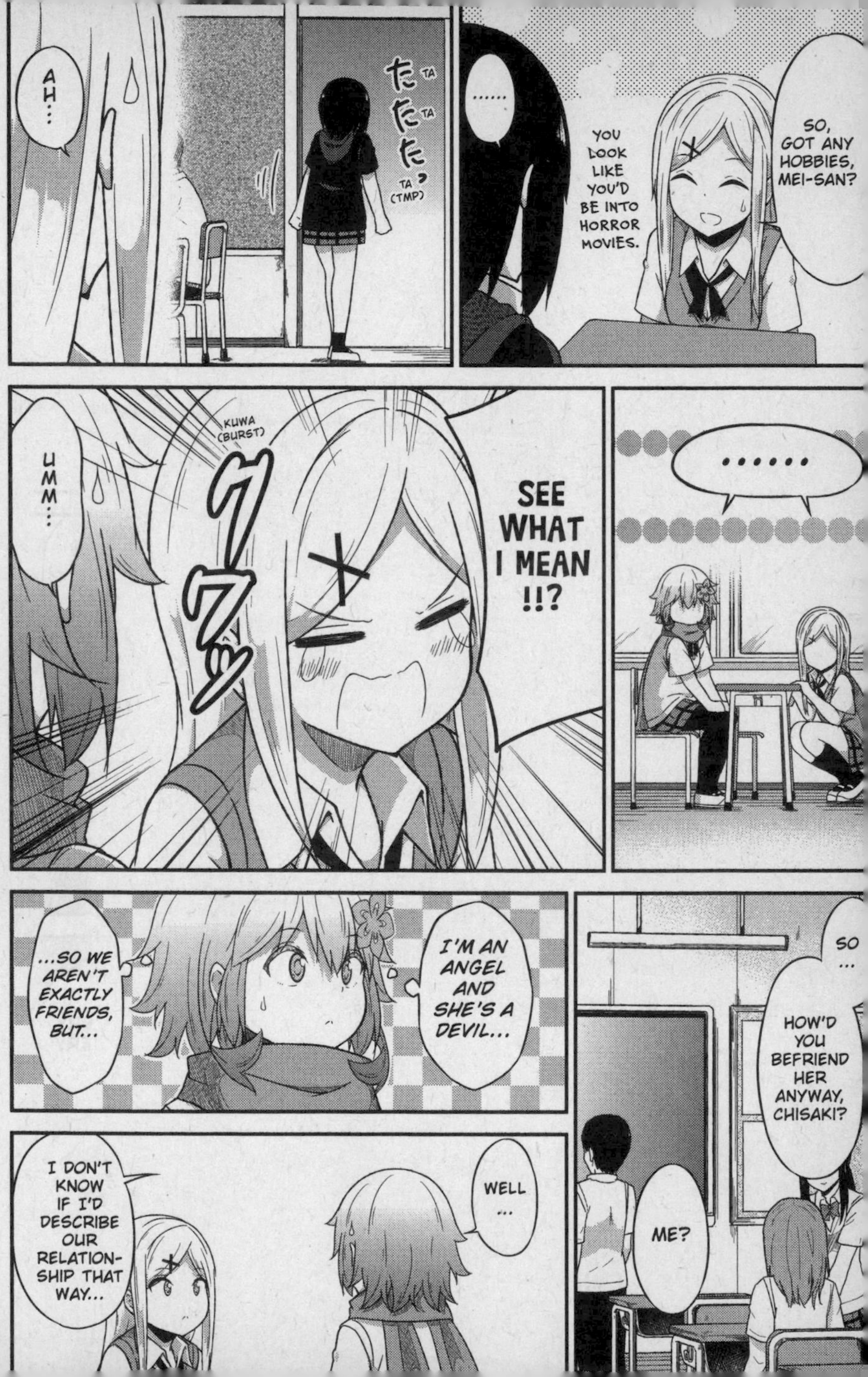
SO, GOT ANY HOBBIES, MEI-SAN?
YOU LOOK LIKE YOU'D BE INTO HORROR MOVIES.
......
たたた,
TA TA TA (TMP)
AH...
......
SEE WHAT I MEAN!!?
クワッ
KUWA (BURST)
UMM...
SO...
HOW'D YOU BEFRIEND HER ANYWAY, CHISAKI?
ME?
I'M AN ANGEL AND SHE'S A DEVIL...
...SO WE AREN'T EXACTLY FRIENDS, BUT...
WELL...
I DON'T KNOW IF I'D DESCRIBE OUR RELATIONSHIP THAT WAY...

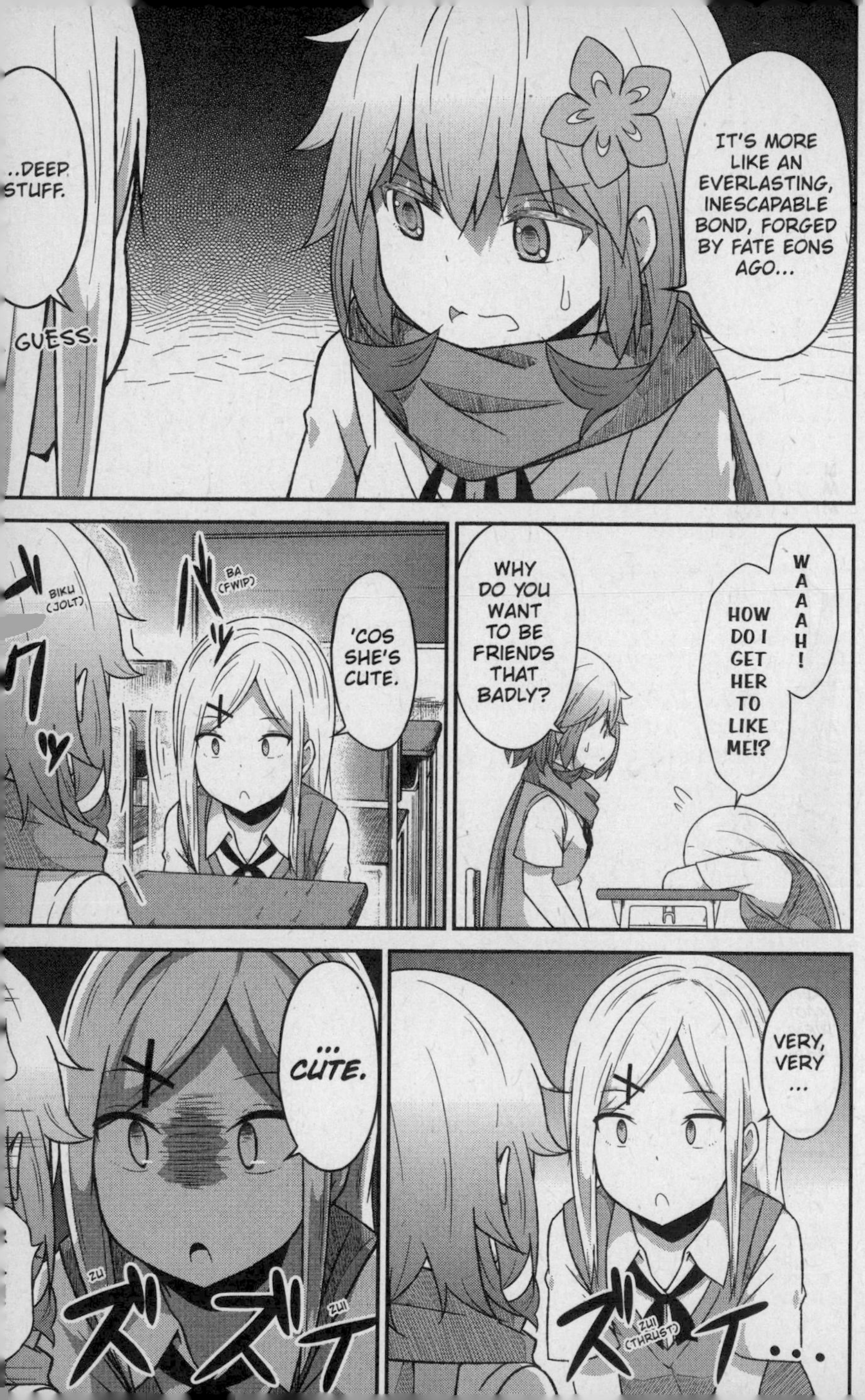

IT'S MORE LIKE AN EVERLASTING, INESCAPABLE BOND, FORGED BY FATE EONS AGO...
...DEEP STUFF.
GUESS.
WAAAH! HOW DO I GET HER TO LIKE ME!?
WHY DO YOU WANT TO BE FRIENDS THAT BADLY?
'COS SHE'S CUTE.
BA (FWIP)
BIKU (JOLT)
VERY, VERY ...
ZUI (THRUST)
...
... CUTE.
ZUI
ZU

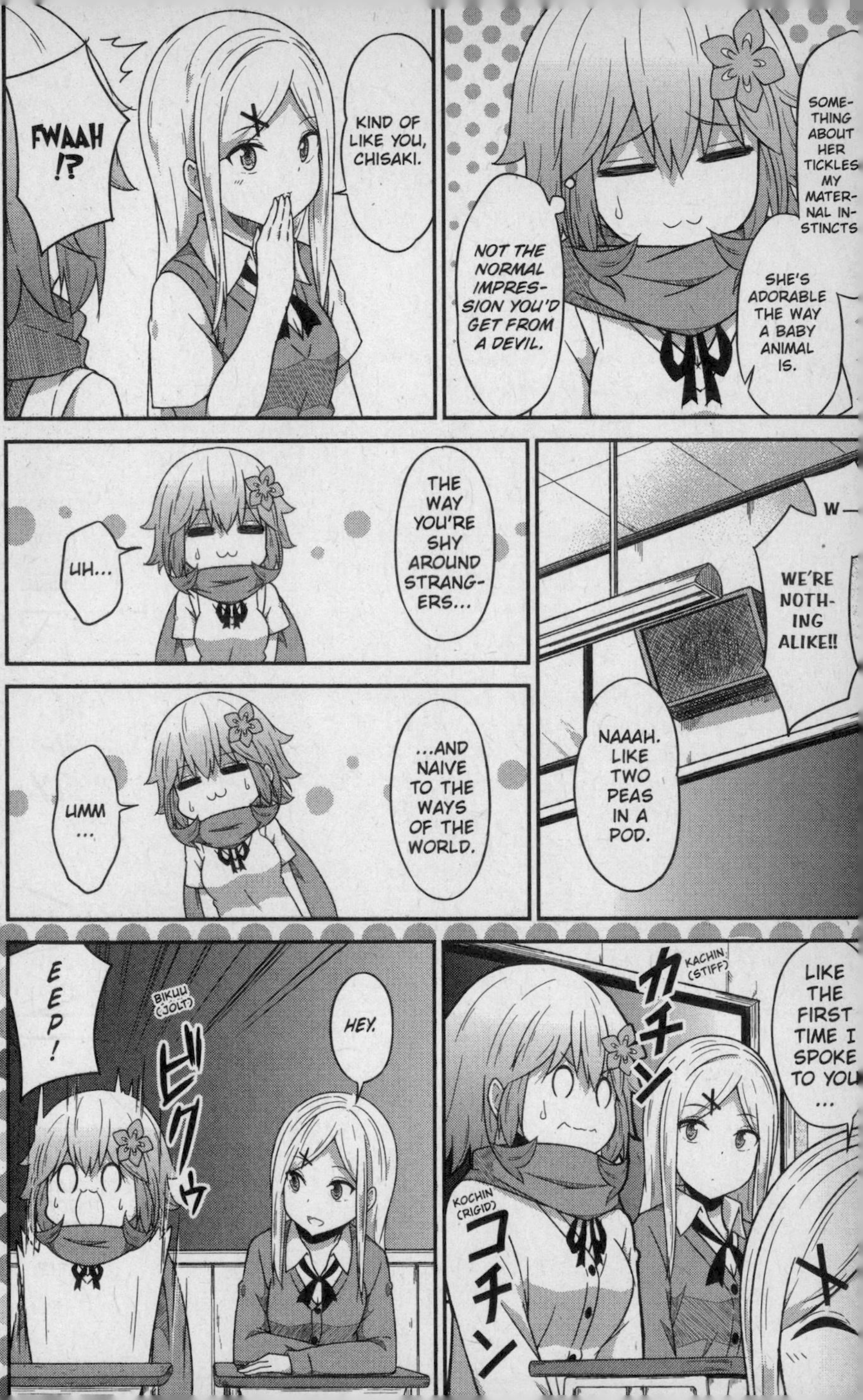

SOMETHING ABOUT HER TICKLES MY MATERNAL INSTINCTS
SHE'S ADORABLE THE WAY A BABY ANIMAL IS.
NOT THE NORMAL IMPRESSION YOU'D GET FROM A DEVIL.
KIND OF LIKE YOU, CHISAKI.
FWAAH!?
W—
WE'RE NOTHING ALIKE!!
NAAAH. LIKE TWO PEAS IN A POD.
THE WAY YOU'RE SHY AROUND STRANGERS...
UH...
...AND NAIVE TO THE WAYS OF THE WORLD.
UMM...
LIKE THE FIRST TIME I SPOKE TO YOU...
KACHIN (STIFF)
カチン
KOCHIN (RIGID)
コチン
HEY.
BIKUU (JOLT)
ビクゥ
EEP!

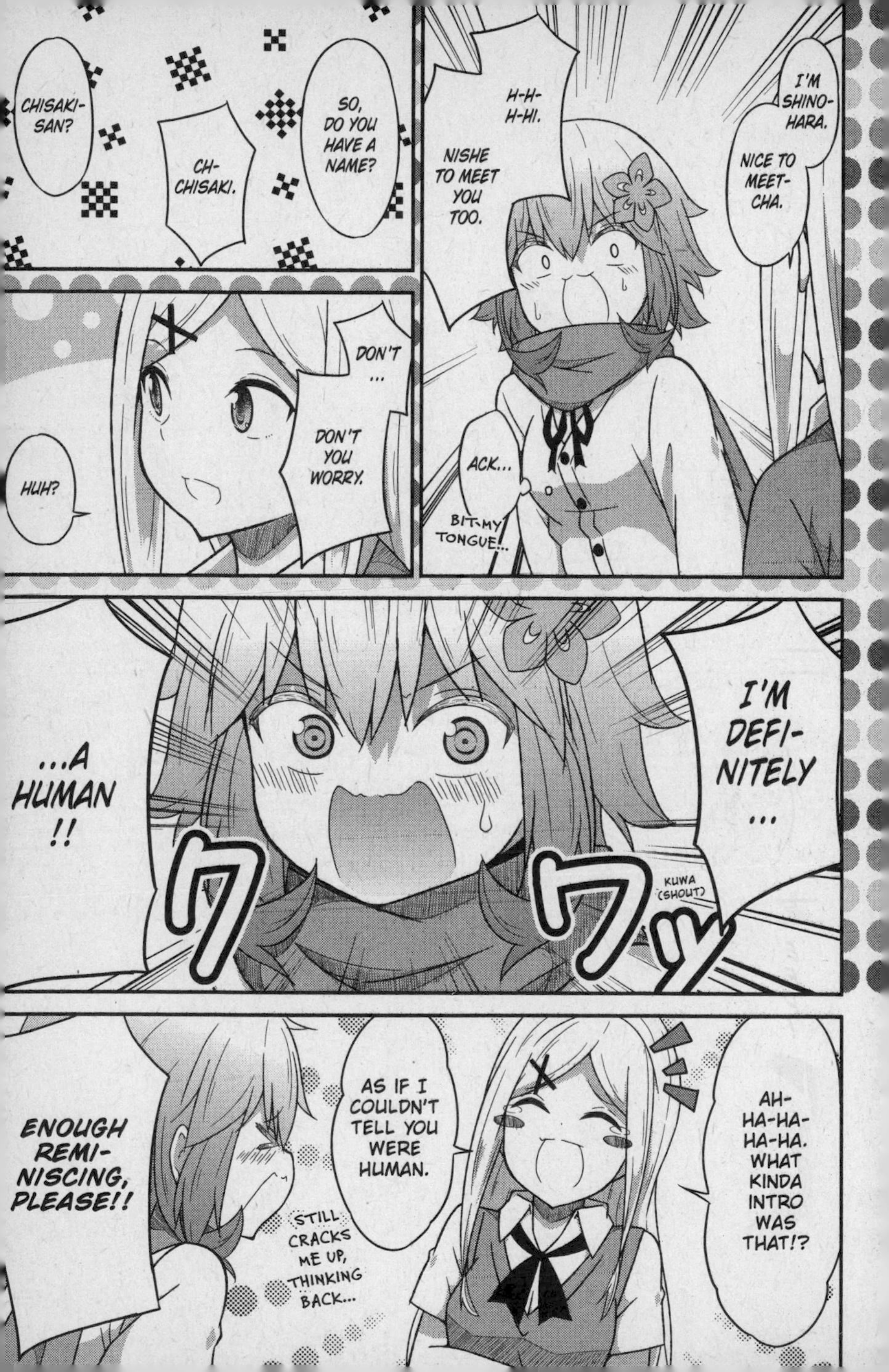
I'M SHINOHARA.
NICE TO MEET-CHA.
H-H-H-HI.
NISHE TO MEET YOU TOO.
ACK...
BIT MY TONGUE...
SO, DO YOU HAVE A NAME?
CH-CHISAKI.
CHISAKI-SAN?
DON'T ...
DON'T YOU WORRY.
HUH?
I'M DEFINITELY...
クワッ
KUWA (SHOUT)
...A HUMAN!!
AH-HA-HA-HA-HA. WHAT KINDA INTRO WAS THAT!?
AS IF I COULDN'T TELL YOU WERE HUMAN.
STILL CRACKS ME UP, THINKING BACK...
ENOUGH REMINISCING, PLEASE!!

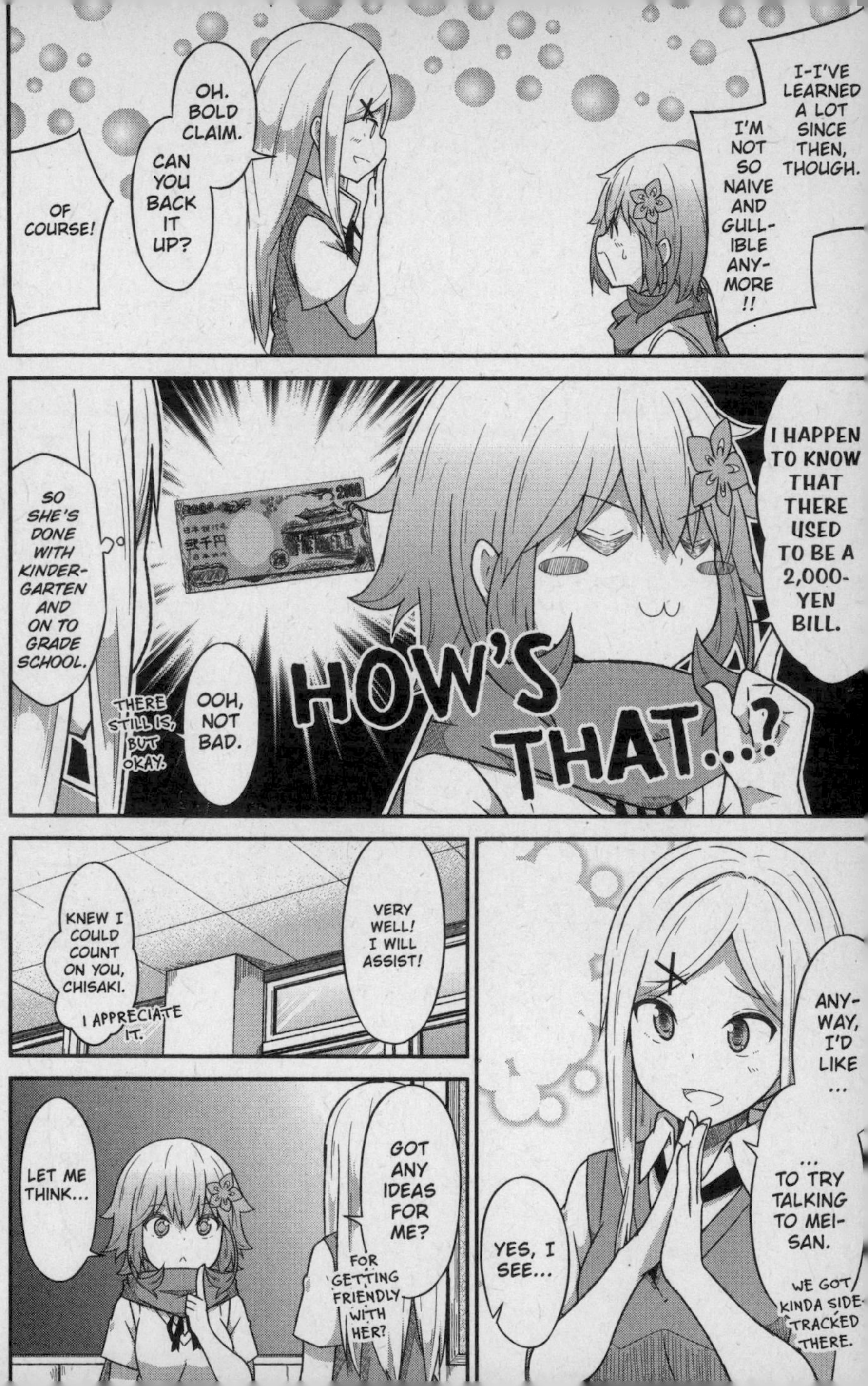
I-I'VE LEARNED A LOT SINCE THEN, THOUGH.
I'M NOT SO NAIVE AND GULLIBLE ANYMORE!!
OH. BOLD CLAIM.
CAN YOU BACK IT UP?
OF COURSE!
I HAPPEN TO KNOW THAT THERE USED TO BE A 2,000-YEN BILL.
HOW'S THAT...?
OOH, NOT BAD.
THERE STILL IS, BUT OKAY.
SO SHE'S DONE WITH KINDERGARTEN AND ON TO GRADE SCHOOL.
ANYWAY, I'D LIKE...
...TO TRY TALKING TO MEI-SAN.
WE GOT KINDA SIDETRACKED THERE.
YES, I SEE...
VERY WELL! I WILL ASSIST!
KNEW I COULD COUNT ON YOU, CHISAKI.
I APPRECIATE IT.
GOT ANY IDEAS FOR ME?
FOR GETTING FRIENDLY WITH HER?
LET ME THINK...

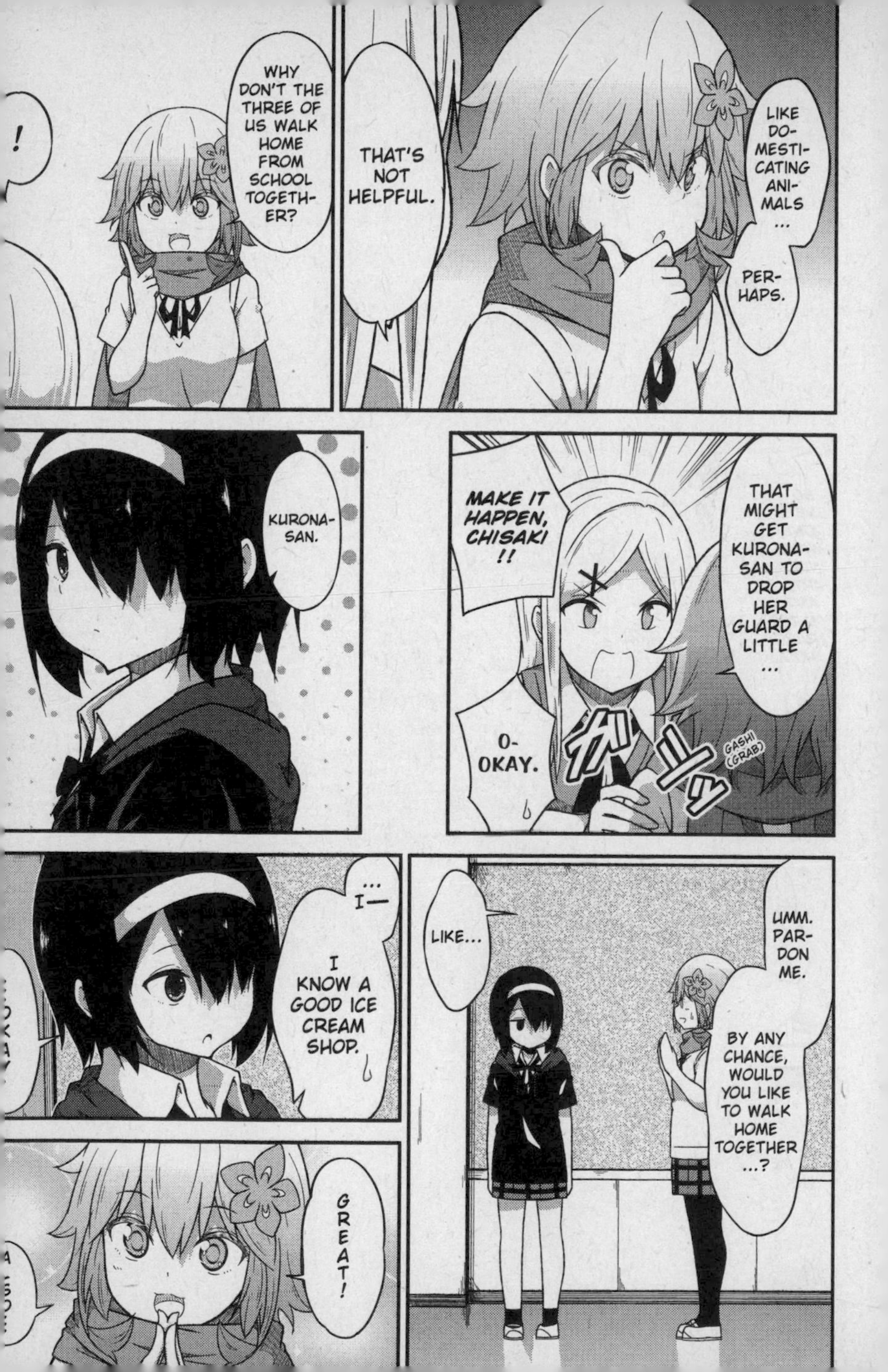
LIKE DO-MESTI-CATING ANI-MALS ...
PER-HAPS.
THAT'S NOT HELPFUL.
WHY DON'T THE THREE OF US WALK HOME FROM SCHOOL TOGETH-ER?
!
THAT MIGHT GET KURONA-SAN TO DROP HER GUARD A LITTLE ...
MAKE IT HAPPEN, CHISAKI !!
GASHI (GRAB)
O-OKAY.
KURONA-SAN.
UMM. PAR-DON ME.
BY ANY CHANCE, WOULD YOU LIKE TO WALK HOME TOGETHER ...?
LIKE...
... I—
I KNOW A GOOD ICE CREAM SHOP.
GREAT!

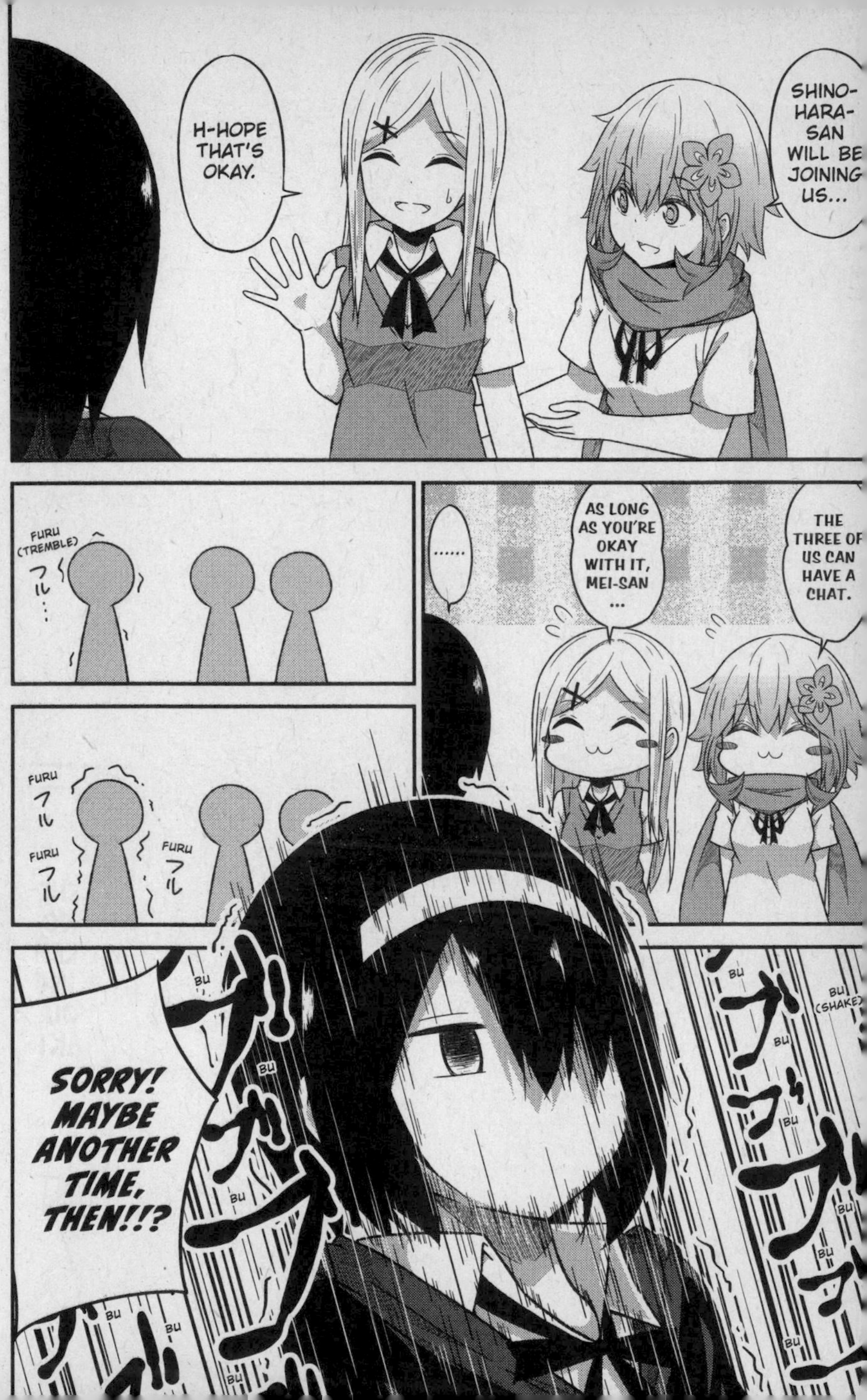
SHINO-HARA-SAN WILL BE JOINING US...
H-HOPE THAT'S OKAY.
THE THREE OF US CAN HAVE A CHAT.
AS LONG AS YOU'RE OKAY WITH IT, MEI-SAN ...
......
FURU (TREMBLE)
フル…
FURU
フル
FURU
フル
FURU
フル
BU (SHAKE)
BU
SORRY! MAYBE ANOTHER TIME, THEN!!?

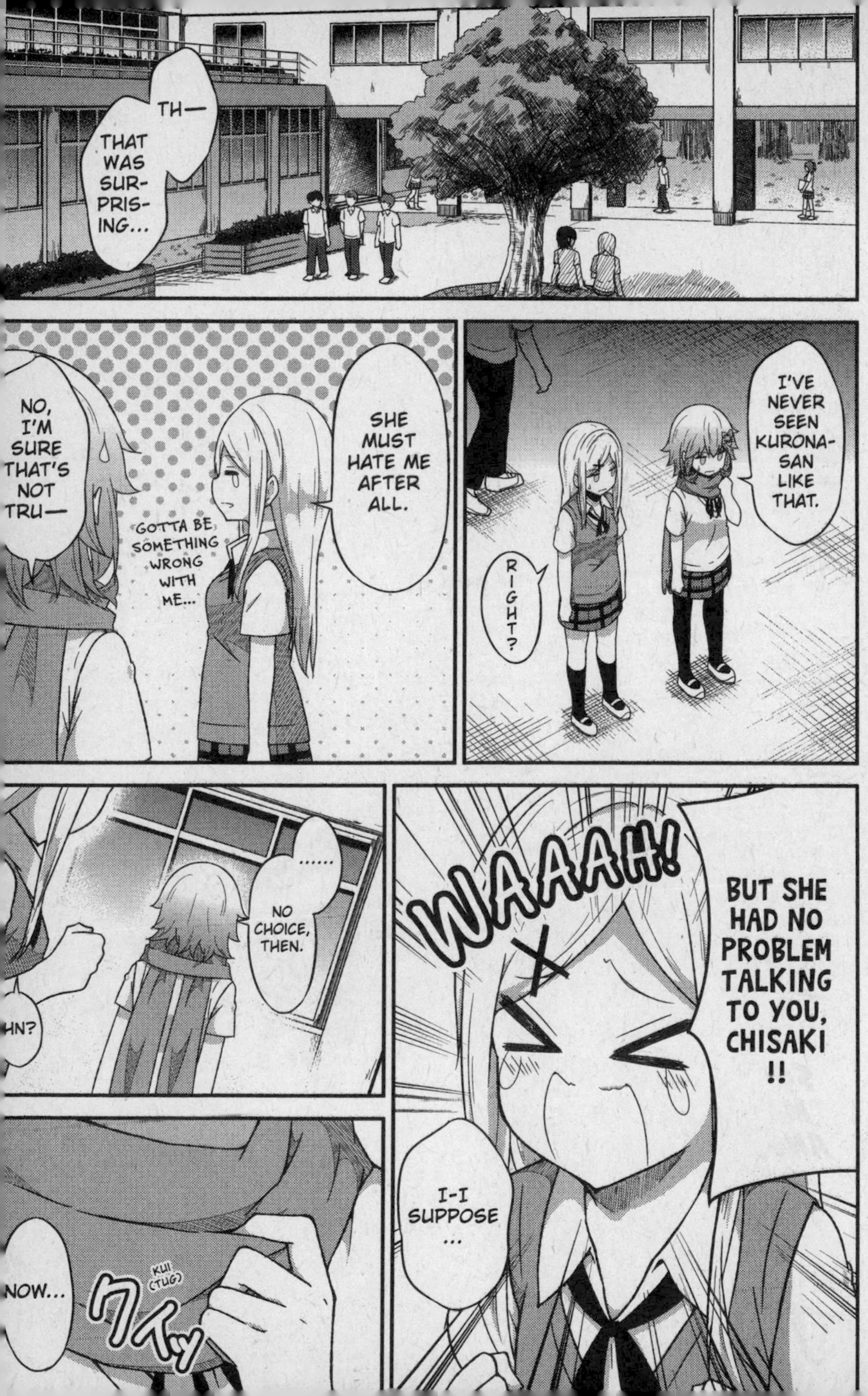
TH—
THAT WAS SURPRISING...
I'VE NEVER SEEN KURONA-SAN LIKE THAT.
RIGHT?
SHE MUST HATE ME AFTER ALL.
GOTTA BE SOMETHING WRONG WITH ME...
NO, I'M SURE THAT'S NOT TRU—
WAAAAH!
BUT SHE HAD NO PROBLEM TALKING TO YOU, CHISAKI!!
I-I SUPPOSE...
......
NO CHOICE, THEN.
HN?
KUI (TUG)
NOW...

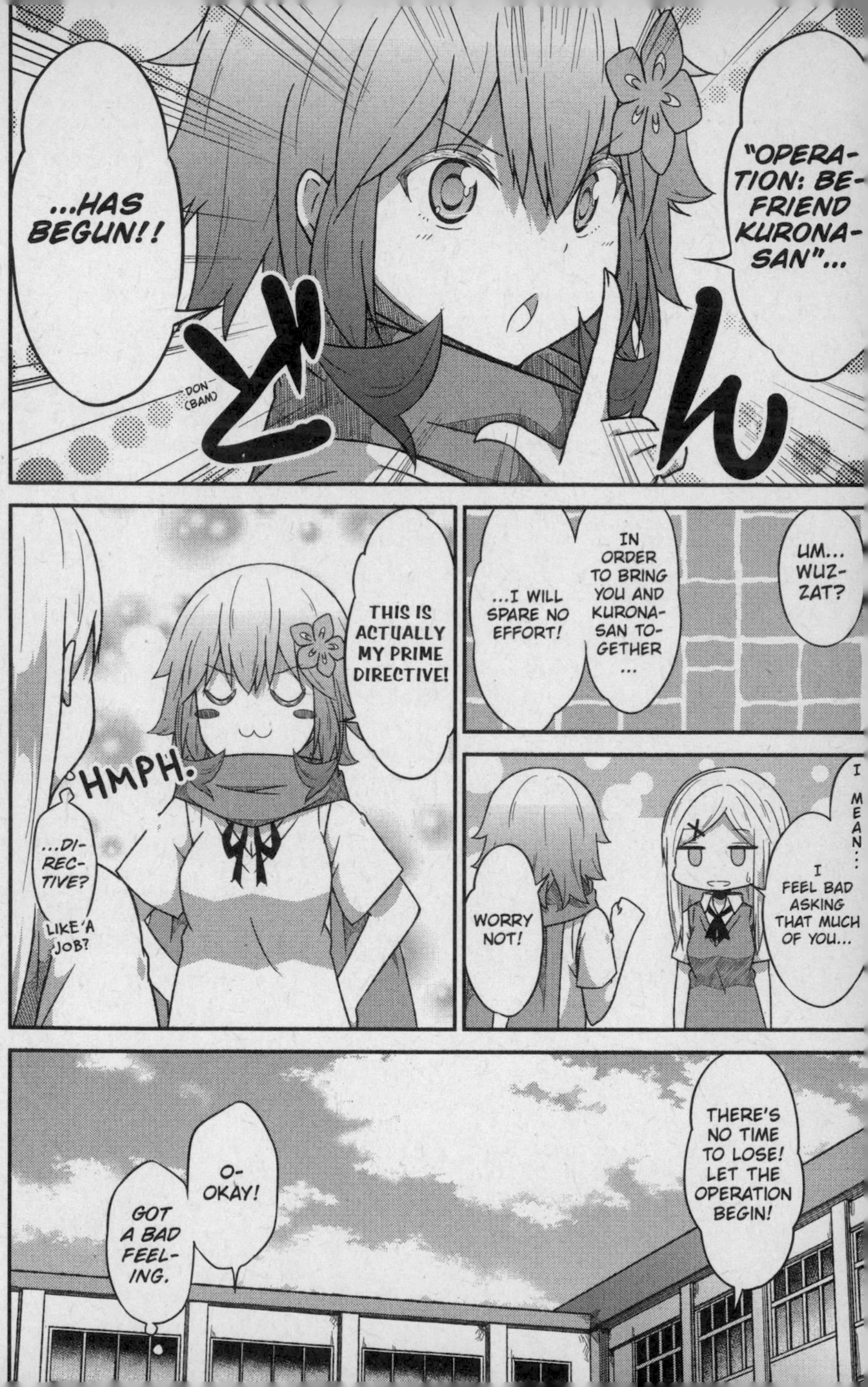
"OPERATION: BEFRIEND KURONA-SAN"...
...HAS BEGUN!!
DON (BAM)
UM... WUZZAT?
IN ORDER TO BRING YOU AND KURONA-SAN TOGETHER...
...I WILL SPARE NO EFFORT!
I MEAN... I FEEL BAD ASKING THAT MUCH OF YOU...
WORRY NOT!
THIS IS ACTUALLY MY PRIME DIRECTIVE!
HMPH.
...DIRECTIVE?
LIKE A JOB?
THERE'S NO TIME TO LOSE! LET THE OPERATION BEGIN!
O-OKAY!
GOT A BAD FEELING.

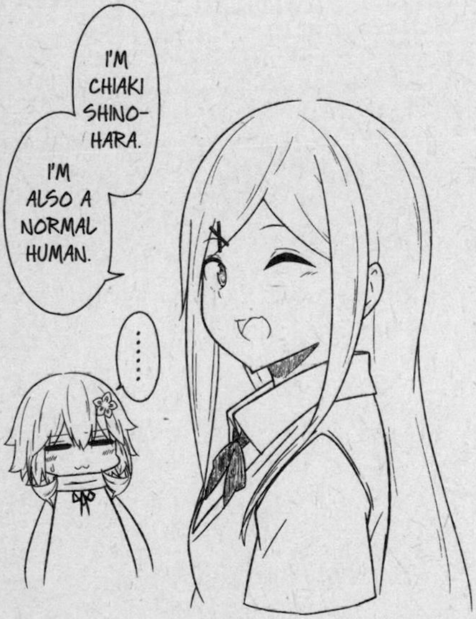
I'M CHIAKI SHINO-HARA.
I'M ALSO A NORMAL HUMAN.
......

Gabriel Dropout

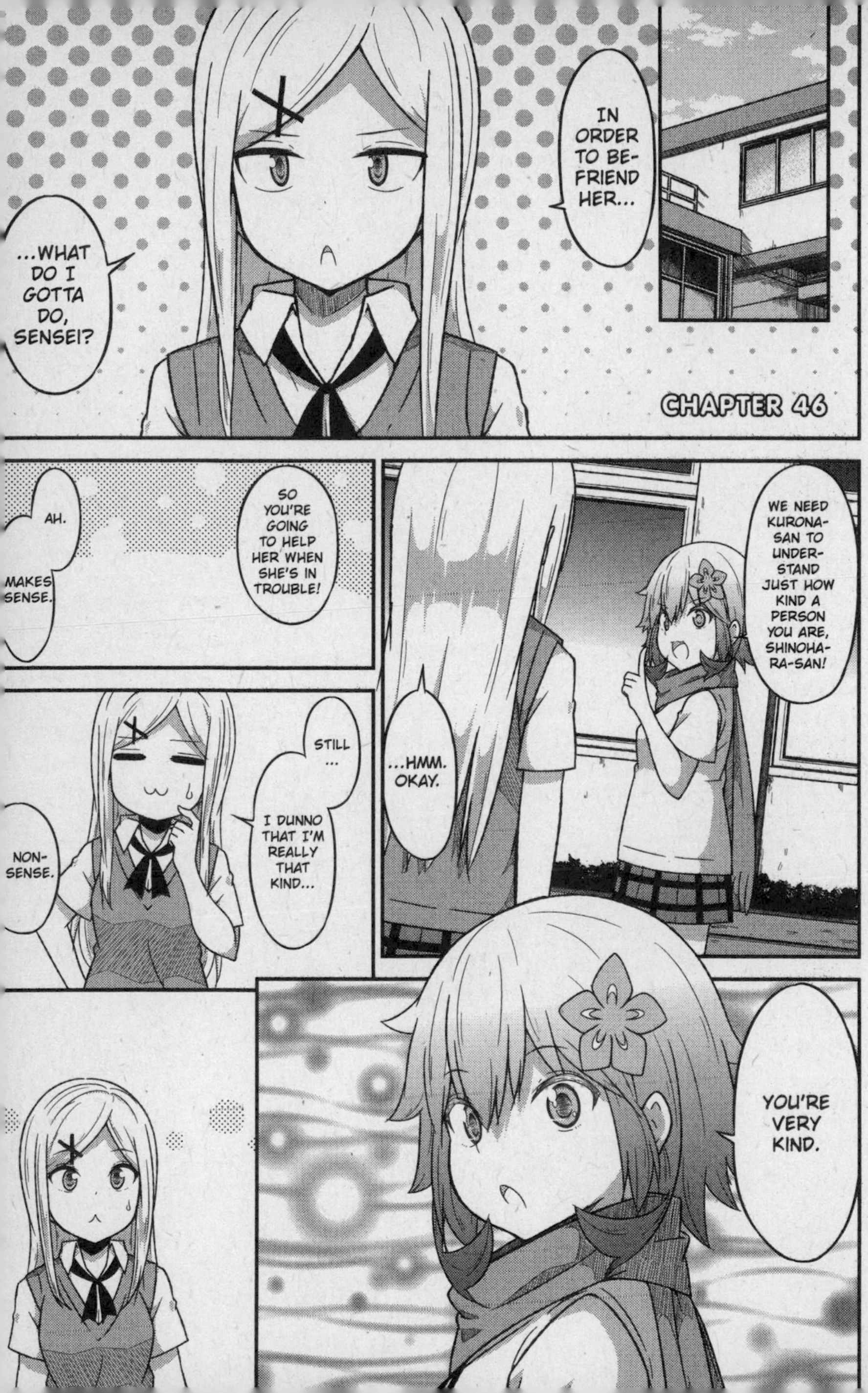
IN ORDER TO BE-FRIEND HER...
...WHAT DO I GOTTA DO, SENSEI?
CHAPTER 46
WE NEED KURONA-SAN TO UNDER-STAND JUST HOW KIND A PERSON YOU ARE, SHINOHARA-SAN!
...HMM. OKAY.
SO YOU'RE GOING TO HELP HER WHEN SHE'S IN TROUBLE!
AH.
MAKES SENSE.
STILL ...
I DUNNO THAT I'M REALLY THAT KIND...
NON-SENSE.
YOU'RE VERY KIND.

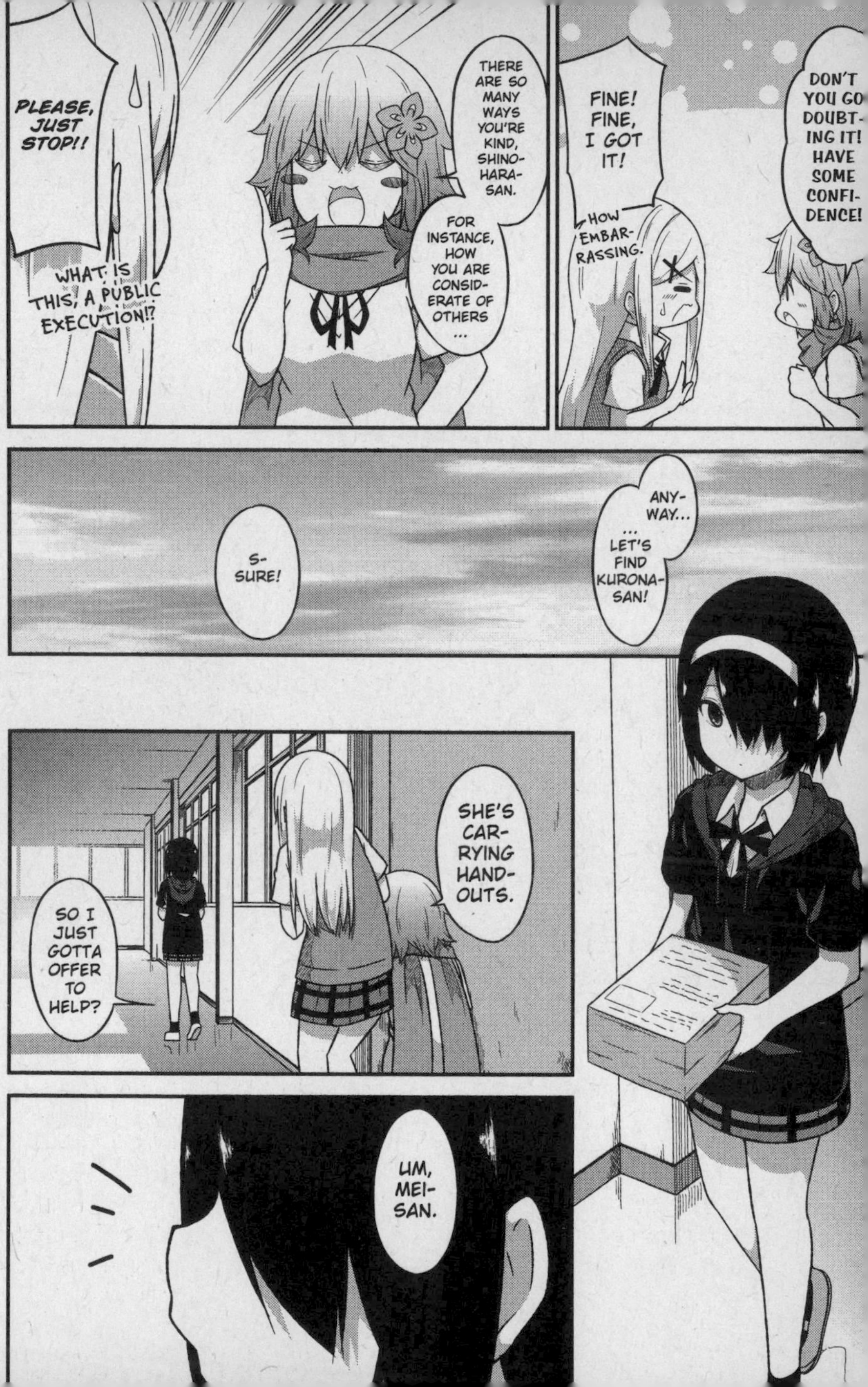
DON'T YOU GO DOUBTING IT! HAVE SOME CONFIDENCE!
FINE! FINE, I GOT IT!
HOW EMBARRASSING.
THERE ARE SO MANY WAYS YOU'RE KIND, SHINOHARA-SAN.
FOR INSTANCE, HOW YOU ARE CONSIDERATE OF OTHERS ...
PLEASE, JUST STOP!!
WHAT IS THIS, A PUBLIC EXECUTION!?
ANYWAY... ... LET'S FIND KURONA-SAN!
S-SURE!
SHE'S CARRYING HANDOUTS.
SO I JUST GOTTA OFFER TO HELP?
UM, MEI-SAN.

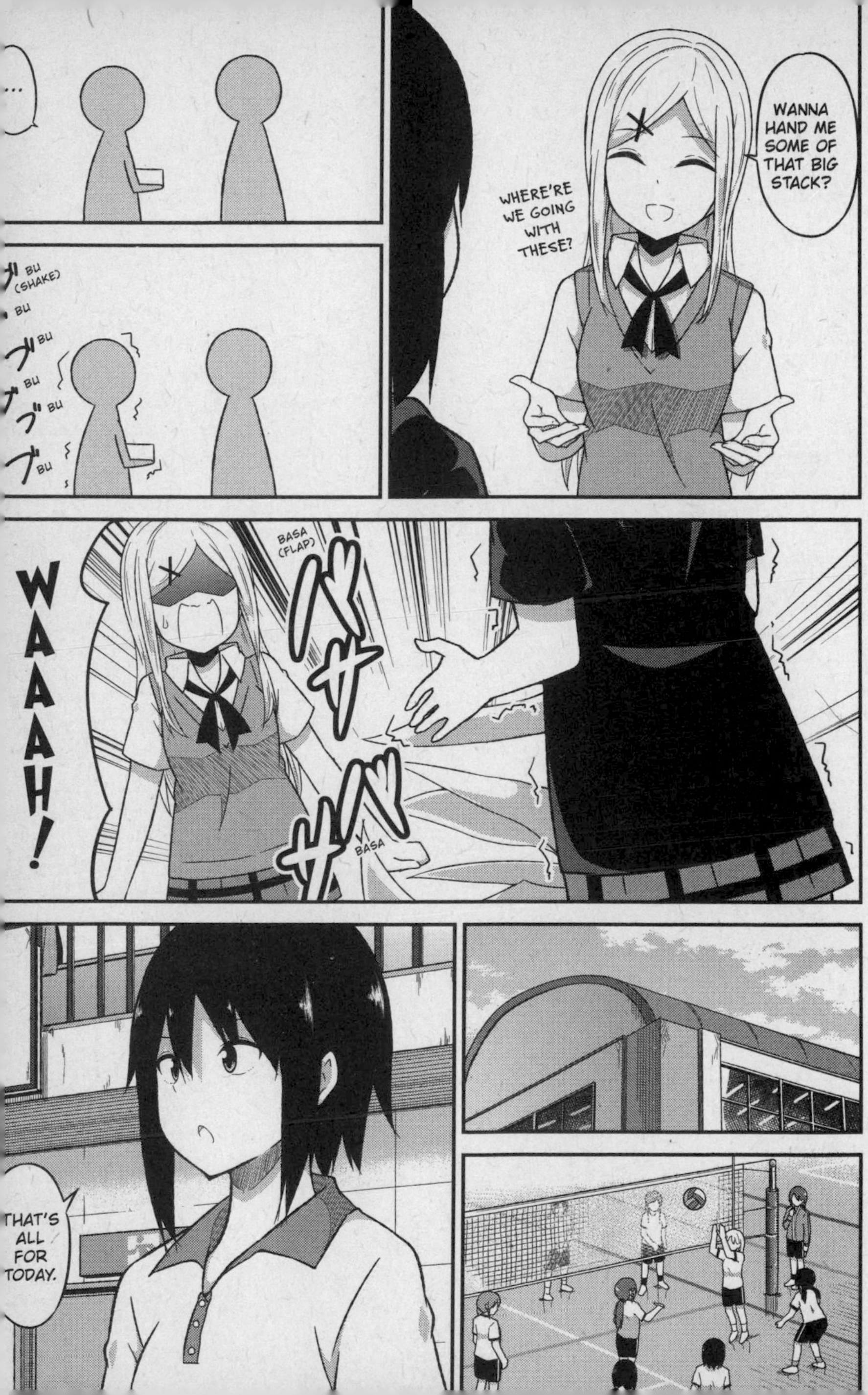

WANNA HAND ME SOME OF THAT BIG STACK?
WHERE'RE WE GOING WITH THESE?
...
BU (SHAKE)
BU
BU
BU
BU
BU
BASA (FLAP)
WAAAH!
BASA
THAT'S ALL FOR TODAY.

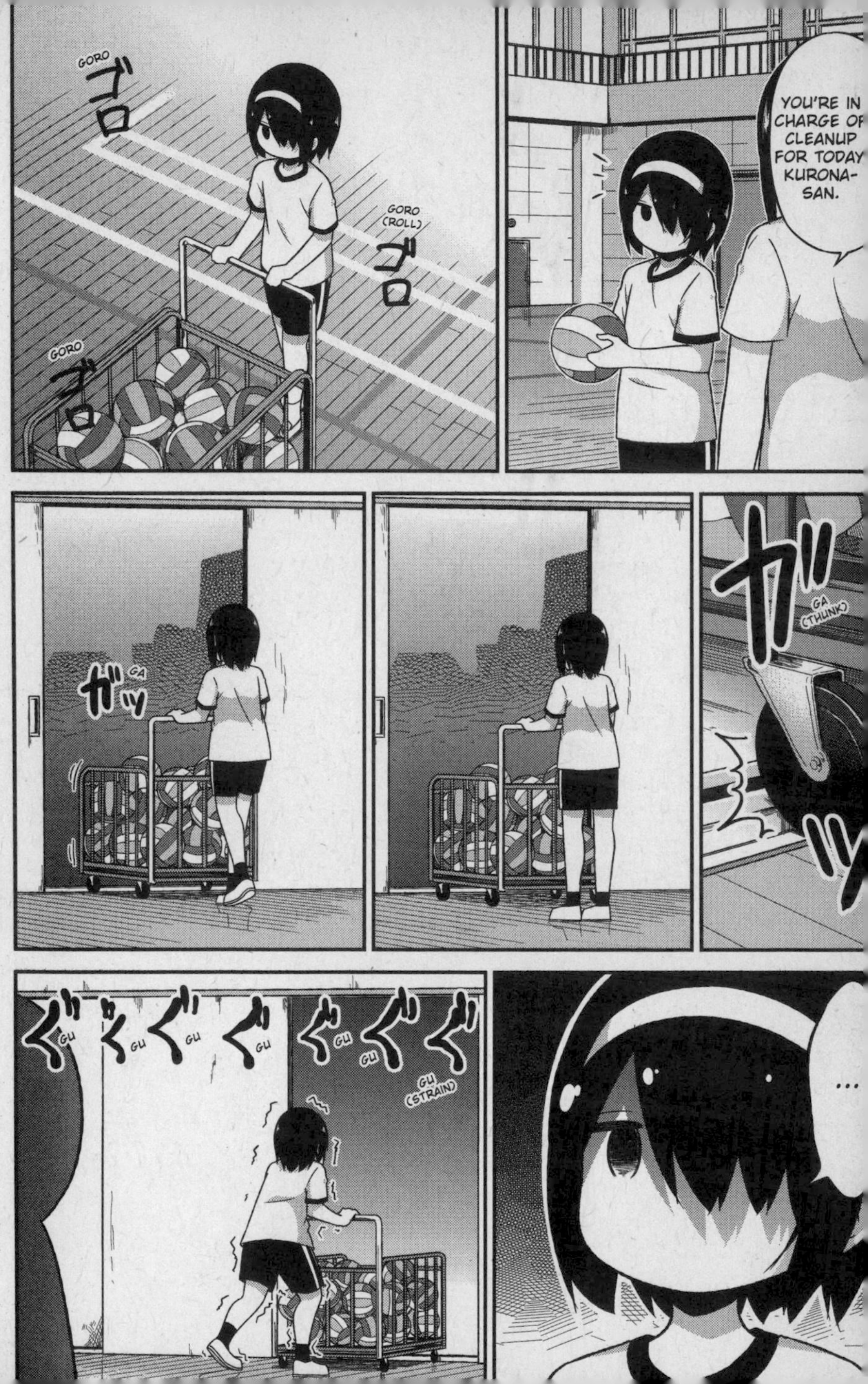
YOU'RE IN CHARGE OF CLEANUP FOR TODAY KURONA-SAN.
GORO
ゴロ
GORO (ROLL)
ゴロ
GORO
ゴロ
ガッ
GA (THUNK)
ガッ
GA
...
ぐ GU
ぐ GU
ぐ GU
ぐ GU
ぐ GU
ぐ GU
ぐ
GU (STRAIN)

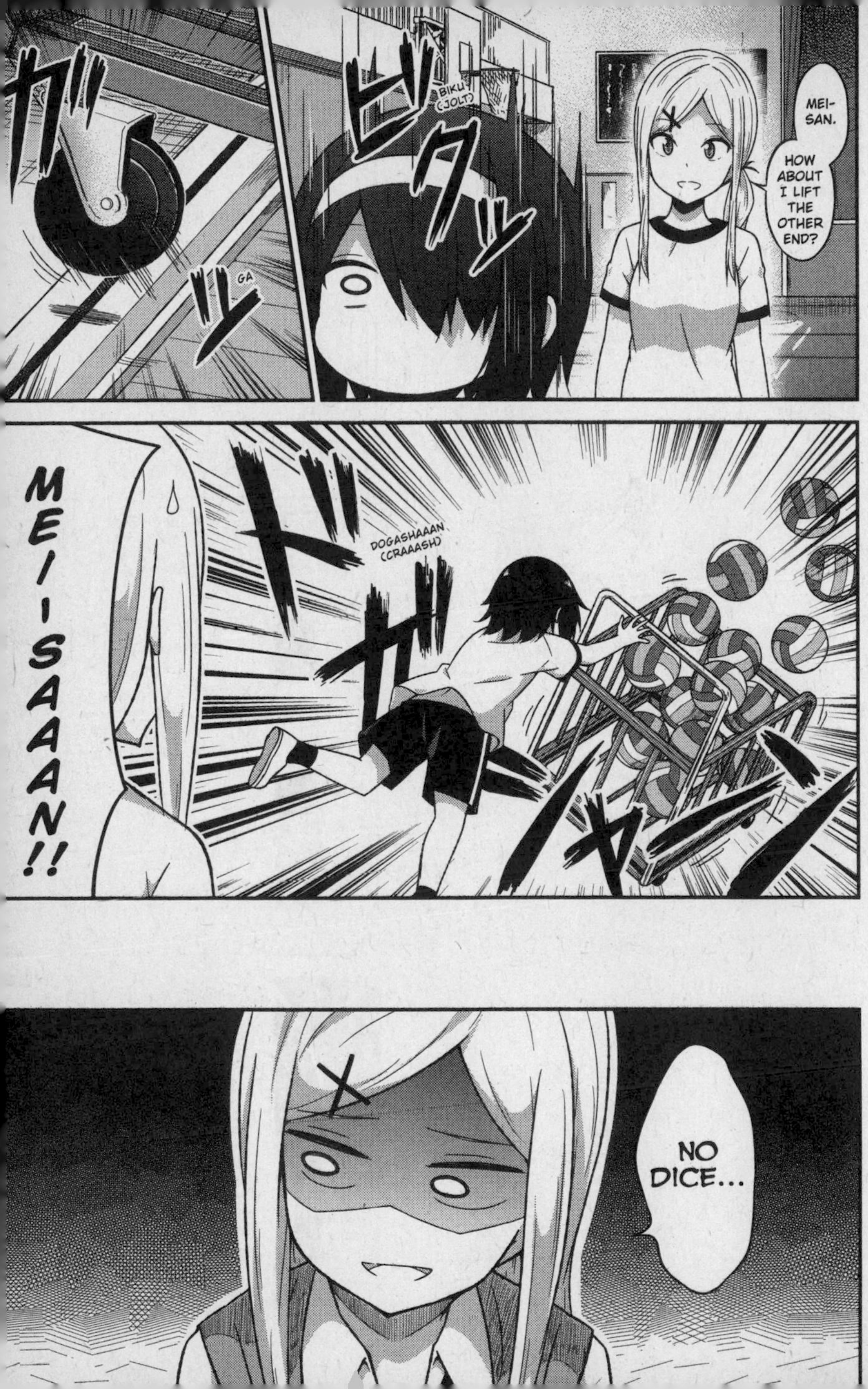
MEI-SAN.
HOW ABOUT I LIFT THE OTHER END?
BIKU (JOLT)
GA
MEI-I-SAAAAN!!
DOGASHAAAN (CRAAASH)
NO DICE...

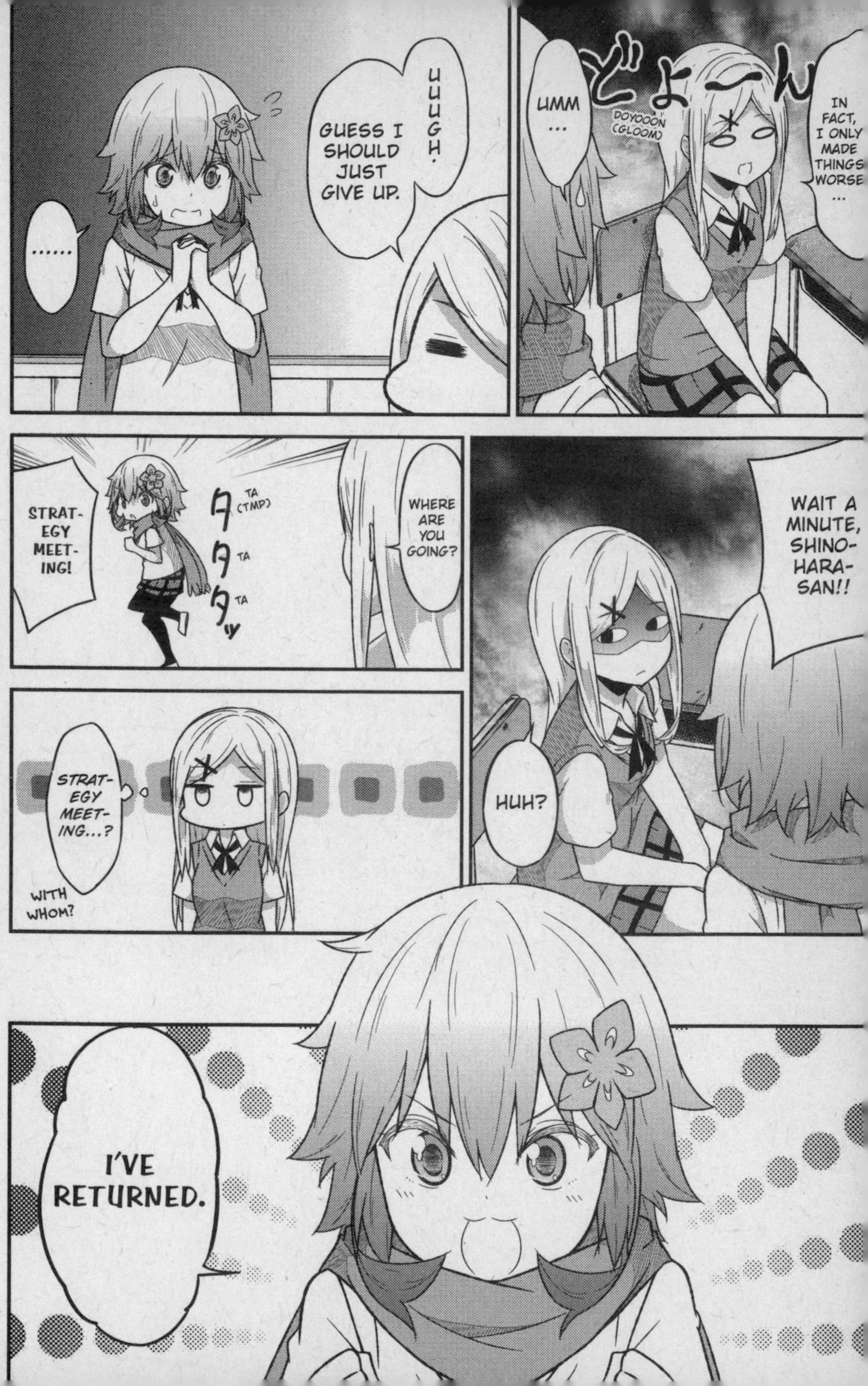
IN FACT, I ONLY MADE THINGS WORSE...
どよ〜ん
DOYOOON (GLOOM)
UMM...
UUUGH.
GUESS I SHOULD JUST GIVE UP.
......
WAIT A MINUTE, SHINOHARA-SAN!!
HUH?
WHERE ARE YOU GOING?
タ TA (TMP) タ TA タッ TA
STRATEGY MEETING!
STRATEGY MEETING...?
WITH WHOM?
I'VE RETURNED.

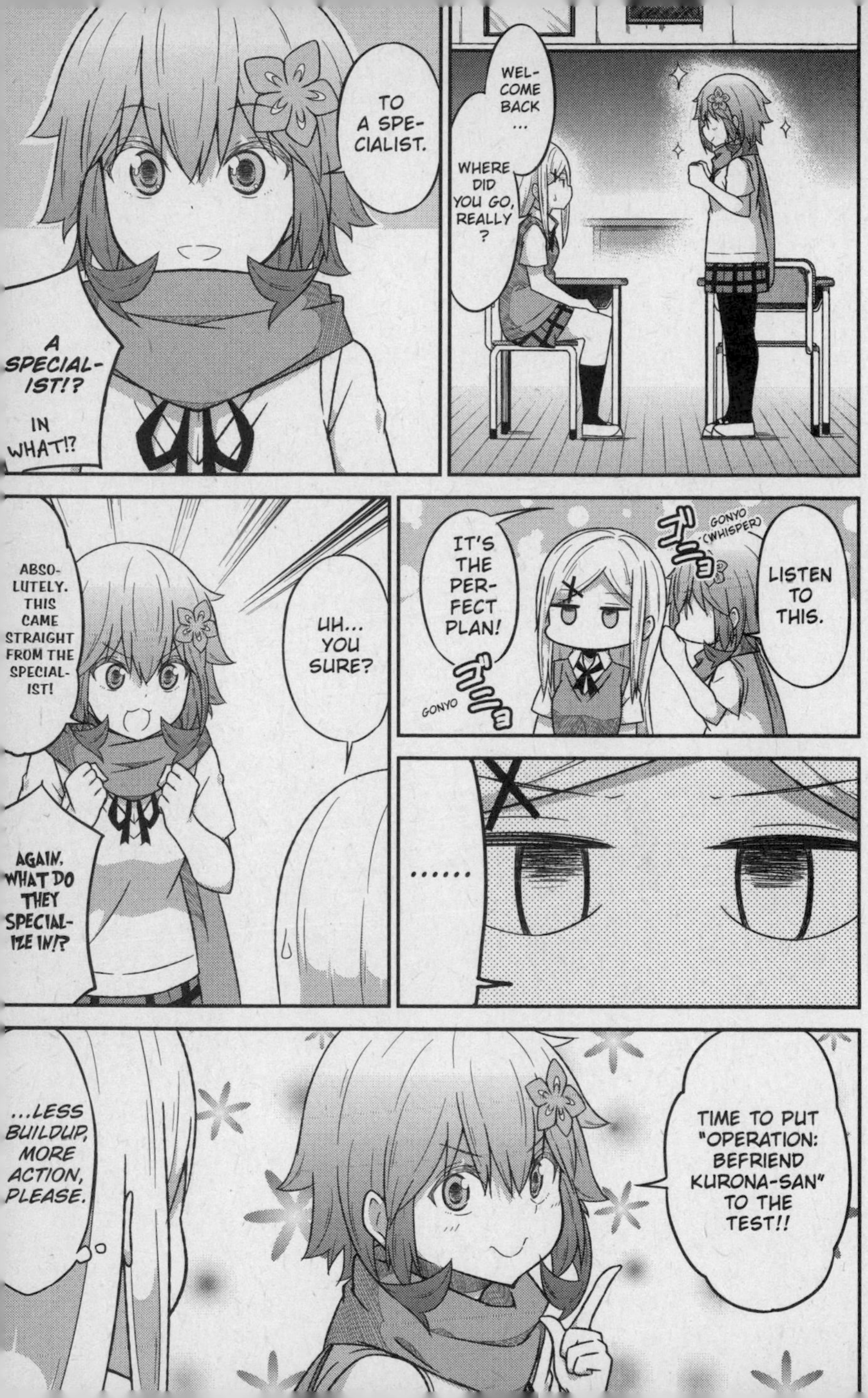
WEL-COME BACK ...
WHERE DID YOU GO, REALLY ?
TO A SPE-CIALIST.
A SPECIAL-IST!?
IN WHAT!?
GONYO (WHISPER)
LISTEN TO THIS.
IT'S THE PER-FECT PLAN!
GONYO
......
UH... YOU SURE?
ABSO-LUTELY. THIS CAME STRAIGHT FROM THE SPECIAL-IST!
AGAIN, WHAT DO THEY SPECIAL-IZE IN!?
TIME TO PUT "OPERATION: BEFRIEND KURONA-SAN" TO THE TEST!!
...LESS BUILDUP, MORE ACTION, PLEASE.

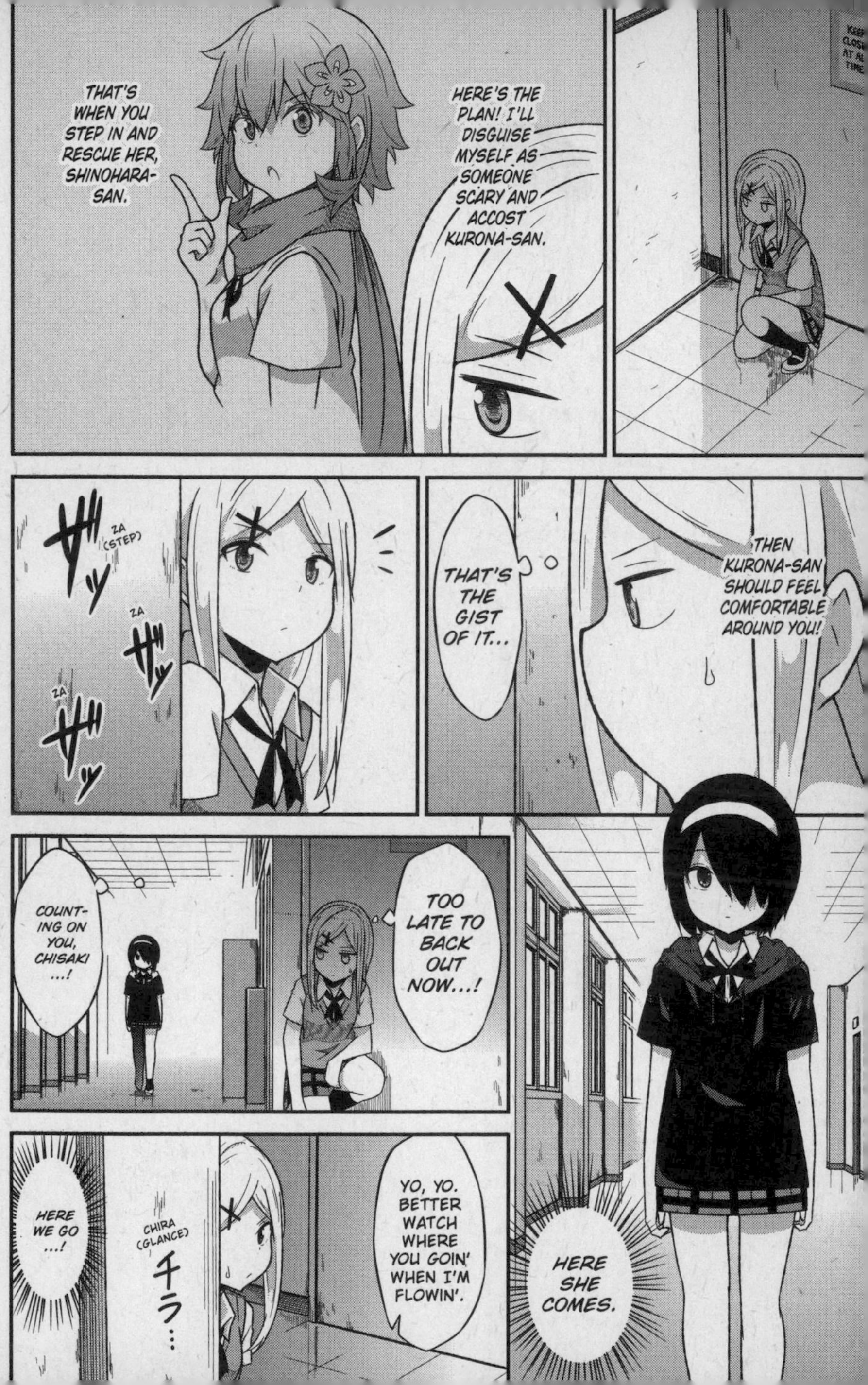
HERE'S THE PLAN! I'LL DISGUISE MYSELF AS SOMEONE SCARY AND ACCOST KURONA-SAN.
THAT'S WHEN YOU STEP IN AND RESCUE HER, SHINOHARA-SAN.
THEN KURONA-SAN SHOULD FEEL COMFORTABLE AROUND YOU!
THAT'S THE GIST OF IT...
ザッ
ZA (STEP)
ザッ
ZA
ザッ
ZA
HERE SHE COMES.
TOO LATE TO BACK OUT NOW...!
COUNTING ON YOU, CHISAKI...!
YO, YO. BETTER WATCH WHERE YOU GOIN' WHEN I'M FLOWIN'.
チラ…
CHIRA (GLANCE)
HERE WE GO...!

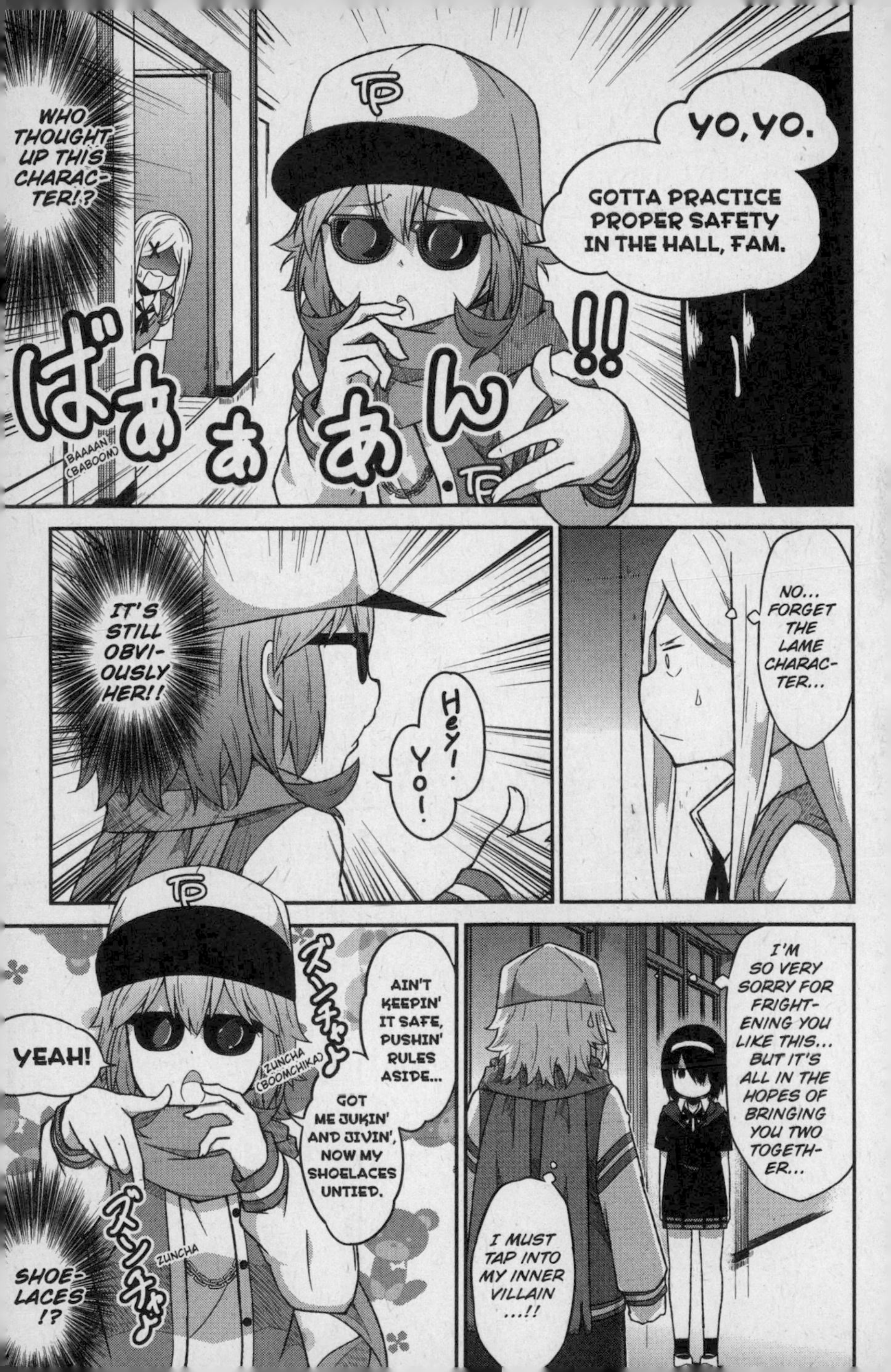

YO, YO.
GOTTA PRACTICE PROPER SAFETY IN THE HALL, FAM.
ばぁぁあん!!
BAAAAN (BABOOM)
WHO THOUGHT UP THIS CHARAC-TER!?
NO... FORGET THE LAME CHARAC-TER...
Hey! Yo!
IT'S STILL OBVI-OUSLY HER!!
I'M SO VERY SORRY FOR FRIGHT-ENING YOU LIKE THIS... BUT IT'S ALL IN THE HOPES OF BRINGING YOU TWO TOGETH-ER...
I MUST TAP INTO MY INNER VILLAIN ...!!
AIN'T KEEPIN' IT SAFE, PUSHIN' RULES ASIDE...
GOT ME JUKIN' AND JIVIN', NOW MY SHOELACES UNTIED.
ZUNCHA (BOOMCHIKA)
YEAH!
ZUNCHA
SHOE-LACES!?

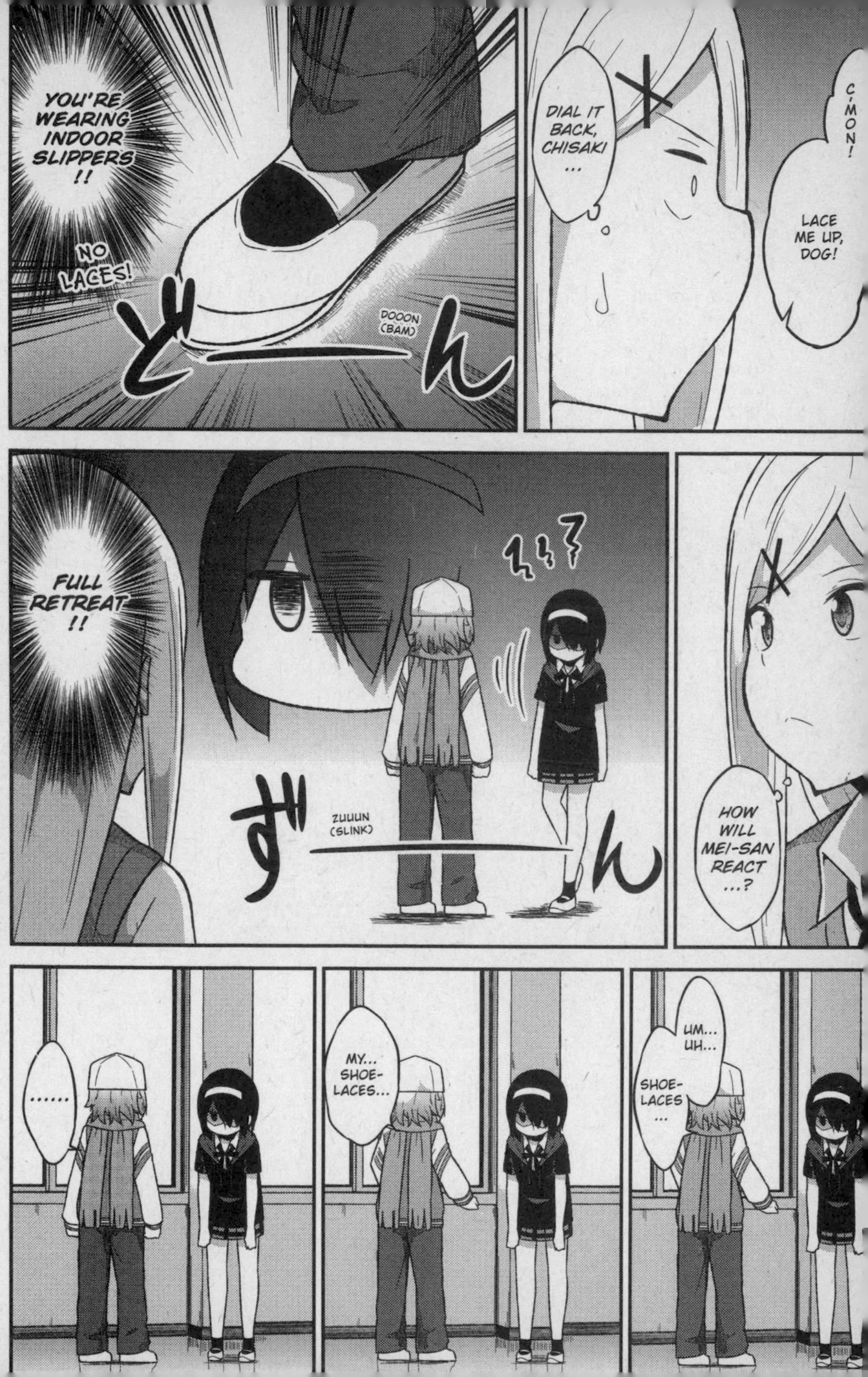
C-MON!
LACE ME UP, DOG!
DIAL IT BACK, CHISAKI...
YOU'RE WEARING INDOOR SLIPPERS!!
NO LACES!
どーん
DOOON (BAM)
HOW WILL MEI-SAN REACT...?
FULL RETREAT!!
ずーん
ZUUUN (SLINK)
UM... UH...
SHOE-LACES...
MY... SHOE-LACES...
......

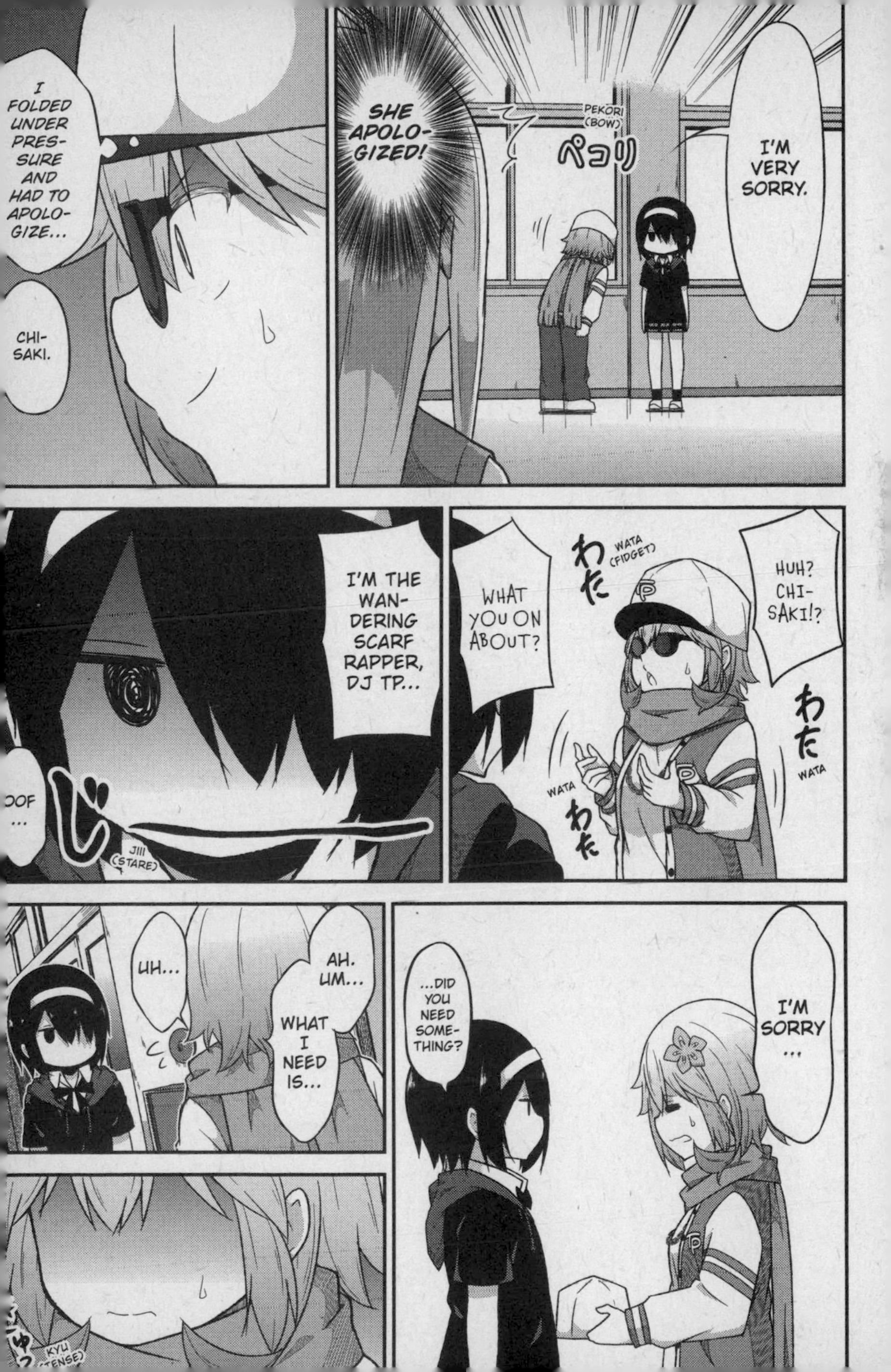

I'M VERY SORRY.
PEKORI (BOW)
ペコリ
SHE APOLOGIZED!
I FOLDED UNDER PRESSURE AND HAD TO APOLOGIZE...
CHISAKI.
HUH? CHISAKI!?
わた
WATA (FIDGET)
WHAT YOU ON ABOUT?
わた
WATA
わた
WATA
I'M THE WANDERING SCARF RAPPER, DJ TP...
OOF...
じ
JIII (STARE)
I'M SORRY...
...DID YOU NEED SOMETHING?
AH. UM... WHAT I NEED IS...
UH...
KYU (TENSE)

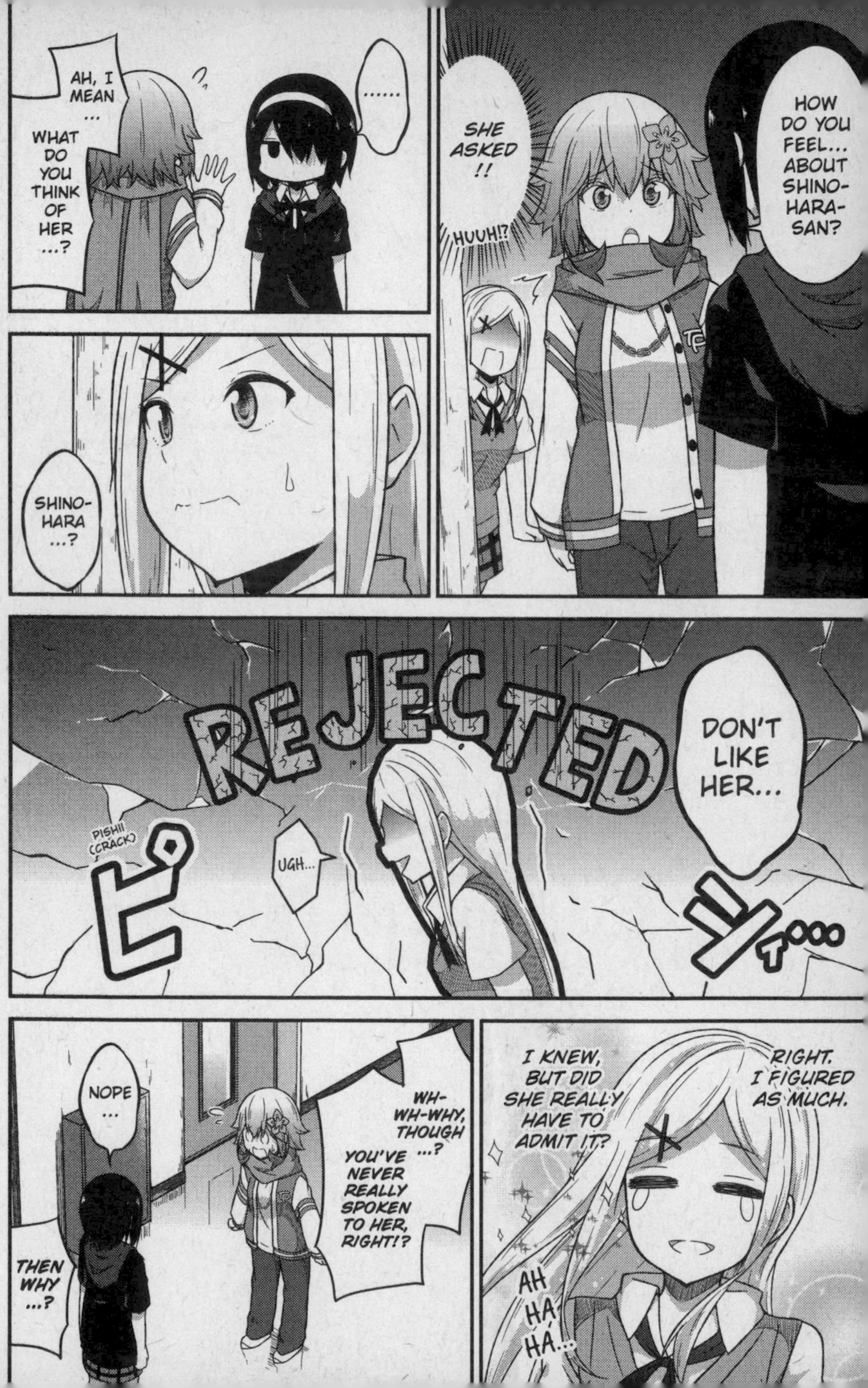
HOW DO YOU FEEL... ABOUT SHINOHARA-SAN?
SHE ASKED!!
HUUH!?
AH, I MEAN... WHAT DO YOU THINK OF HER...?
......
SHINOHARA...?
DON'T LIKE HER...
ッ T...
REJECTED
UGH...
PISHII (CRACK)
ピ
RIGHT. I FIGURED AS MUCH.
I KNEW, BUT DID SHE REALLY HAVE TO ADMIT IT?
AH HA HA...
WH-WH-WHY, THOUGH...?
YOU'VE NEVER REALLY SPOKEN TO HER, RIGHT!?
NOPE...
THEN WHY...?

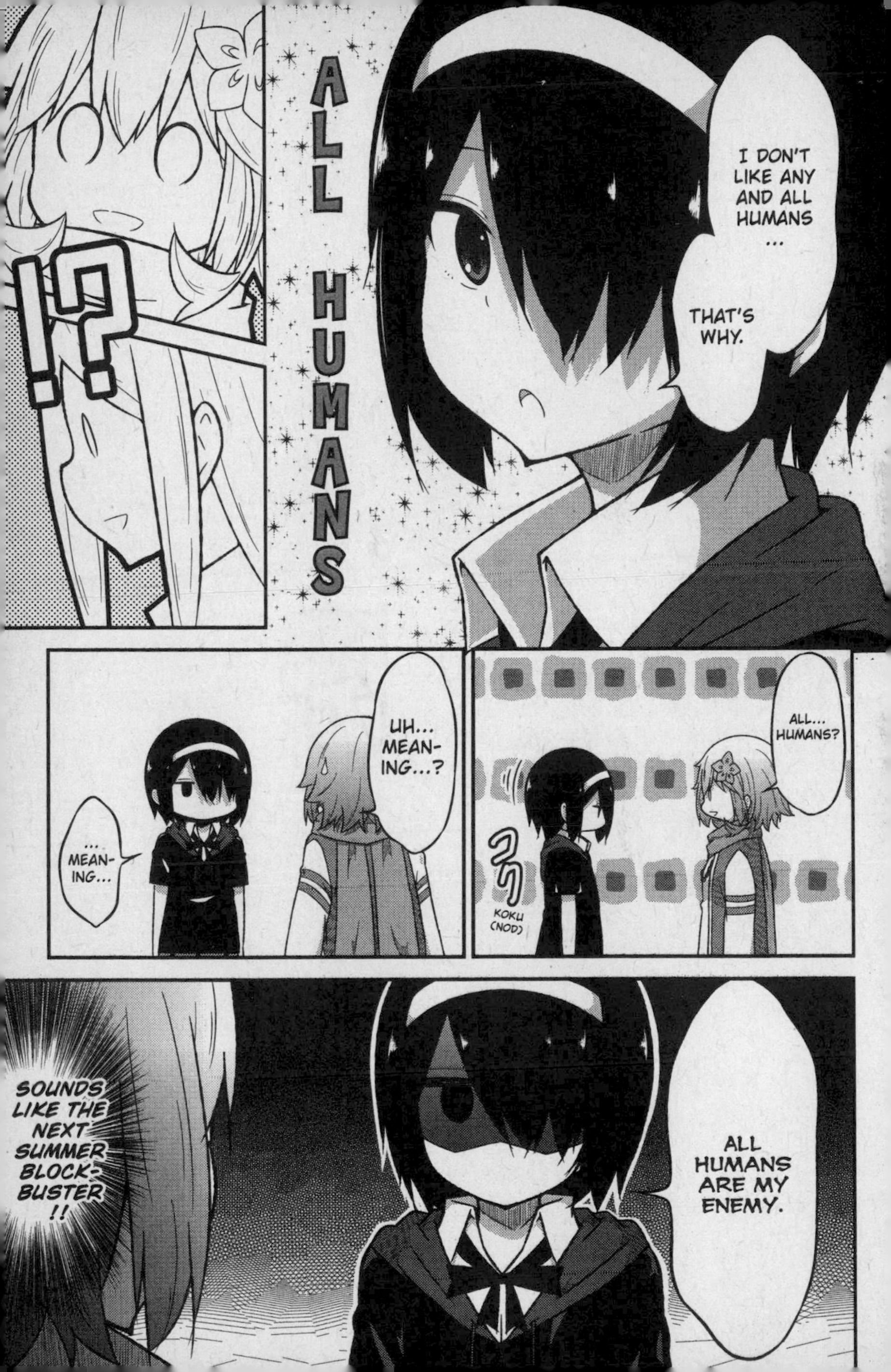
I DON'T LIKE ANY AND ALL HUMANS ...
THAT'S WHY.
ALL HUMANS
!?
ALL... HUMANS?
KOKU (NOD)
UH... MEAN-ING...?
... MEAN-ING...
ALL HUMANS ARE MY ENEMY.
SOUNDS LIKE THE NEXT SUMMER BLOCK-BUSTER !!

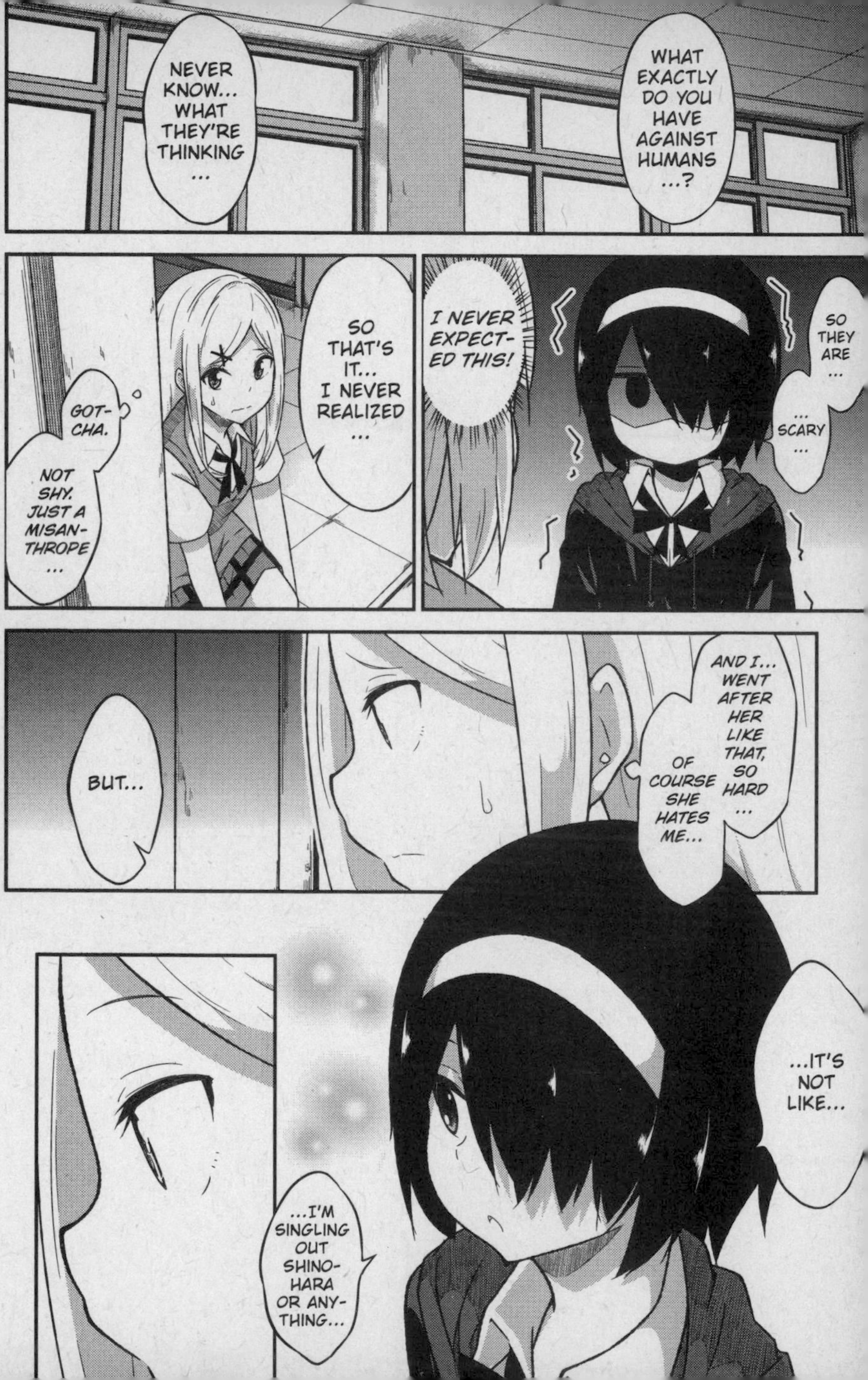
WHAT EXACTLY DO YOU HAVE AGAINST HUMANS ...?
NEVER KNOW... WHAT THEY'RE THINKING ...
SO THEY ARE ...
... SCARY ...
I NEVER EXPECTED THIS!
SO THAT'S IT... I NEVER REALIZED ...
GOTCHA.
NOT SHY. JUST A MISANTHROPE ...
AND I... WENT AFTER HER LIKE THAT, SO HARD ...
OF COURSE SHE HATES ME...
BUT...
...IT'S NOT LIKE...
...I'M SINGLING OUT SHINOHARA OR ANYTHING...

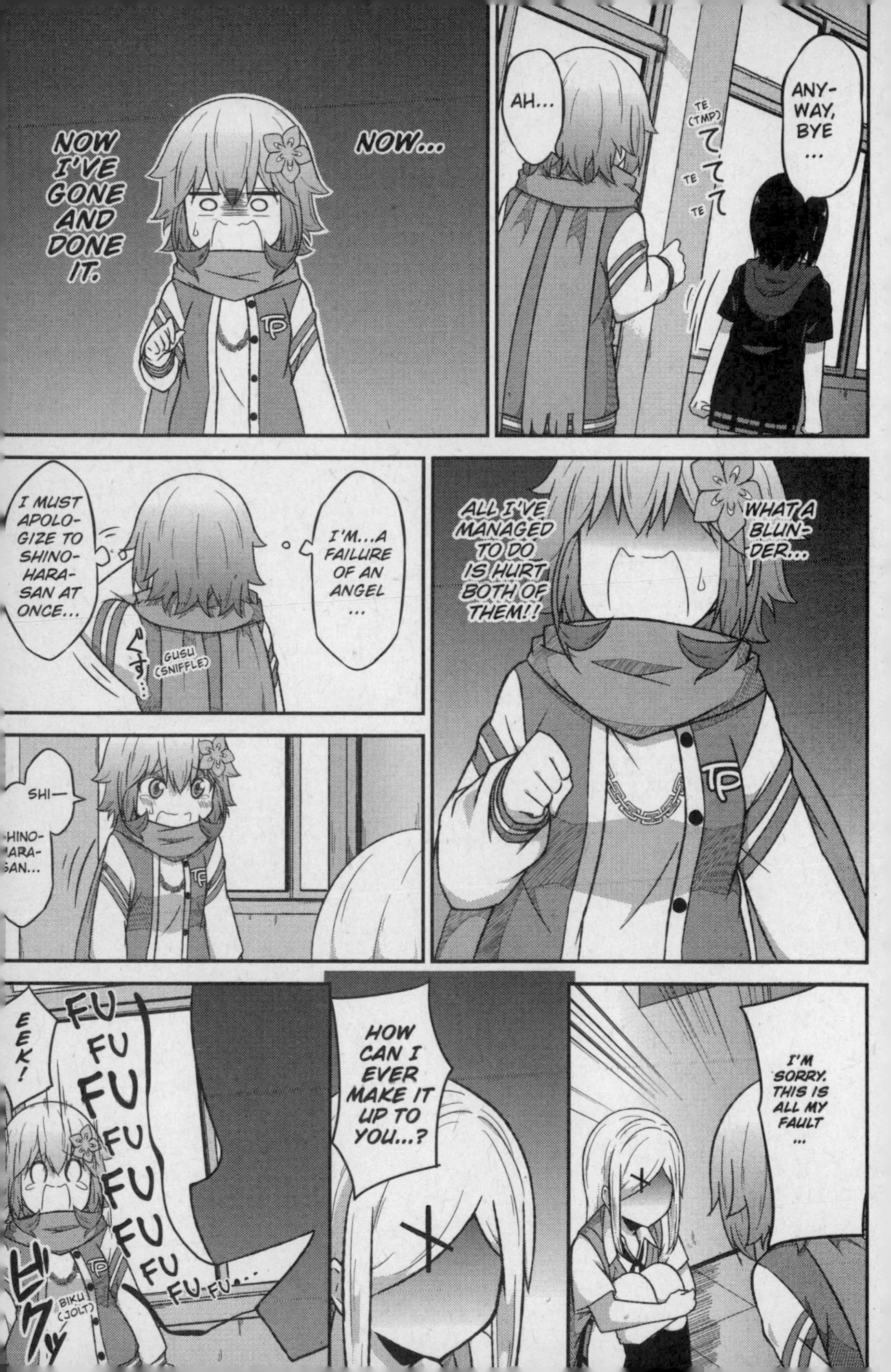
ANY-WAY, BYE ...
TE (TMP) て TE て TE て
AH...
NOW...
NOW I'VE GONE AND DONE IT.
WHAT A BLUN-DER...
ALL I'VE MANAGED TO DO IS HURT BOTH OF THEM!!
I'M...A FAILURE OF AN ANGEL ...
I MUST APOLO-GIZE TO SHINO-HARA-SAN AT ONCE...
ぐす... GUSU (SNIFFLE)
SHI—
HINO- HARA- SAN...
I'M SORRY. THIS IS ALL MY FAULT ...
HOW CAN I EVER MAKE IT UP TO YOU...?
EEK!
FU FU FU FU FU FU FU FU FU FU FU...
ビクッ BIKU (JOLT)

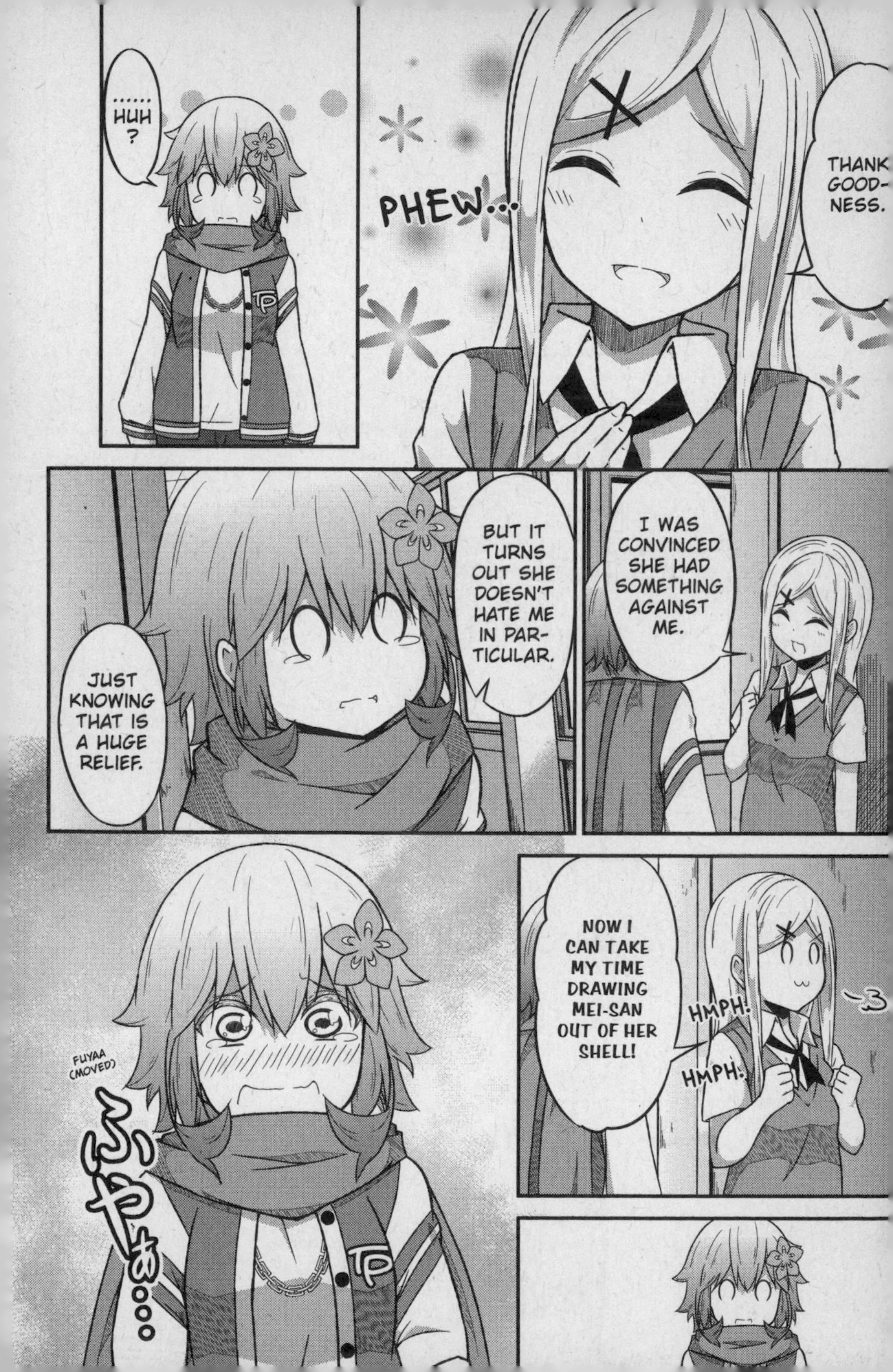
THANK GOOD-NESS.
PHEW...
......HUH?
I WAS CONVINCED SHE HAD SOMETHING AGAINST ME.
BUT IT TURNS OUT SHE DOESN'T HATE ME IN PAR-TICULAR.
JUST KNOWING THAT IS A HUGE RELIEF.
NOW I CAN TAKE MY TIME DRAWING MEI-SAN OUT OF HER SHELL!
HMPH!
HMPH!
FUYAA (MOVED)
ふやぁooo

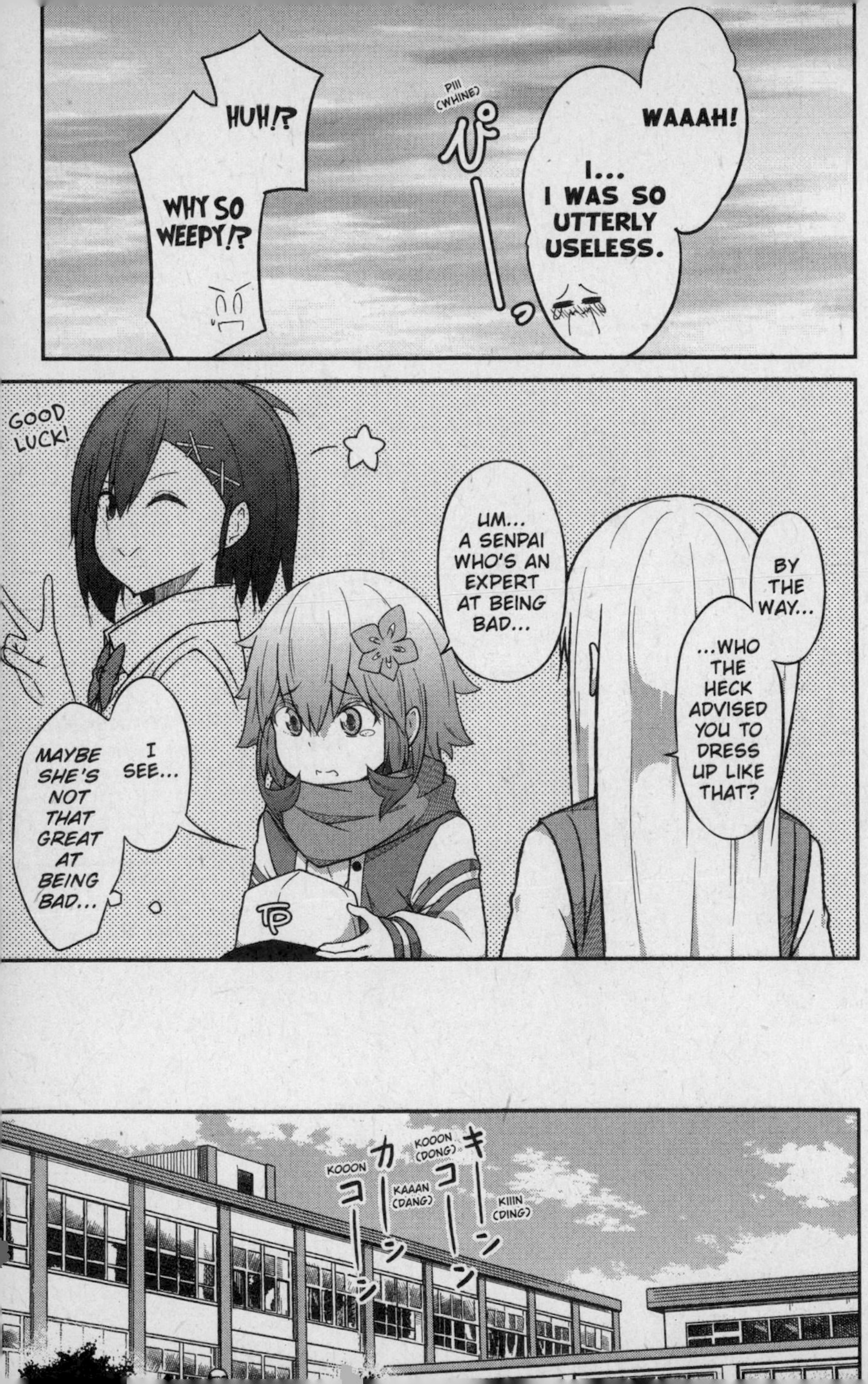
WAAAH!
I... I WAS SO UTTERLY USELESS.
PIII (WHINE)
HUH!?
WHY SO WEEPY!?
BY THE WAY...
...WHO THE HECK ADVISED YOU TO DRESS UP LIKE THAT?
UM... A SENPAI WHO'S AN EXPERT AT BEING BAD...
I SEE...
MAYBE SHE'S NOT THAT GREAT AT BEING BAD...
GOOD LUCK!
KIIIN (DING)
KOOON (DONG)
KAAAN (DANG)
KOOON

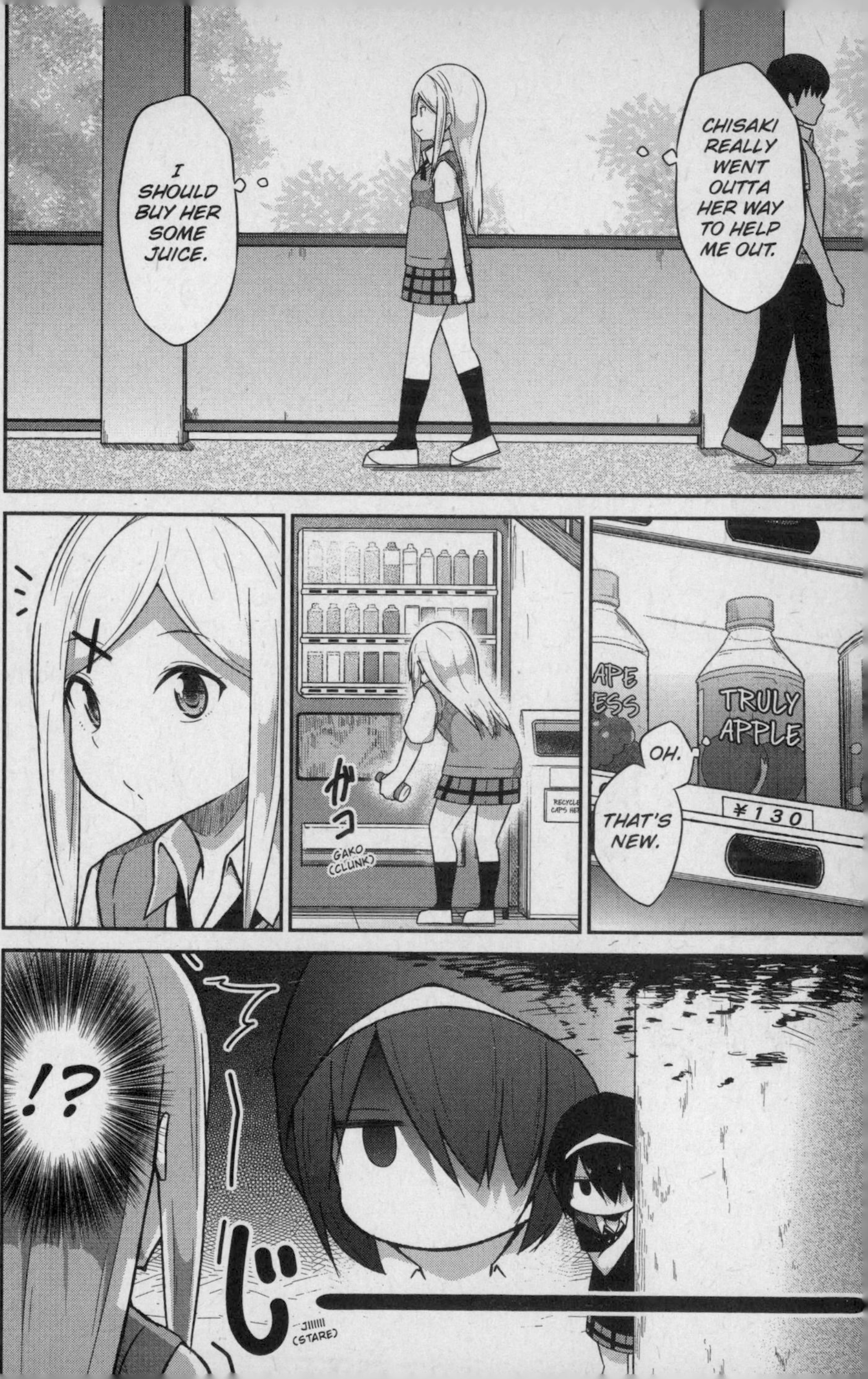
CHISAKI REALLY WENT OUTTA HER WAY TO HELP ME OUT.
I SHOULD BUY HER SOME JUICE.
TRULY APPLE
¥130
OH. THAT'S NEW.
GAKO (CLUNK)
!?
JIIIIII (STARE)

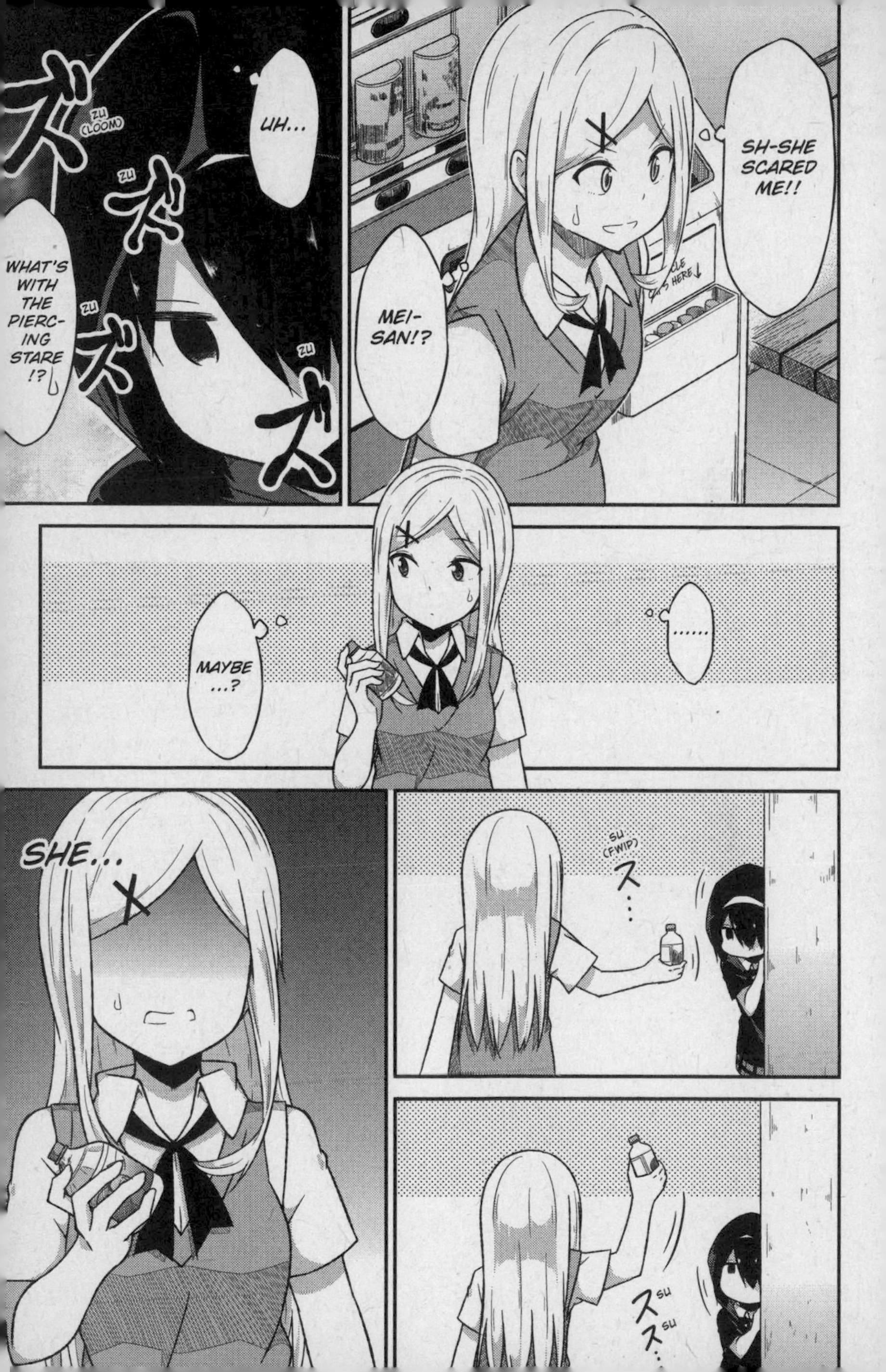
SH-SHE SCARED ME!!
MEI-SAN!?
UH...
ZU (LOOM)
ZU
ZU
ZU
WHAT'S WITH THE PIERC-ING STARE!?
......
MAYBE...?
SU (FWIP)
ス...
SU SU
スス...
SHE...

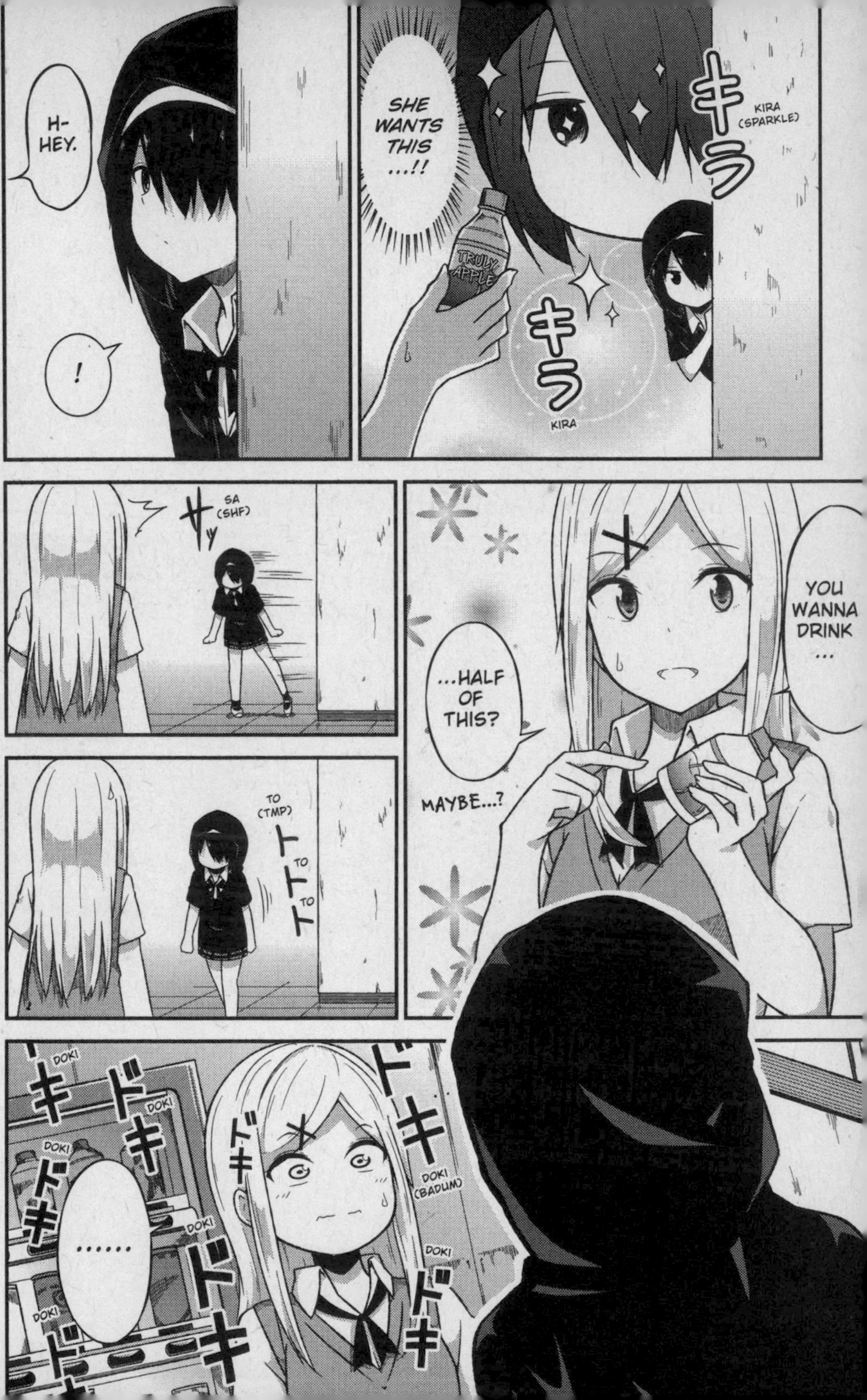

キラ
KIRA (SPARKLE)
SHE WANTS THIS ...!!
TRULY APPLE
キラ
KIRA
H-HEY.
!
YOU WANNA DRINK ...
...HALF OF THIS?
MAYBE...?
サッ
SA (SHF)
TO (TMP)
TO
TO
ドキ
DOKI (BADUM)
DOKI
DOKI
DOKI
......
DOKI
DOKI
DOKI

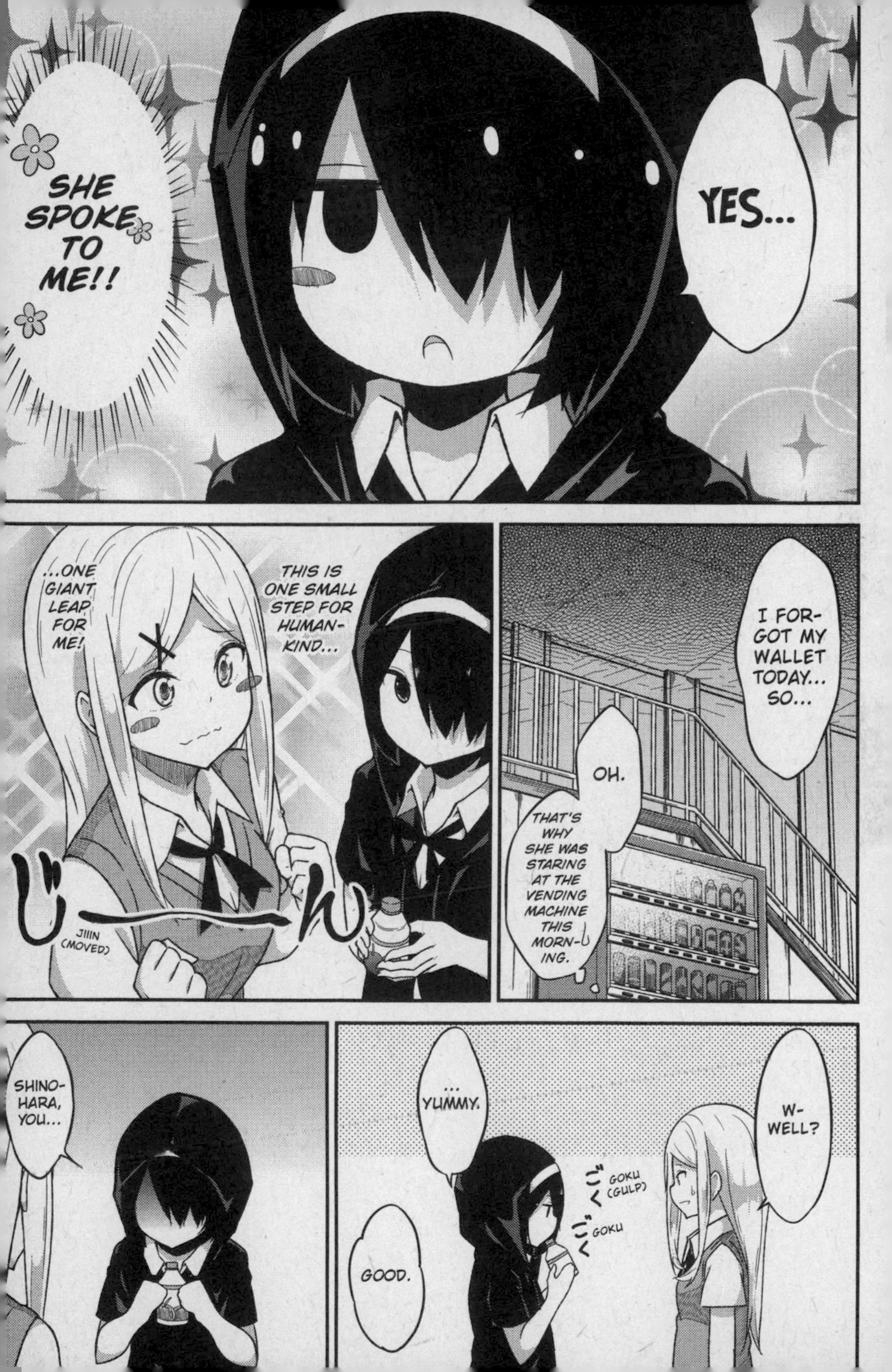
YES...
SHE SPOKE TO ME!!
I FORGOT MY WALLET TODAY... SO...
OH.
THAT'S WHY SHE WAS STARING AT THE VENDING MACHINE THIS MORNING.
THIS IS ONE SMALL STEP FOR HUMANKIND...
...ONE GIANT LEAP FOR ME!
じーん
JIIIN (MOVED)
W-WELL?
... YUMMY.
ごく
GOKU (GULP)
ごく
GOKU
GOOD.
SHINOHARA, YOU...

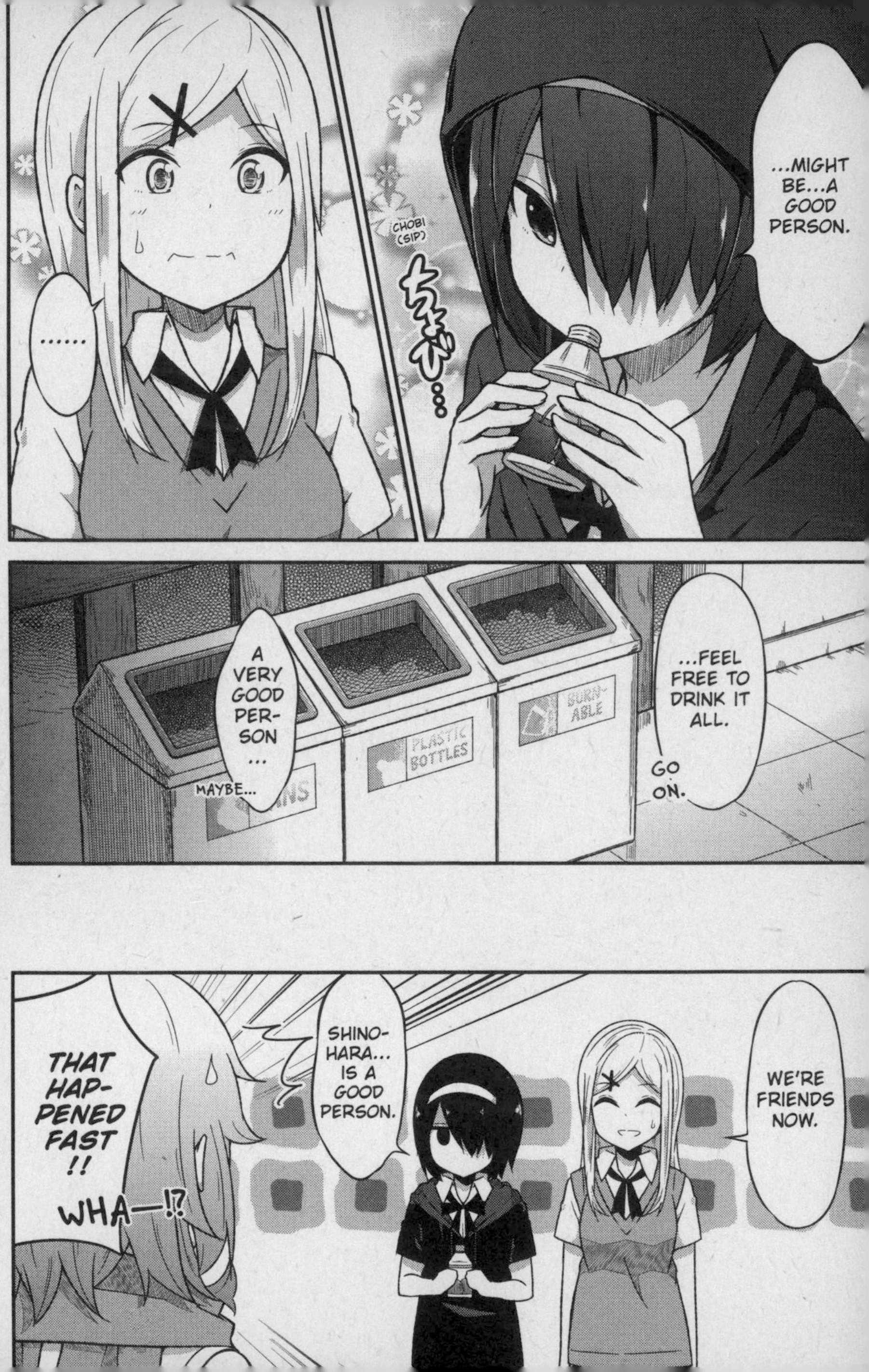
...MIGHT BE...A GOOD PERSON.
CHOBI (SIP)
ちょび…
......
...FEEL FREE TO DRINK IT ALL.
GO ON.
A VERY GOOD PER-SON...
MAYBE...
PLASTIC BOTTLES
BURN-ABLE
WE'RE FRIENDS NOW.
SHINO-HARA... IS A GOOD PERSON.
WHA—!?
THAT HAP-PENED FAST!!

WHEN
ONE GIRL
DARES TO
STAND
AGAINST
AN ENTIRE
SPECIES...

ALL HUMANS ARE MY ENEMY

Gabriel Dropout

CHAPTER 47

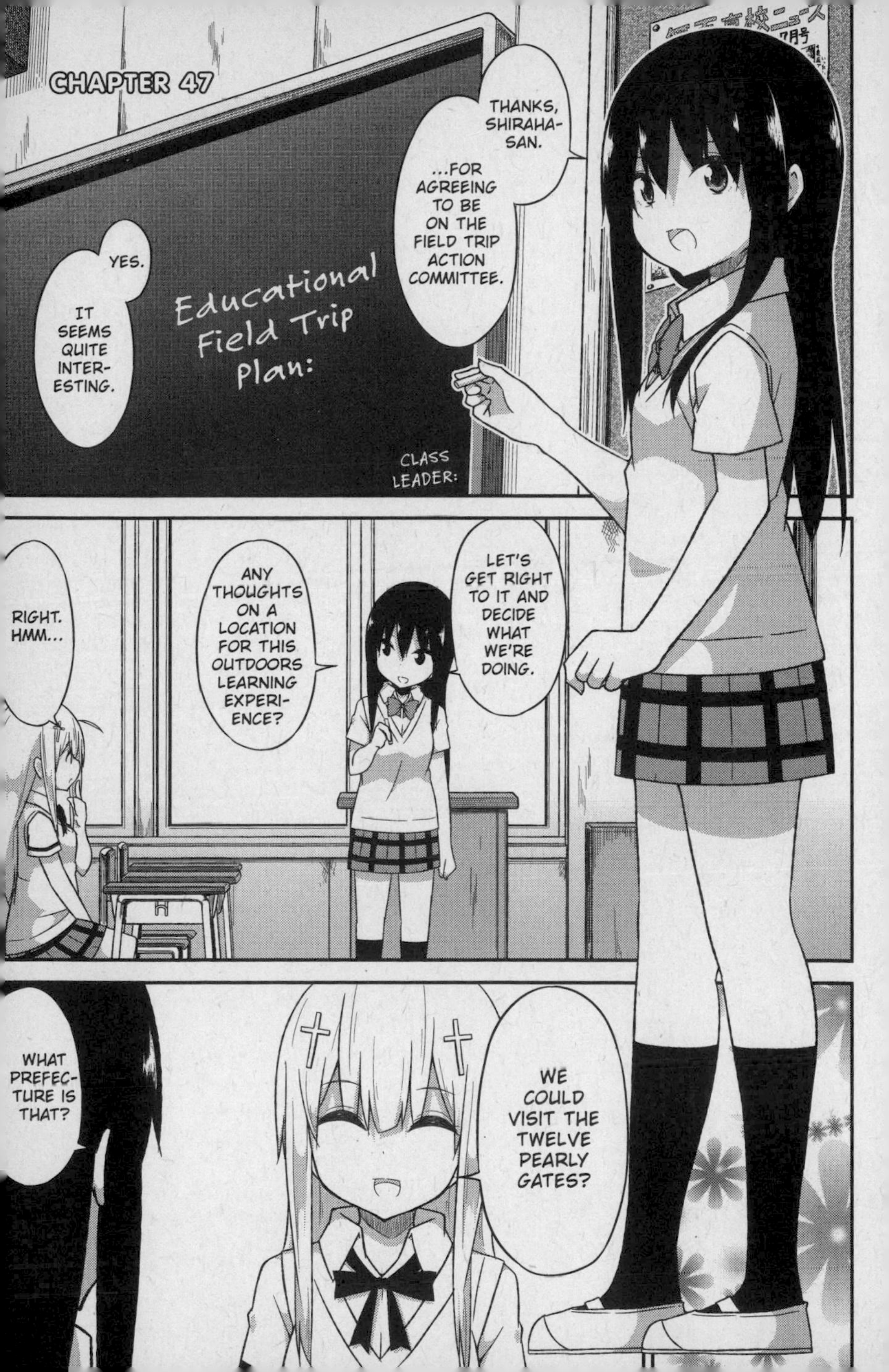
THANKS, SHIRAHA-SAN.
...FOR AGREEING TO BE ON THE FIELD TRIP ACTION COMMITTEE.
Educational Field Trip Plan:
CLASS LEADER:
YES.
IT SEEMS QUITE INTER-ESTING.
LET'S GET RIGHT TO IT AND DECIDE WHAT WE'RE DOING.
ANY THOUGHTS ON A LOCATION FOR THIS OUTDOORS LEARNING EXPERI-ENCE?
RIGHT. HMM...
WE COULD VISIT THE TWELVE PEARLY GATES?
WHAT PREFEC-TURE IS THAT?

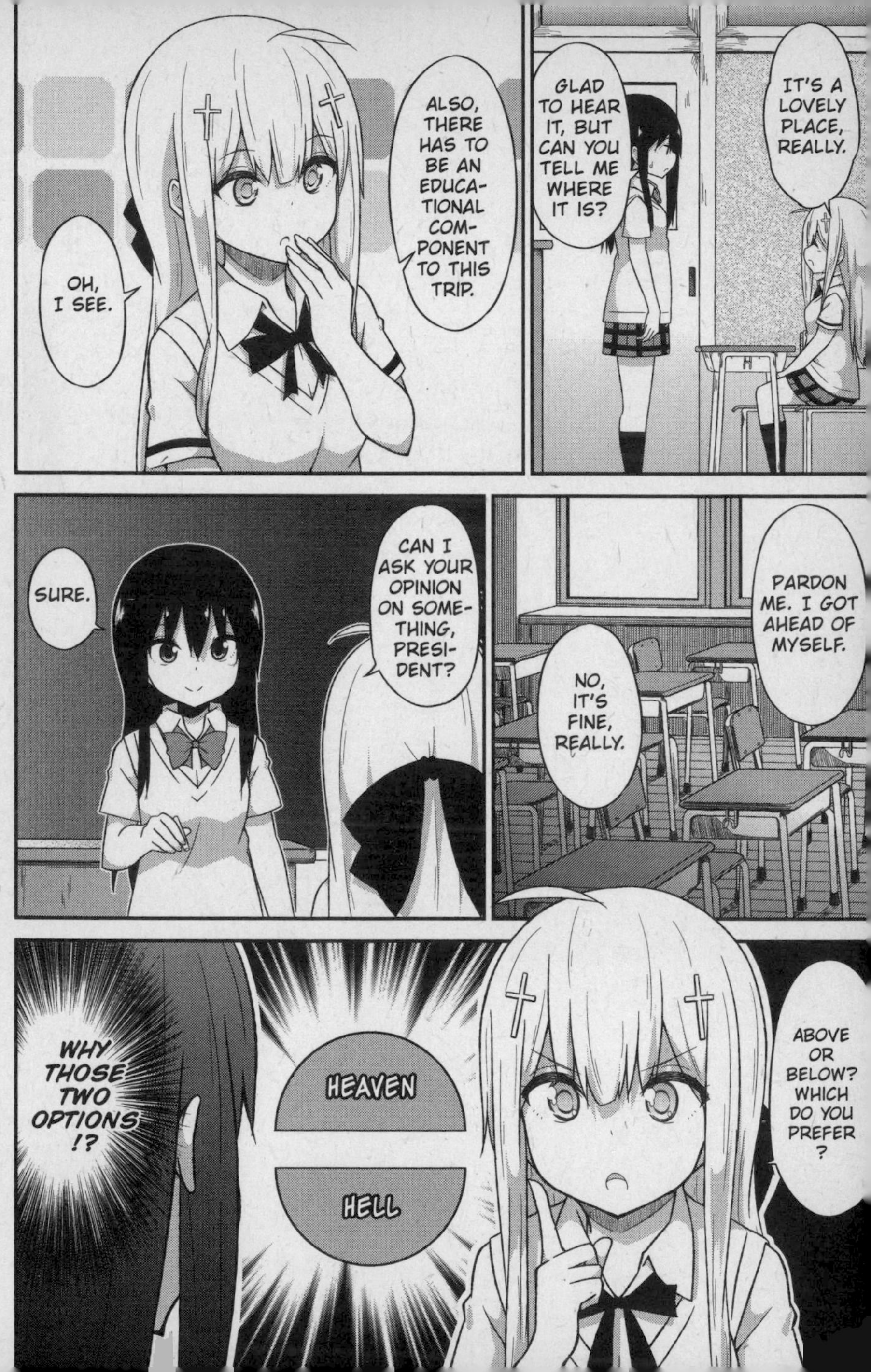

IT'S A LOVELY PLACE, REALLY.
GLAD TO HEAR IT, BUT CAN YOU TELL ME WHERE IT IS?
ALSO, THERE HAS TO BE AN EDUCATIONAL COMPONENT TO THIS TRIP.
OH, I SEE.
PARDON ME. I GOT AHEAD OF MYSELF.
NO, IT'S FINE, REALLY.
CAN I ASK YOUR OPINION ON SOMETHING, PRESIDENT?
SURE.
ABOVE OR BELOW? WHICH DO YOU PREFER?
HEAVEN
HELL
WHY THOSE TWO OPTIONS!?

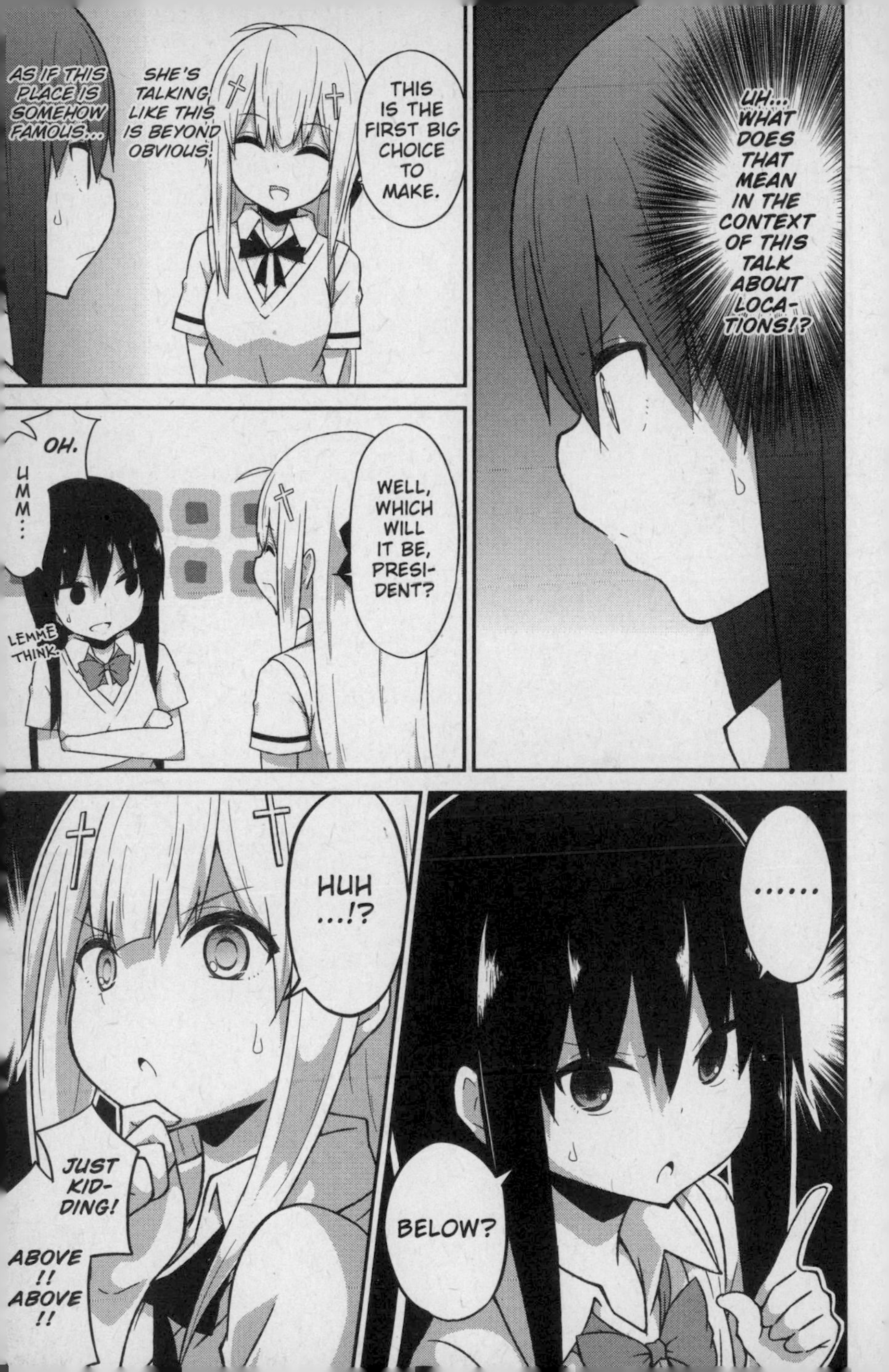
UH... WHAT DOES THAT MEAN IN THE CONTEXT OF THIS TALK ABOUT LOCATIONS!?
THIS IS THE FIRST BIG CHOICE TO MAKE.
SHE'S TALKING LIKE THIS IS BEYOND OBVIOUS!
AS IF THIS PLACE IS SOMEHOW FAMOUS...
WELL, WHICH WILL IT BE, PRESIDENT?
OH.
UMM...
LEMME THINK.
......
BELOW?
HUH ...!?
JUST KIDDING!
ABOVE!! ABOVE!!

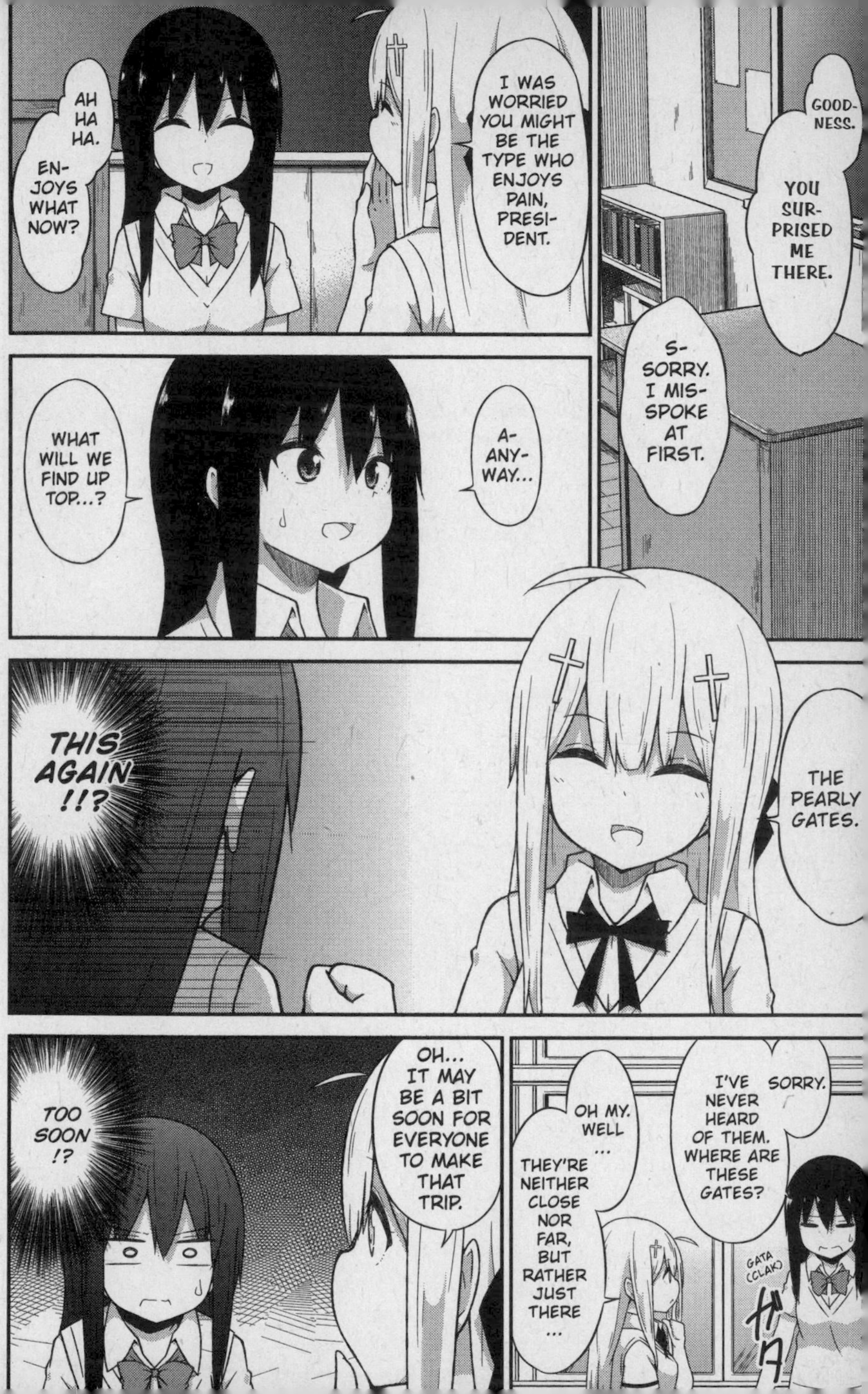
GOODNESS.
YOU SURPRISED ME THERE.
S-SORRY. I MISSPOKE AT FIRST.
I WAS WORRIED YOU MIGHT BE THE TYPE WHO ENJOYS PAIN, PRESIDENT.
AH HA HA. ENJOYS WHAT NOW?
A-ANYWAY...
WHAT WILL WE FIND UP TOP...?
THE PEARLY GATES.
THIS AGAIN!!?
SORRY.
I'VE NEVER HEARD OF THEM. WHERE ARE THESE GATES?
OH MY. WELL...
THEY'RE NEITHER CLOSE NOR FAR, BUT RATHER JUST THERE...
GATA (CLAK)
OH... IT MAY BE A BIT SOON FOR EVERYONE TO MAKE THAT TRIP.
TOO SOON!?

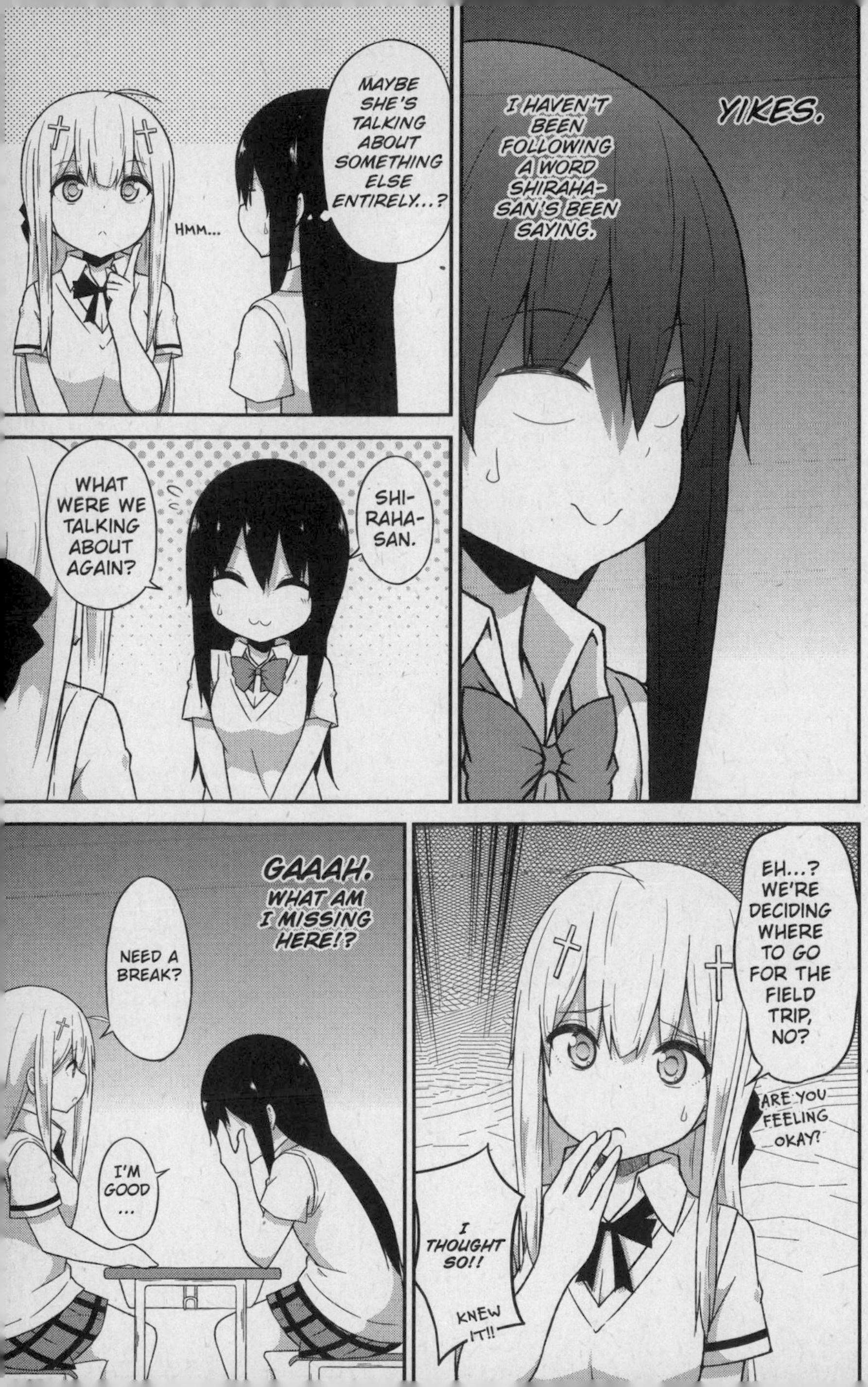
YIKES.
I HAVEN'T BEEN FOLLOWING A WORD SHIRAHA-SAN'S BEEN SAYING.
MAYBE SHE'S TALKING ABOUT SOMETHING ELSE ENTIRELY...?
HMM...
SHI-RAHA-SAN.
WHAT WERE WE TALKING ABOUT AGAIN?
EH...? WE'RE DECIDING WHERE TO GO FOR THE FIELD TRIP, NO?
ARE YOU FEELING OKAY?
I THOUGHT SO!!
KNEW IT!!
GAAAH. WHAT AM I MISSING HERE!?
NEED A BREAK?
I'M GOOD ...

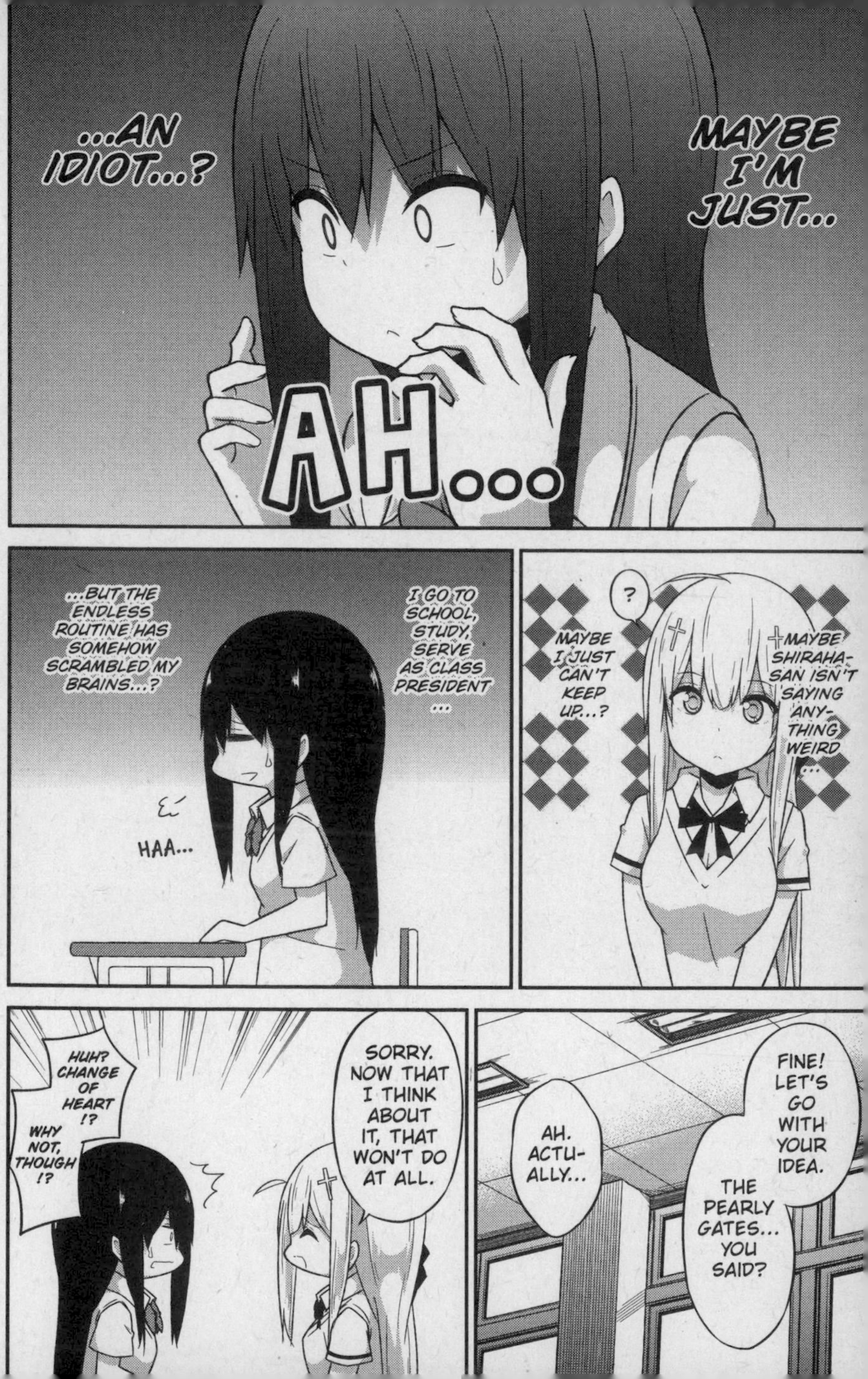
MAYBE I'M JUST...
...AN IDIOT...?
AH...
?
MAYBE SHIRAHA-SAN ISN'T SAYING ANYTHING WEIRD...
MAYBE I JUST CAN'T KEEP UP...?
I GO TO SCHOOL, STUDY, SERVE AS CLASS PRESIDENT...
...BUT THE ENDLESS ROUTINE HAS SOMEHOW SCRAMBLED MY BRAINS...?
HAA...
FINE! LET'S GO WITH YOUR IDEA.
THE PEARLY GATES... YOU SAID?
AH. ACTUALLY...
SORRY. NOW THAT I THINK ABOUT IT, THAT WON'T DO AT ALL.
HUH? CHANGE OF HEART!?
WHY NOT, THOUGH!?

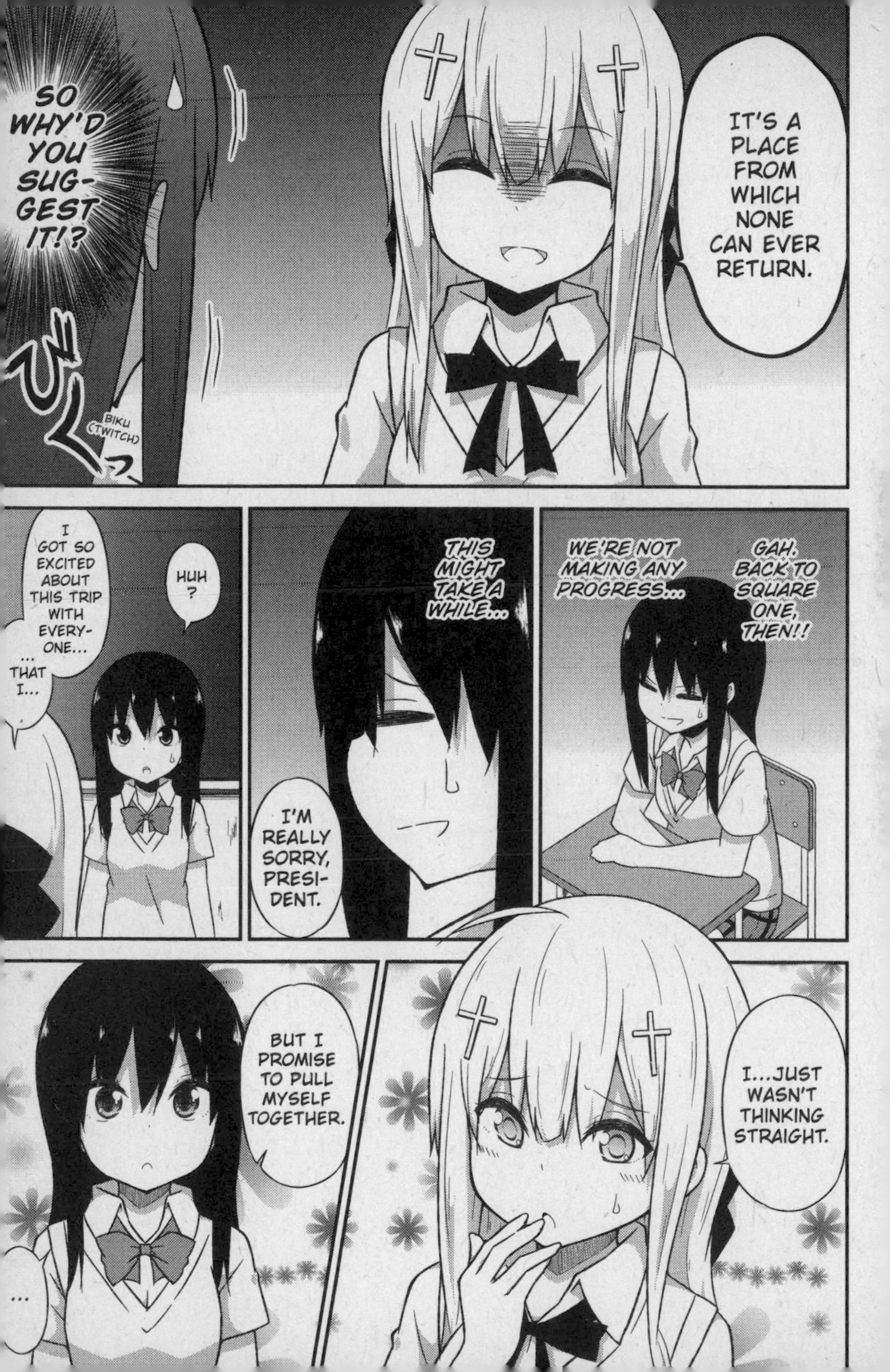
IT'S A PLACE FROM WHICH NONE CAN EVER RETURN.
SO WHY'D YOU SUG-GEST IT!?
BIKU (TWITCH)
GAH. BACK TO SQUARE ONE, THEN!!
WE'RE NOT MAKING ANY PROGRESS...
THIS MIGHT TAKE A WHILE...
I'M REALLY SORRY, PRESI-DENT.
HUH ?
I GOT SO EXCITED ABOUT THIS TRIP WITH EVERY-ONE... ...THAT I...
I...JUST WASN'T THINKING STRAIGHT.
BUT I PROMISE TO PULL MYSELF TOGETHER.
...

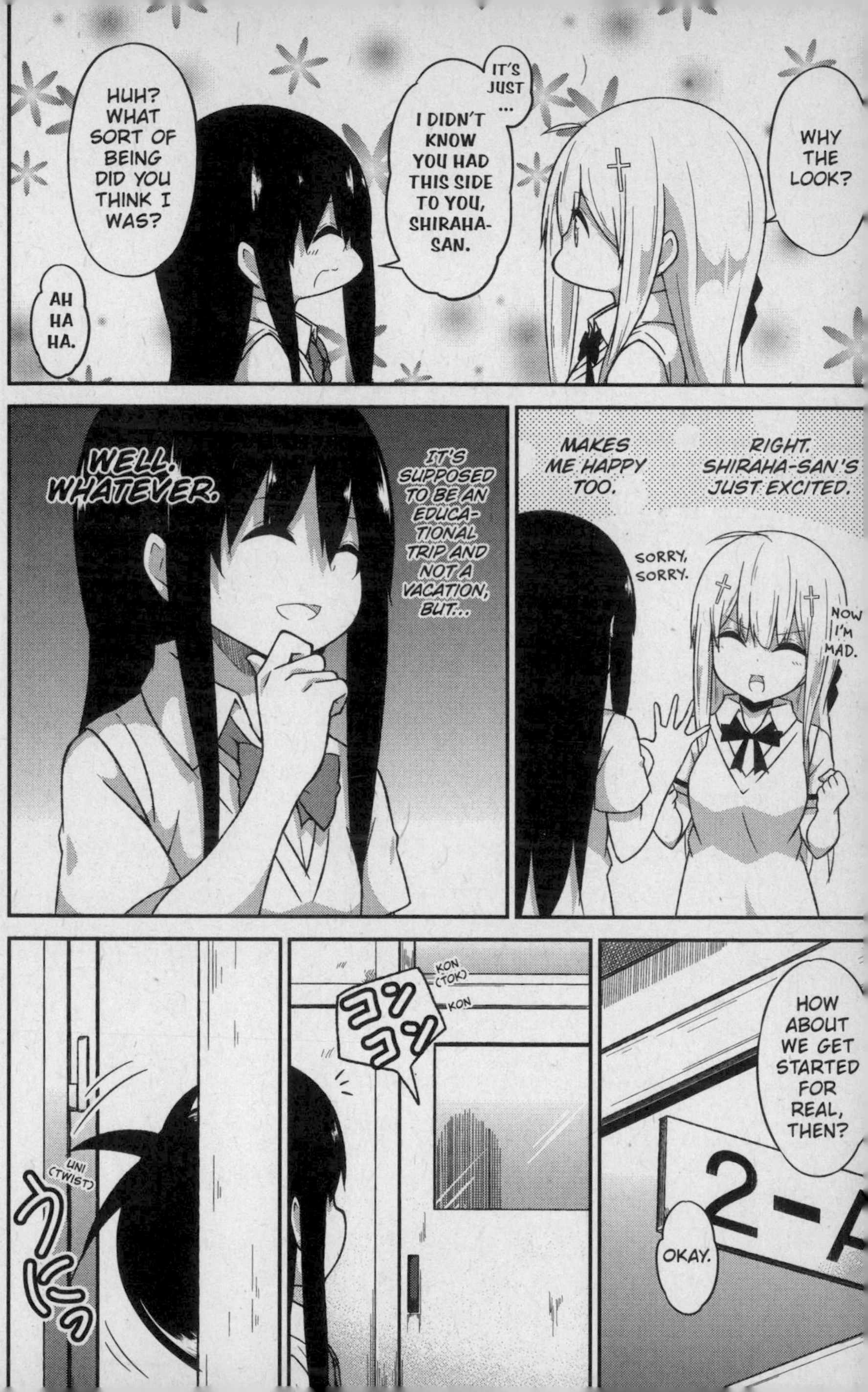
WHY THE LOOK?
IT'S JUST ... I DIDN'T KNOW YOU HAD THIS SIDE TO YOU, SHIRAHA-SAN.
HUH? WHAT SORT OF BEING DID YOU THINK I WAS?
AH HA HA.
RIGHT. SHIRAHA-SAN'S JUST EXCITED.
MAKES ME HAPPY TOO.
NOW I'M MAD.
SORRY, SORRY.
IT'S SUPPOSED TO BE AN EDUCATIONAL TRIP AND NOT A VACATION, BUT...
WELL. WHATEVER.
HOW ABOUT WE GET STARTED FOR REAL, THEN?
2-A
OKAY.
KON (TOK)
KON
UNI (TWIST)

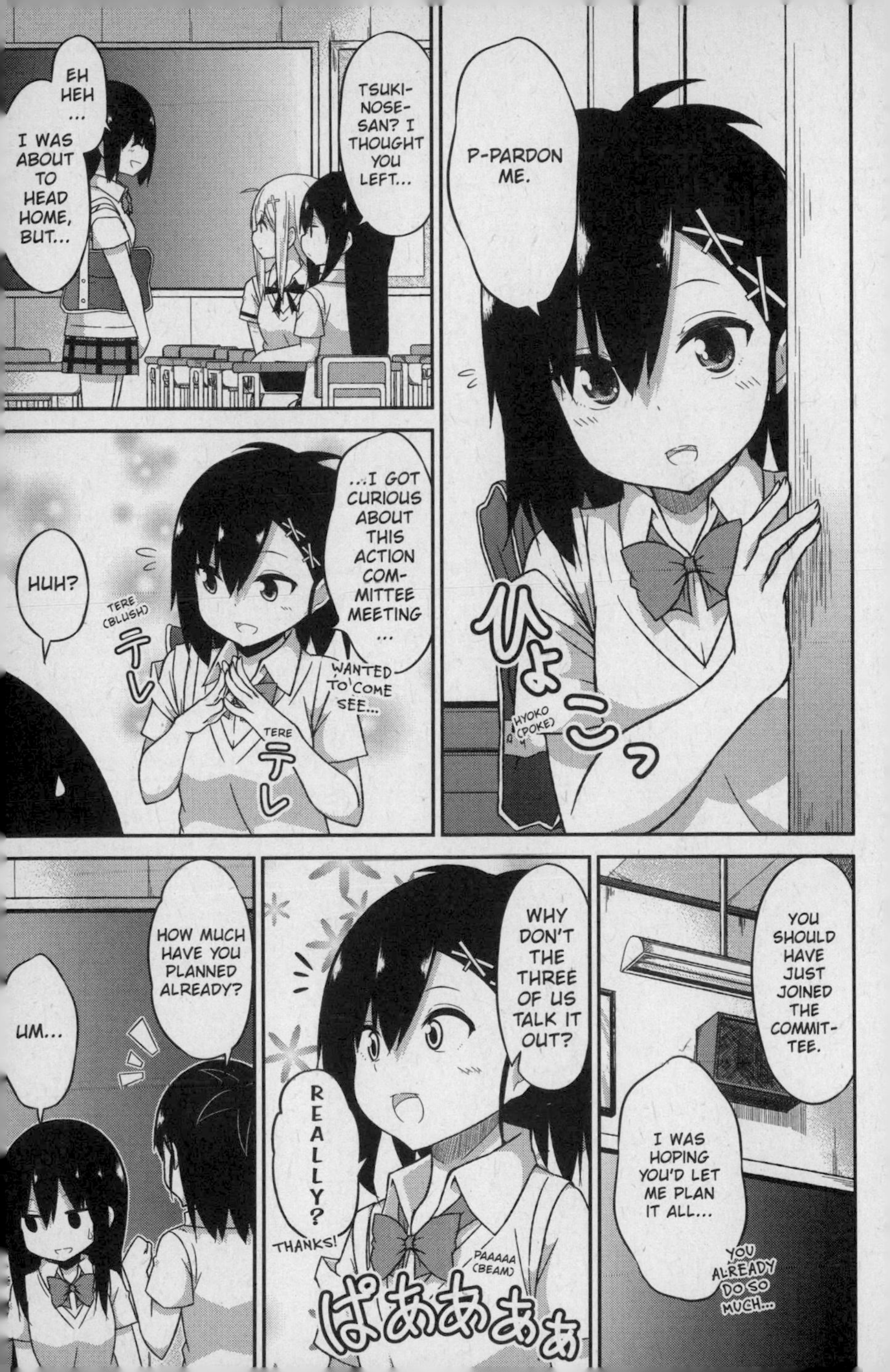
P-PARDON ME.
ひょこっ
HYOKO (POKE)
TSUKI-NOSE-SAN? I THOUGHT YOU LEFT...
EH HEH... I WAS ABOUT TO HEAD HOME, BUT...
...I GOT CURIOUS ABOUT THIS ACTION COM-MITTEE MEETING...
WANTED TO COME SEE...
TERE (BLUSH)
テレ
TERE
テレ
HUH?
YOU SHOULD HAVE JUST JOINED THE COMMIT-TEE.
I WAS HOPING YOU'D LET ME PLAN IT ALL...
YOU ALREADY DO SO MUCH...
WHY DON'T THE THREE OF US TALK IT OUT?
REALLY?
THANKS!
PAAAAA (BEAM)
ぱああああ
HOW MUCH HAVE YOU PLANNED ALREADY?
UM...

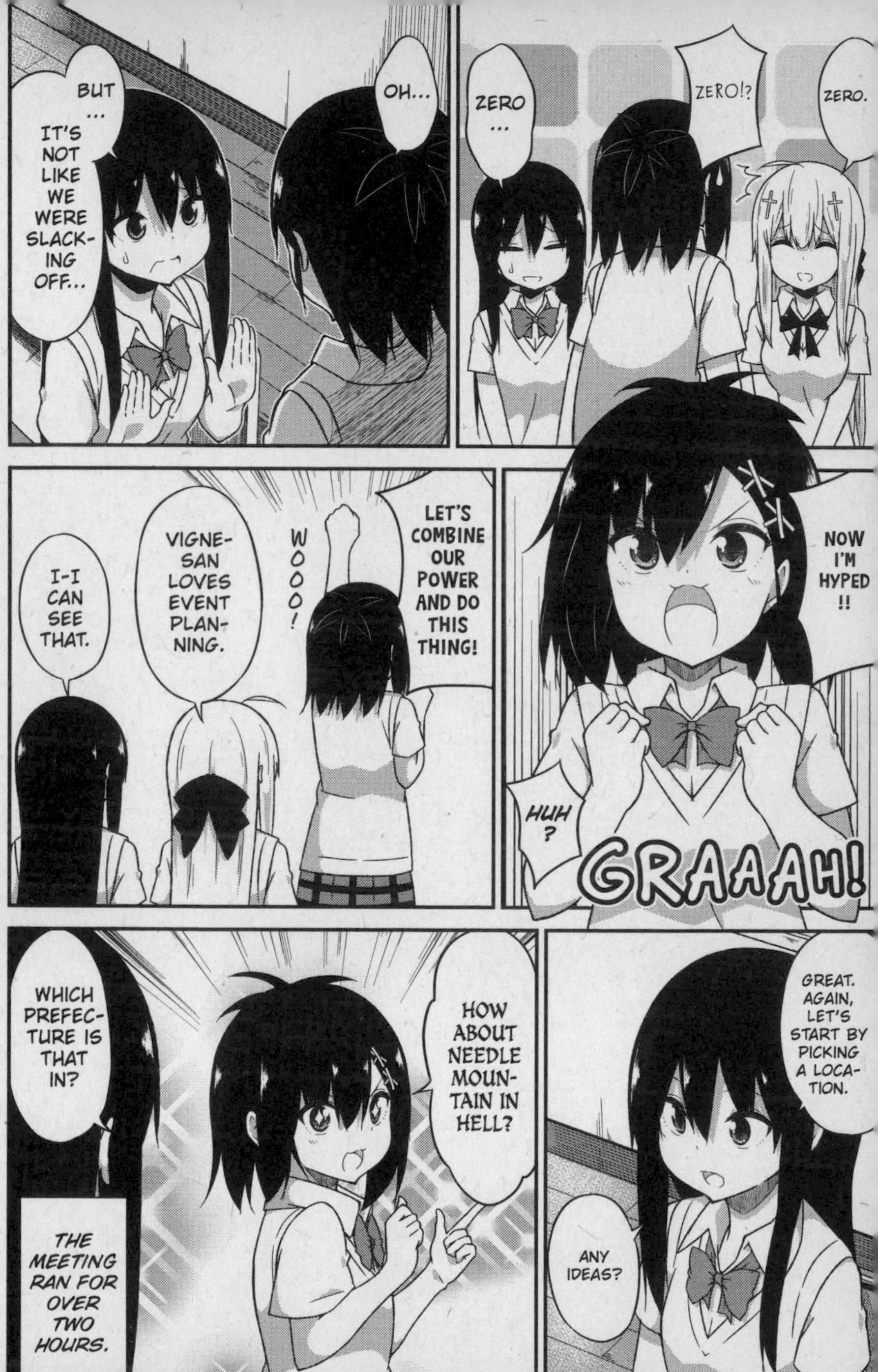
ZERO.
ZERO!?
ZERO ...
OH...
BUT ... IT'S NOT LIKE WE WERE SLACKING OFF...
NOW I'M HYPED !!
GRAAAH!
HUH ?
LET'S COMBINE OUR POWER AND DO THIS THING!
WOOOO!
VIGNE-SAN LOVES EVENT PLANNING.
I-I CAN SEE THAT.
GREAT. AGAIN, LET'S START BY PICKING A LOCATION.
ANY IDEAS?
HOW ABOUT NEEDLE MOUNTAIN IN HELL?
WHICH PREFECTURE IS THAT IN?
THE MEETING RAN FOR OVER TWO HOURS.

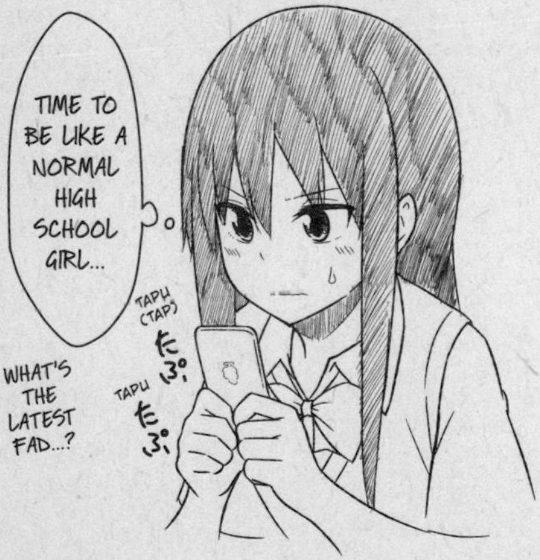
TIME TO BE LIKE A NORMAL HIGH SCHOOL GIRL...
TAPU (TAP) たぷ
TAPU たぷ
WHAT'S THE LATEST FAD...?

Gabriel DropOut

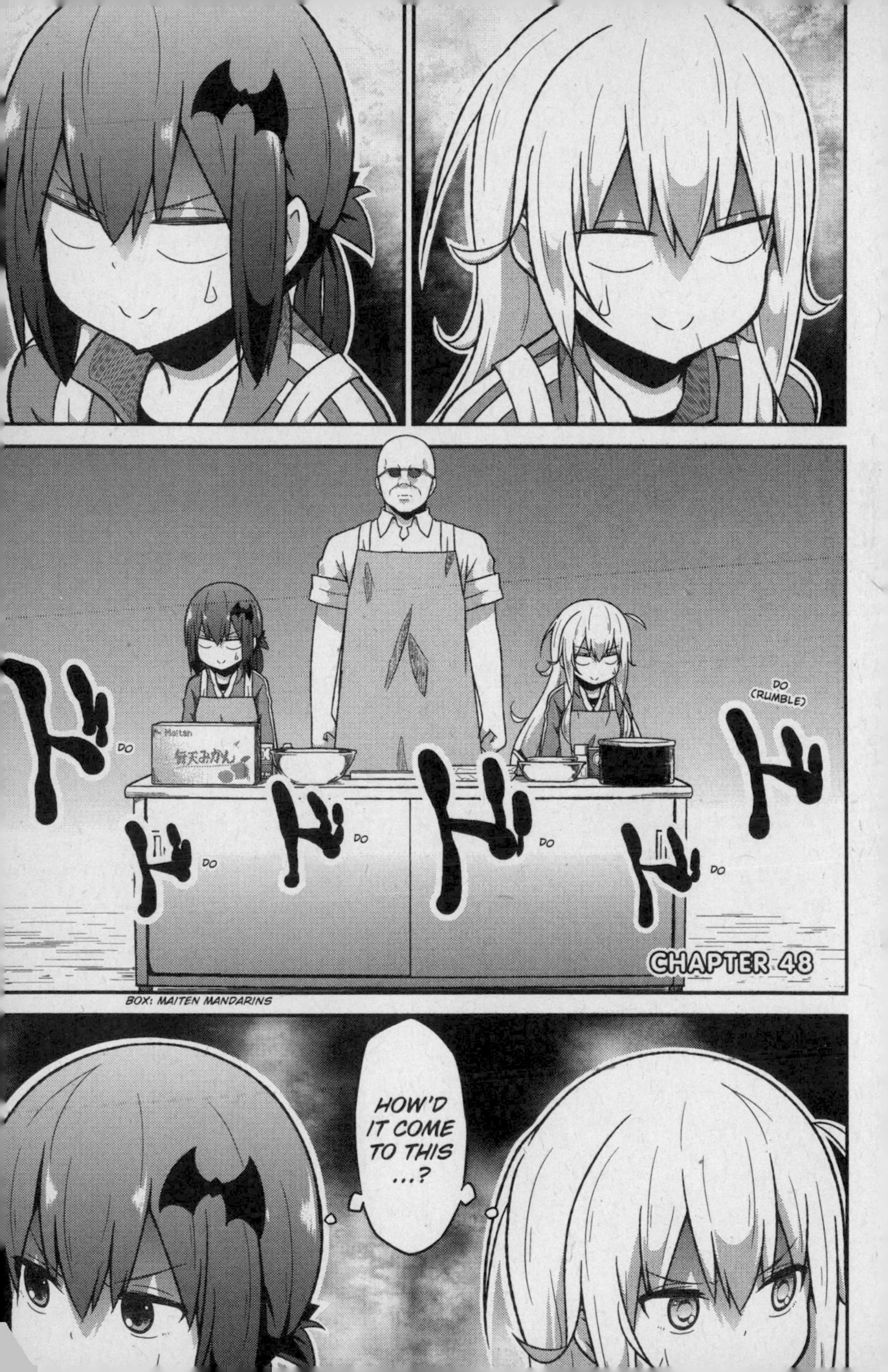
DO
(RUMBLE)
DO
DO
DO
DO
DO
Maiten
CHAPTER 48
HOW'D IT COME TO THIS ...?
BOX: MAITEN MANDARINS

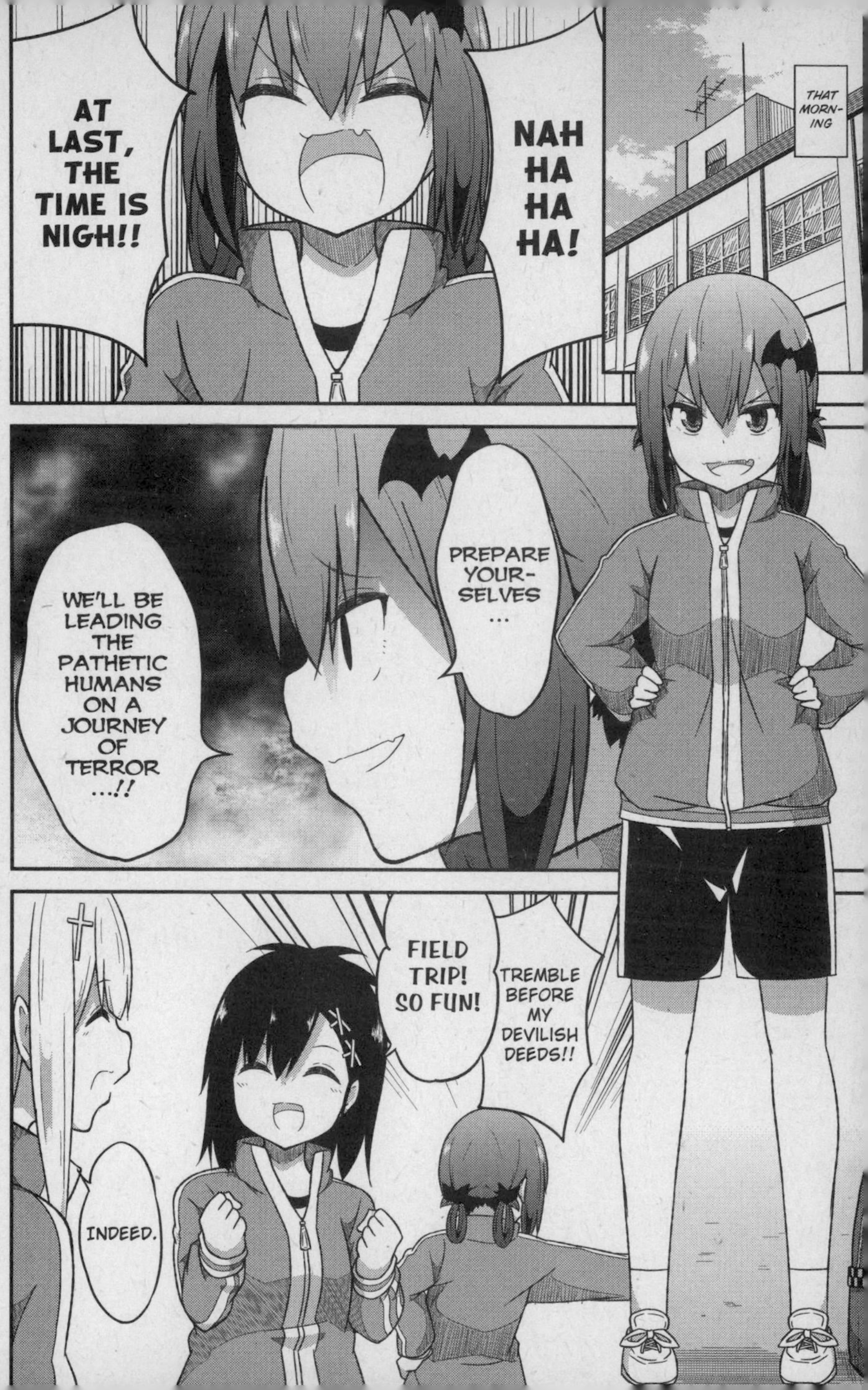
THAT MORNING
NAH HA HA HA!
AT LAST, THE TIME IS NIGH!!
PREPARE YOURSELVES...
WE'LL BE LEADING THE PATHETIC HUMANS ON A JOURNEY OF TERROR...!!
TREMBLE BEFORE MY DEVILISH DEEDS!!
FIELD TRIP! SO FUN!
INDEED.

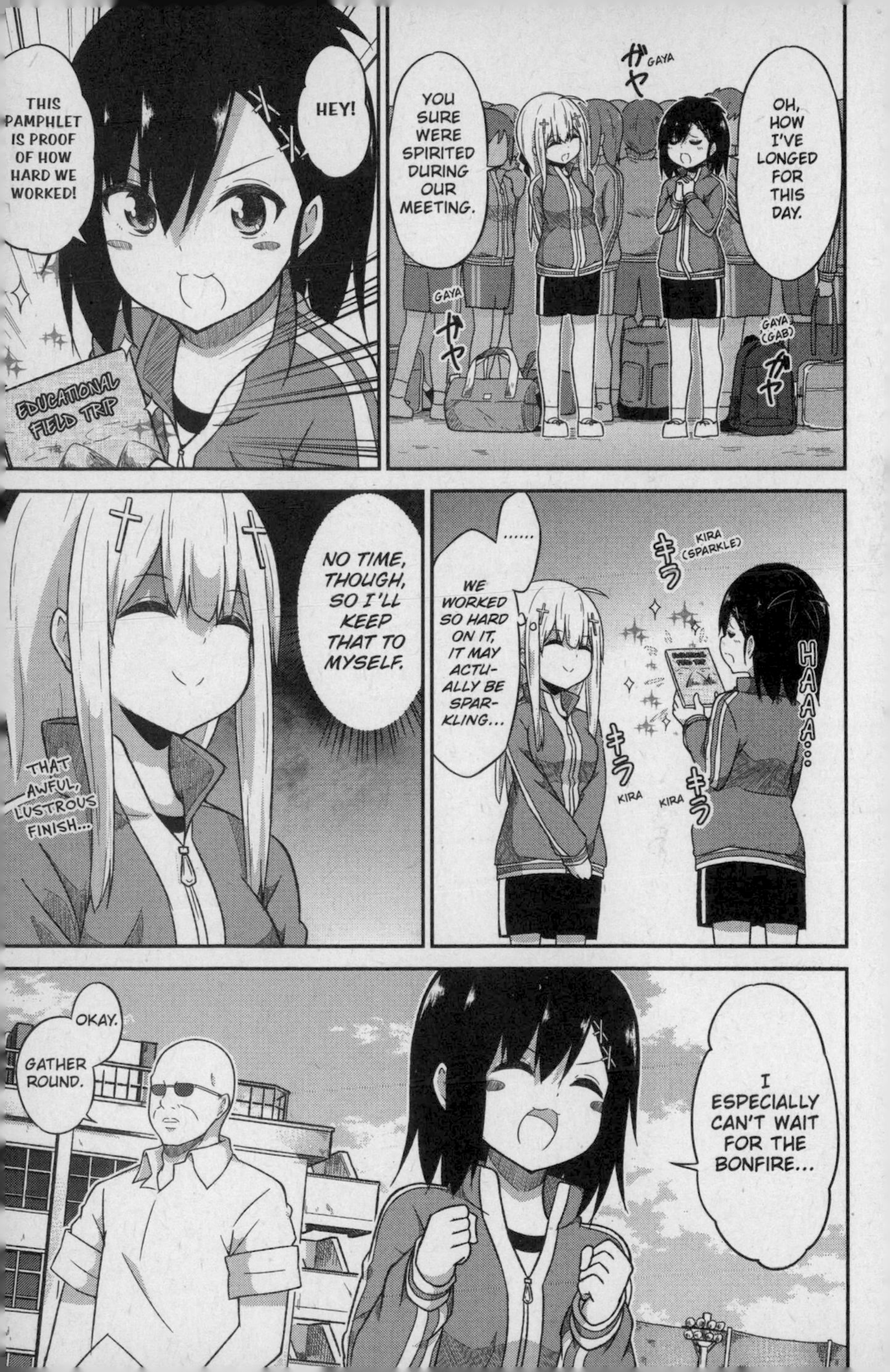
GAYA
OH, HOW I'VE LONGED FOR THIS DAY.
YOU SURE WERE SPIRITED DURING OUR MEETING.
GAYA
GAYA (GAB)
HEY!
THIS PAMPHLET IS PROOF OF HOW HARD WE WORKED!
EDUCATIONAL FIELD TRIP
KIRA (SPARKLE)
HAAAA...
KIRA
KIRA
......
WE WORKED SO HARD ON IT, IT MAY ACTU-ALLY BE SPAR-KLING...
NO TIME, THOUGH, SO I'LL KEEP THAT TO MYSELF.
THAT AWFUL, LUSTROUS FINISH...
I ESPECIALLY CAN'T WAIT FOR THE BONFIRE...
OKAY.
GATHER ROUND.

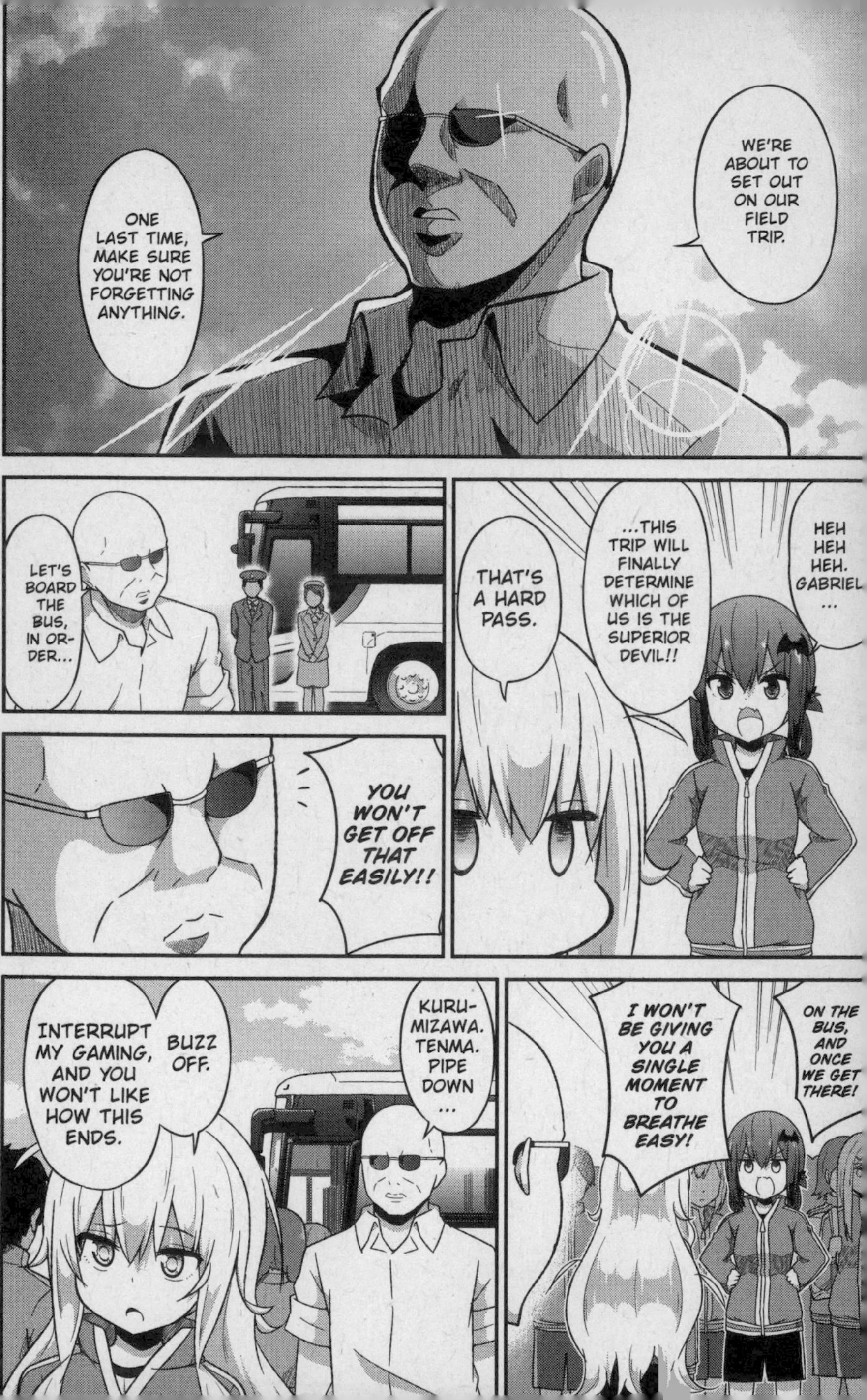
WE'RE ABOUT TO SET OUT ON OUR FIELD TRIP.
ONE LAST TIME, MAKE SURE YOU'RE NOT FORGETTING ANYTHING.
HEH HEH HEH. GABRIEL...
...THIS TRIP WILL FINALLY DETERMINE WHICH OF US IS THE SUPERIOR DEVIL!!
THAT'S A HARD PASS.
LET'S BOARD THE BUS, IN ORDER...
YOU WON'T GET OFF THAT EASILY!!
ON THE BUS, AND ONCE WE GET THERE!
I WON'T BE GIVING YOU A SINGLE MOMENT TO BREATHE EASY!
KURUMIZAWA. TENMA. PIPE DOWN...
BUZZ OFF.
INTERRUPT MY GAMING, AND YOU WON'T LIKE HOW THIS ENDS.

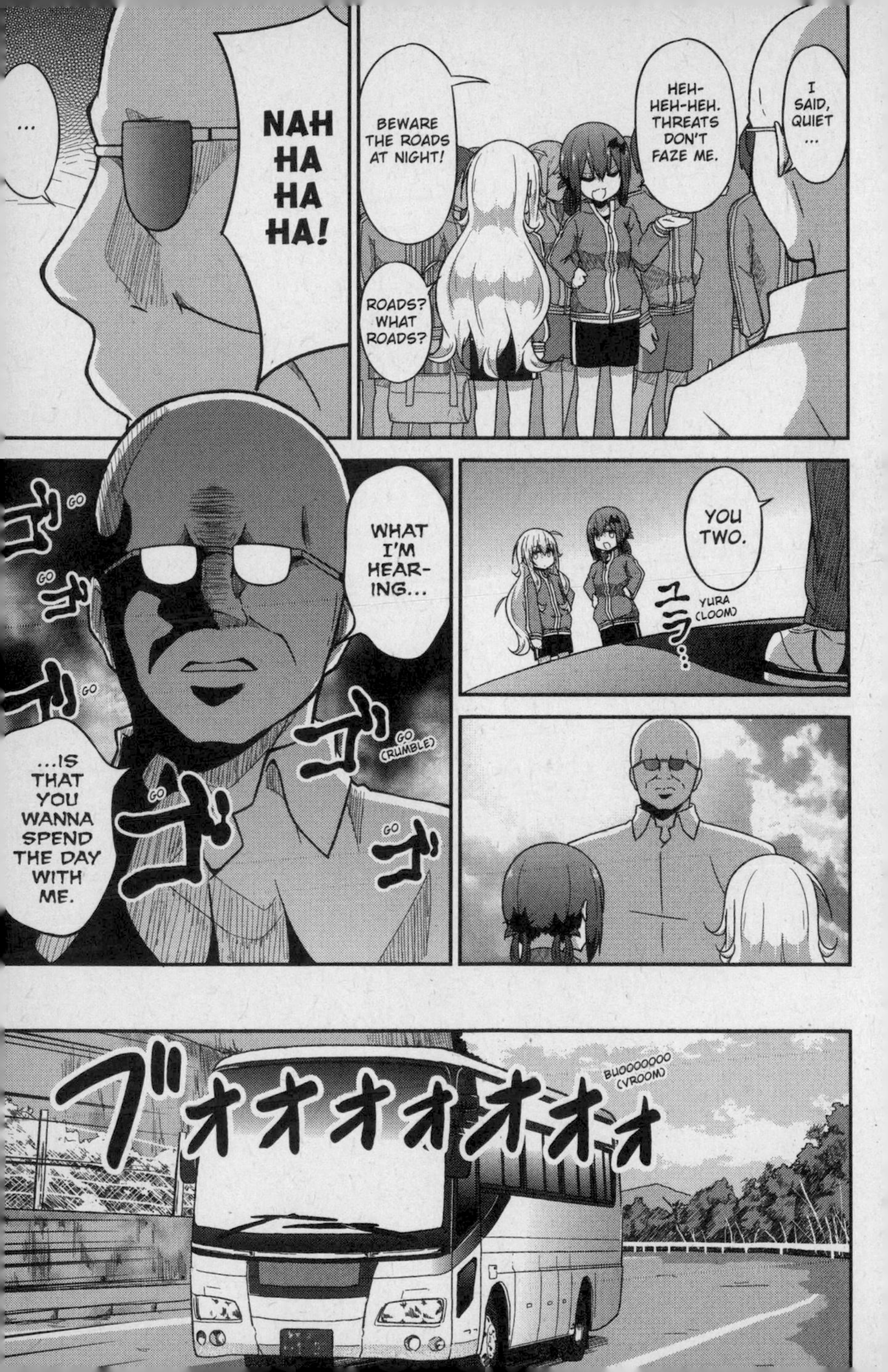
I SAID, QUIET ...
HEH-HEH-HEH. THREATS DON'T FAZE ME.
BEWARE THE ROADS AT NIGHT!
ROADS? WHAT ROADS?
NAH HA HA HA!
...
YOU TWO.
ユラ
YURA (LOOM)
WHAT I'M HEARING...
ゴゴゴ
GO GO GO
ゴゴゴ
GO (RUMBLE) GO GO
...IS THAT YOU WANNA SPEND THE DAY WITH ME.
ブオオオオオオオ
BUOOOOOOO (VROOM)

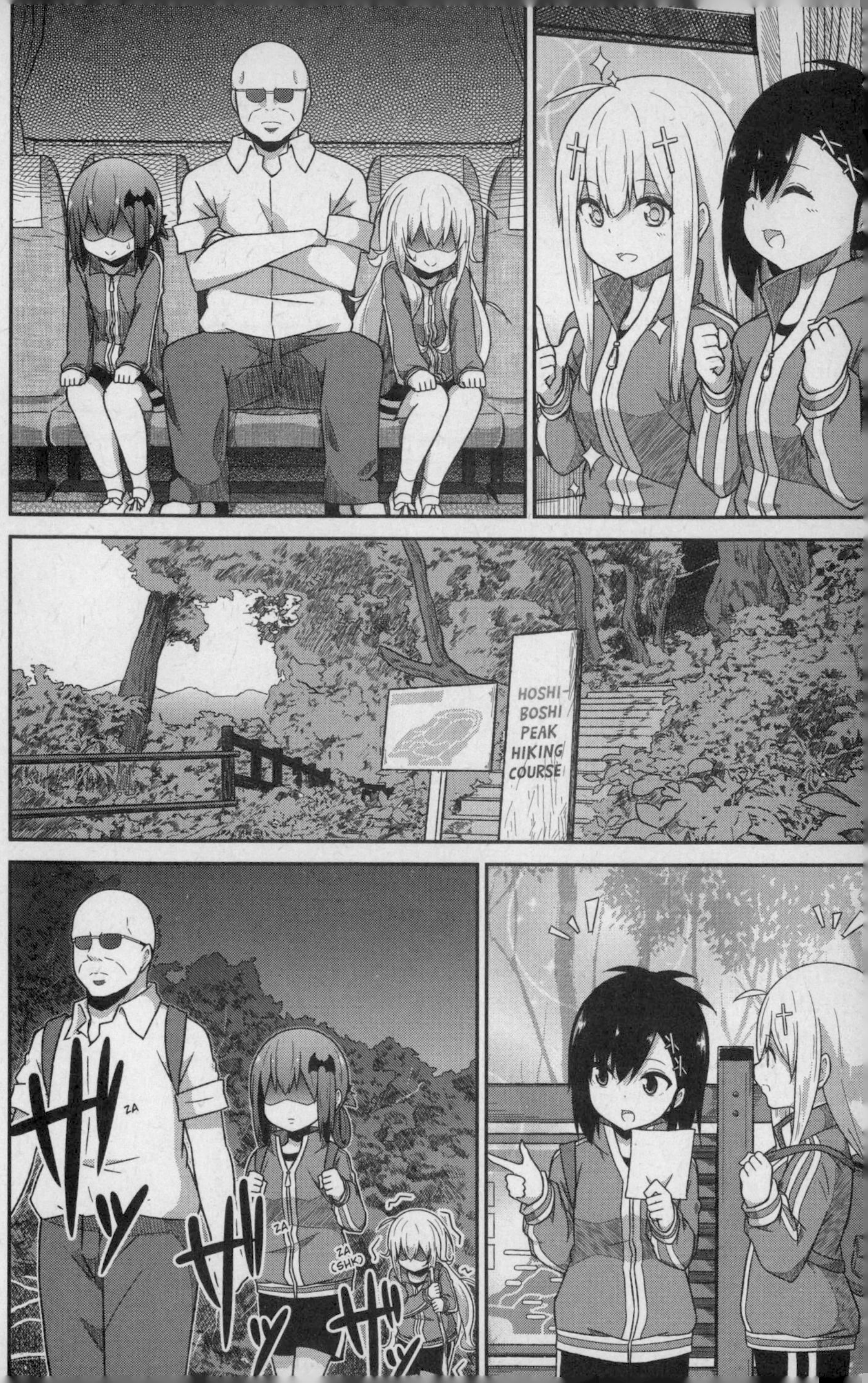
HOSHI-BOSHI PEAK HIKING COURSE
ZA
ザッ
ZA
ザッ
ZA (SHK)
ザッ

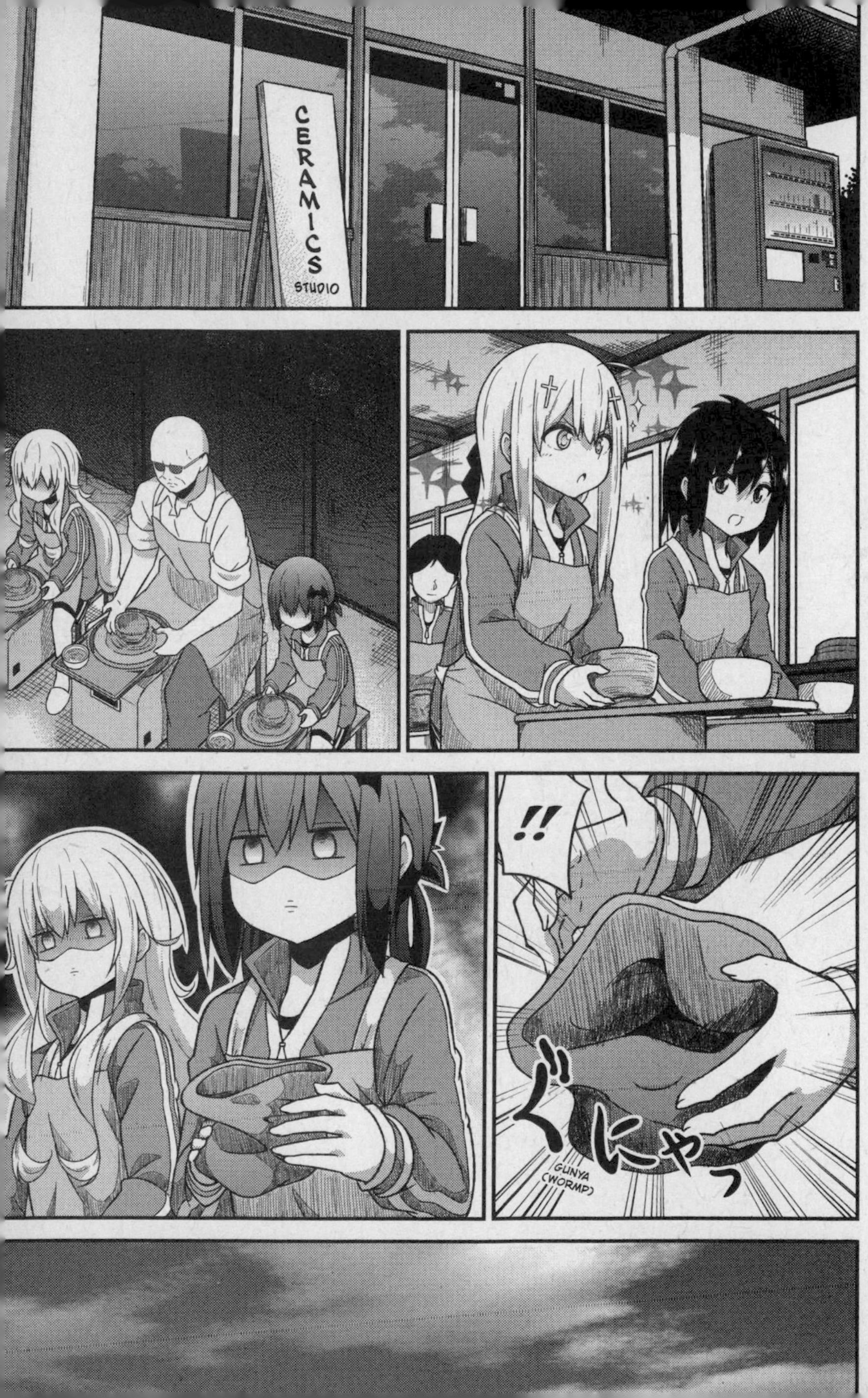
CERAMICS
STUDIO
!!
ぐにゃっ
GUNYA
(WORMP)

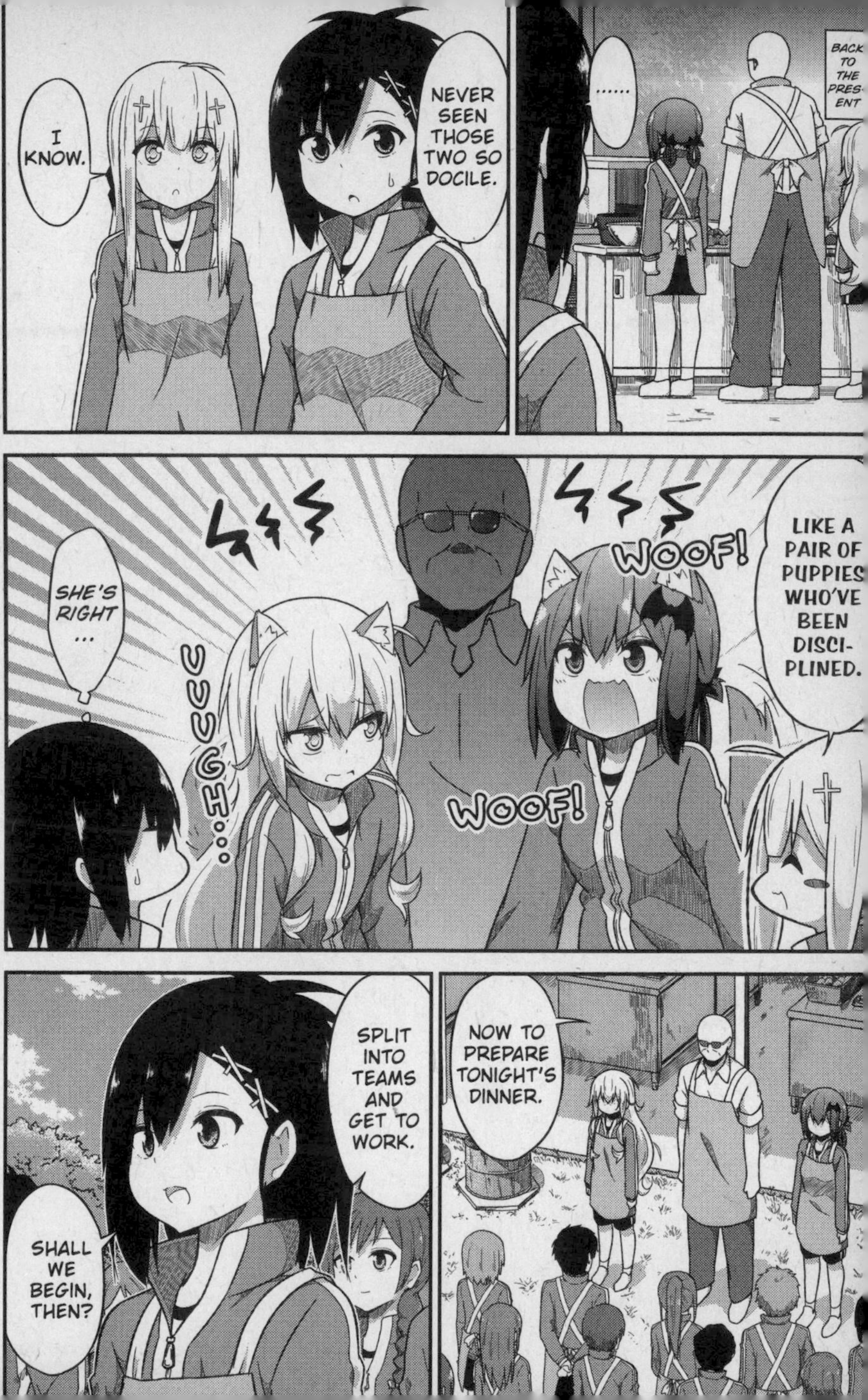
BACK TO THE PRESENT
......
NEVER SEEN THOSE TWO SO DOCILE.
I KNOW.
LIKE A PAIR OF PUPPIES WHO'VE BEEN DISCI-PLINED.
WOOF!
WOOF!
UUUGH...
SHE'S RIGHT ...
NOW TO PREPARE TONIGHT'S DINNER.
SPLIT INTO TEAMS AND GET TO WORK.
SHALL WE BEGIN, THEN?

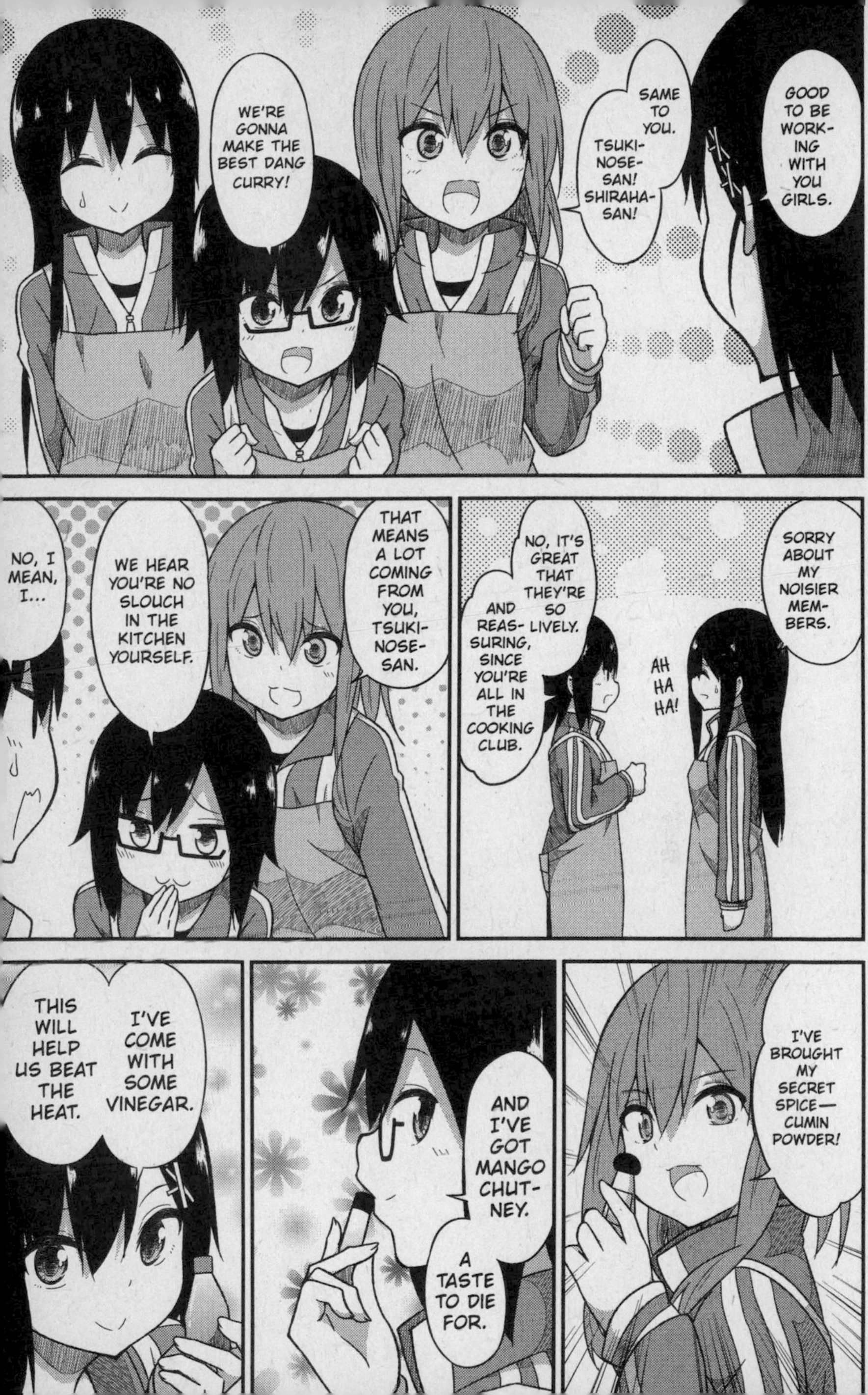
GOOD TO BE WORKING WITH YOU GIRLS.
SAME TO YOU. TSUKINOSE-SAN! SHIRAHA-SAN!
WE'RE GONNA MAKE THE BEST DANG CURRY!
SORRY ABOUT MY NOISIER MEMBERS.
AH HA HA!
NO, IT'S GREAT THAT THEY'RE SO LIVELY.
AND REASSURING, SINCE YOU'RE ALL IN THE COOKING CLUB.
THAT MEANS A LOT COMING FROM YOU, TSUKINOSE-SAN.
WE HEAR YOU'RE NO SLOUCH IN THE KITCHEN YOURSELF.
NO, I MEAN, I...
I'VE BROUGHT MY SECRET SPICE—CUMIN POWDER!
AND I'VE GOT MANGO CHUTNEY.
A TASTE TO DIE FOR.
I'VE COME WITH SOME VINEGAR.
THIS WILL HELP US BEAT THE HEAT.

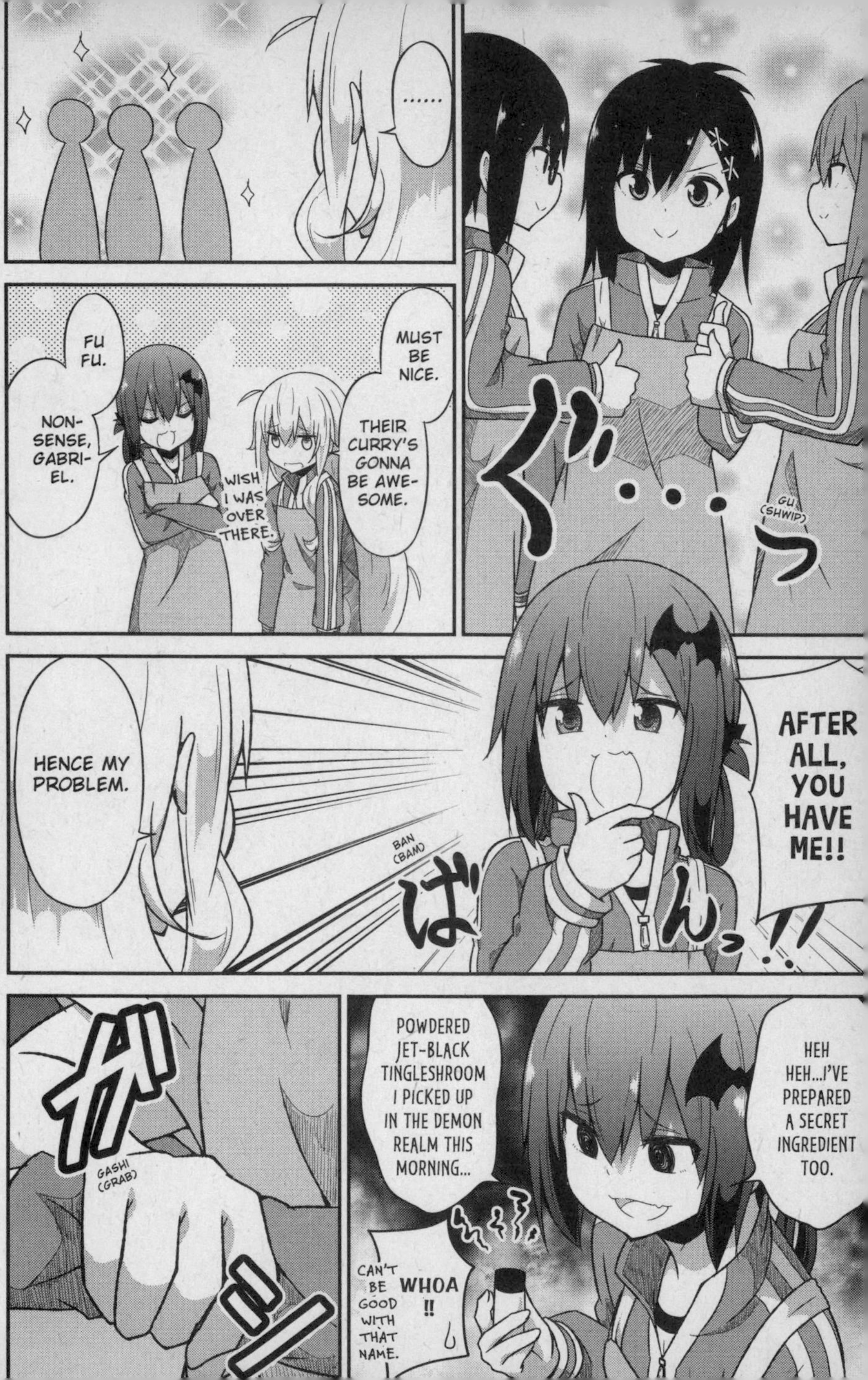
ぐ…っ
GU (SHWIP)
......
MUST BE NICE.
THEIR CURRY'S GONNA BE AWESOME.
WISH I WAS OVER THERE.
FU FU.
NONSENSE, GABRIEL.
AFTER ALL, YOU HAVE ME!!
ばんっ!!
BAN (BAM)
HENCE MY PROBLEM.
HEH HEH...I'VE PREPARED A SECRET INGREDIENT TOO.
POWDERED JET-BLACK TINGLESHROOM I PICKED UP IN THE DEMON REALM THIS MORNING...
WHOA!!
CAN'T BE GOOD WITH THAT NAME.
ガシ
GASHI (GRAB)

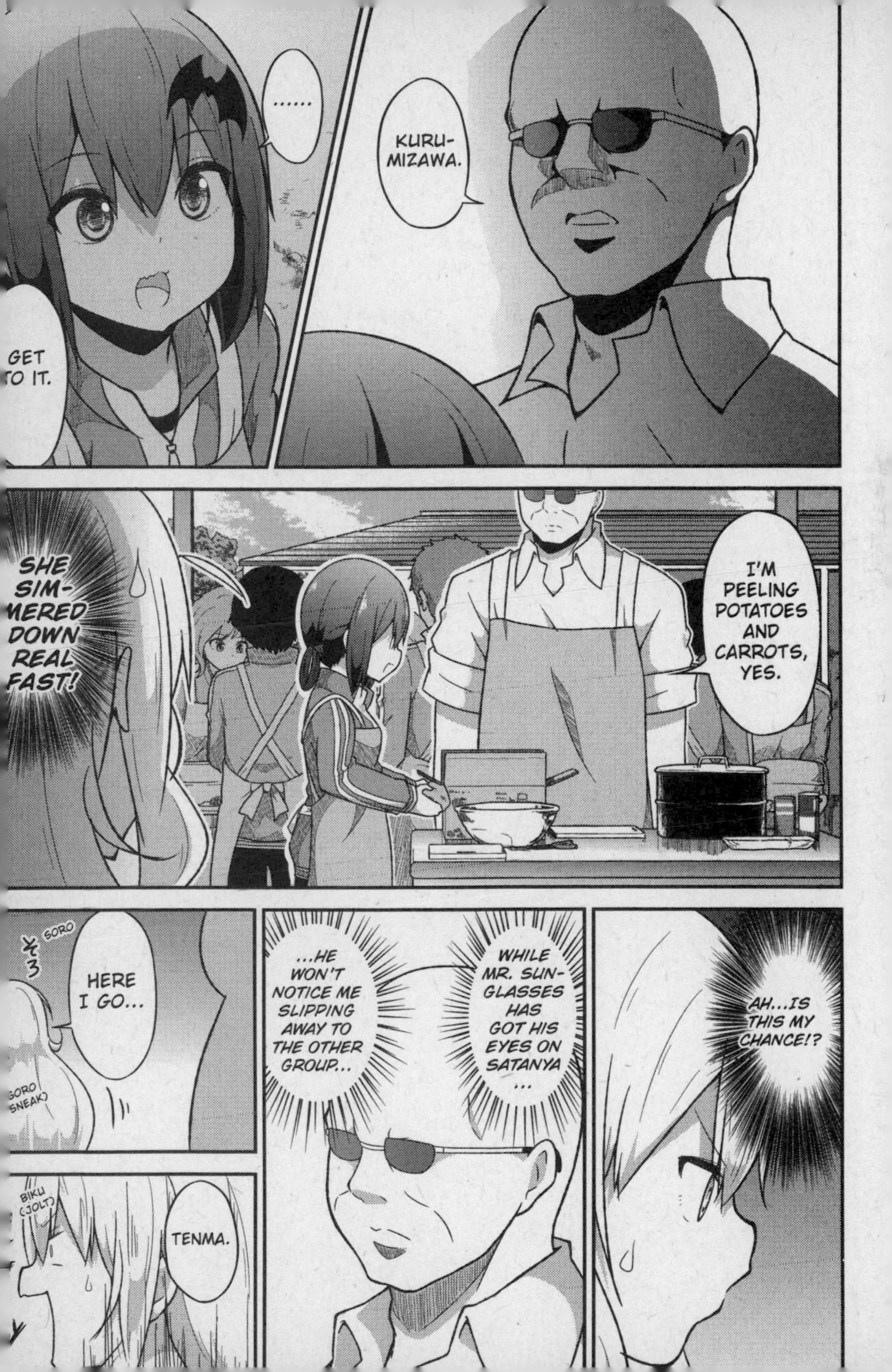
KURU-MIZAWA.
......
GET TO IT.
I'M PEELING POTATOES AND CARROTS, YES.
SHE SIMMERED DOWN REAL FAST!
AH...IS THIS MY CHANCE!?
WHILE MR. SUNGLASSES HAS GOT HIS EYES ON SATANYA...
...HE WON'T NOTICE ME SLIPPING AWAY TO THE OTHER GROUP...
SORO
HERE I GO...
SORO (SNEAK)
BIKU (JOLT)
TENMA.

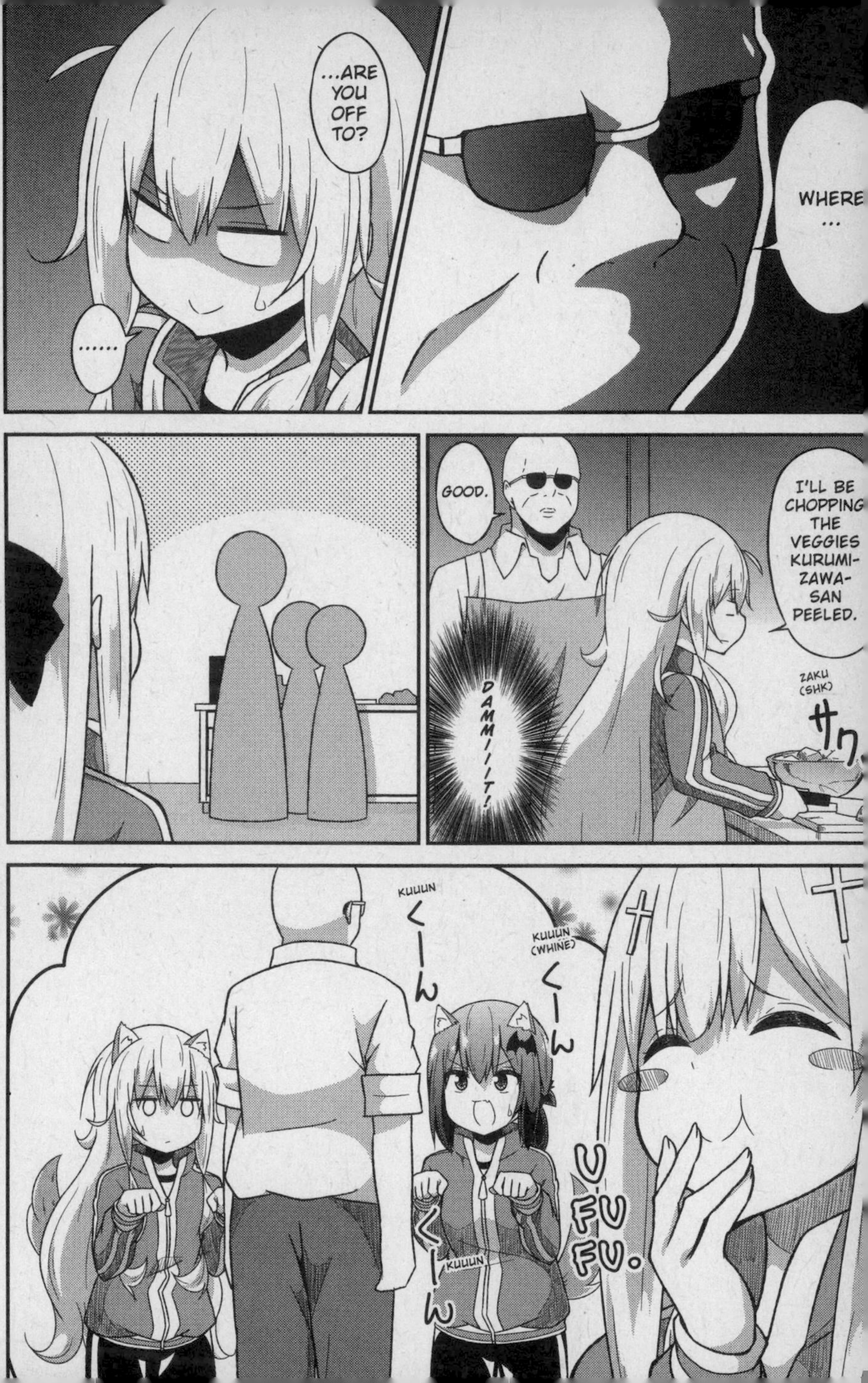
WHERE ...
...ARE YOU OFF TO?
......
I'LL BE CHOPPING THE VEGGIES KURUMIZAWA-SAN PEELED.
ZAKU (SHK)
サク
DAMMIIIT!
GOOD.
U-FU FU FU.
KUUUN (WHINE)
くーん
KUUUN
くーん
KUUUN
くーん

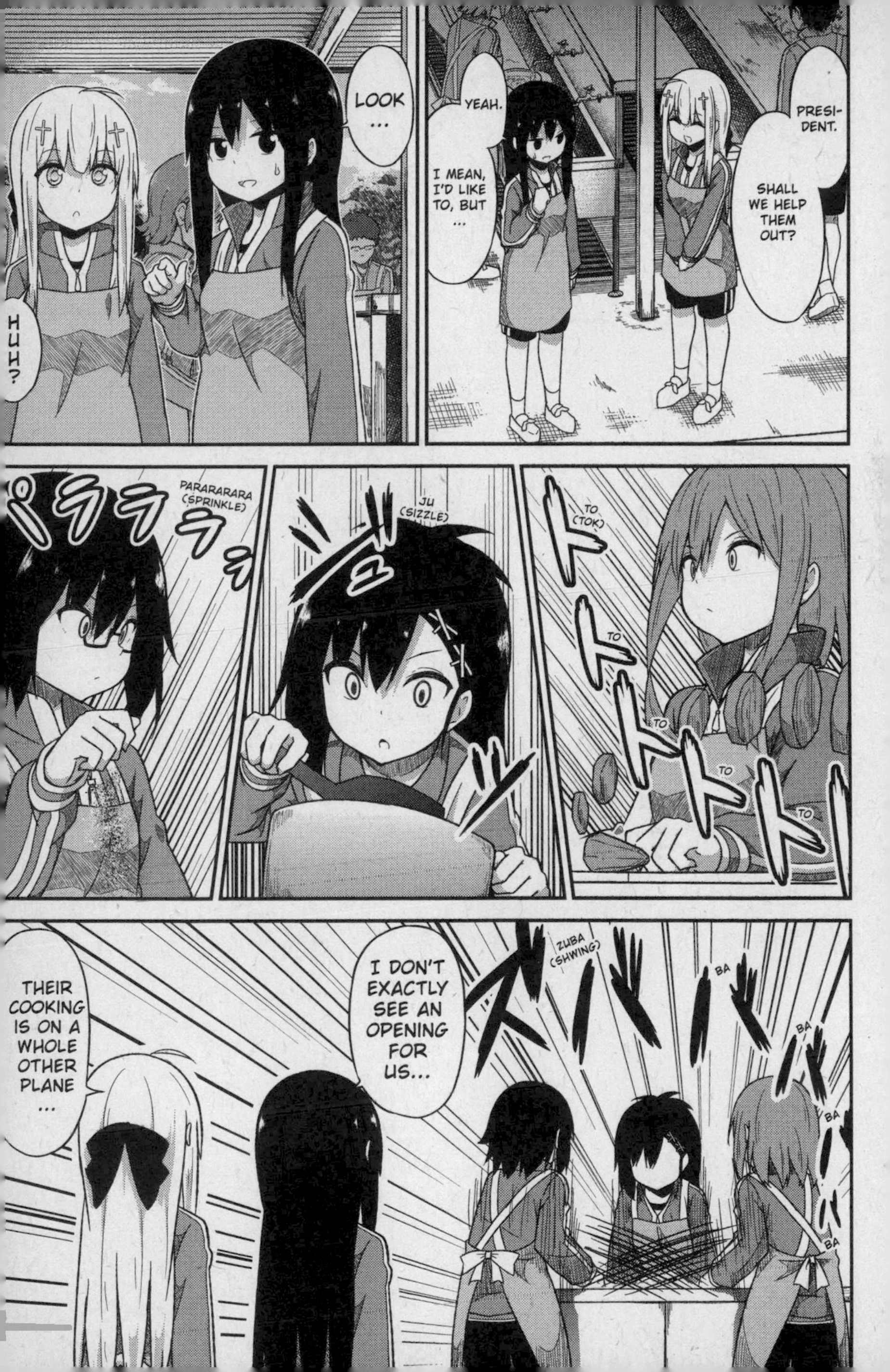
PRESIDENT.
SHALL WE HELP THEM OUT?
YEAH.
I MEAN, I'D LIKE TO, BUT ...
LOOK ...
HUH?
TO (TOK)
TO
TO
TO
TO
JU (SIZZLE)
PARARARARA (SPRINKLE)
ZUBA (SHWING)
BA
BA
BA
BA
I DON'T EXACTLY SEE AN OPENING FOR US...
THEIR COOKING IS ON A WHOLE OTHER PLANE ...

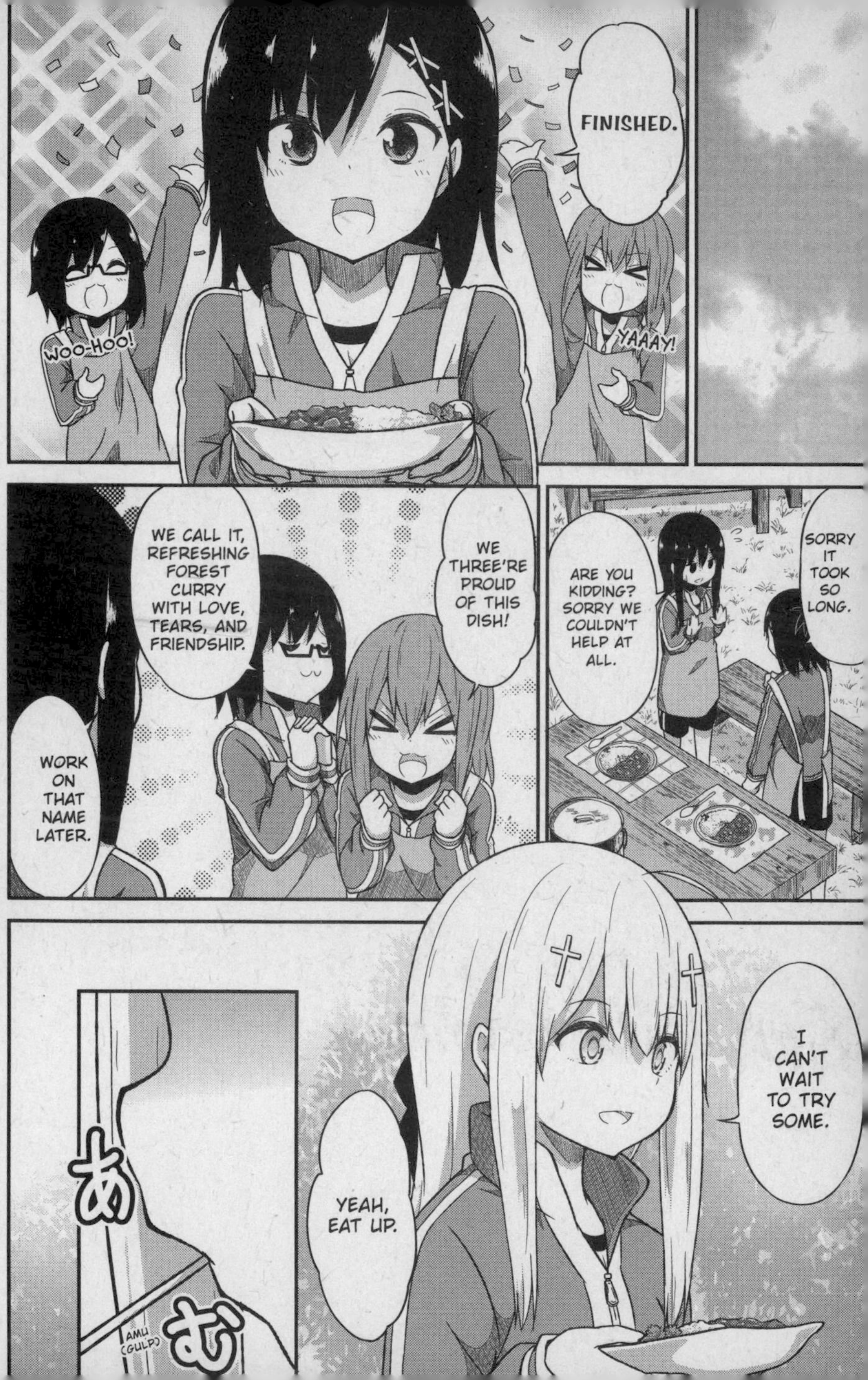
FINISHED.
YAAAY!
WOO-HOO!
SORRY IT TOOK SO LONG.
ARE YOU KIDDING? SORRY WE COULDN'T HELP AT ALL.
WE THREE'RE PROUD OF THIS DISH!
WE CALL IT, REFRESHING FOREST CURRY WITH LOVE, TEARS, AND FRIENDSHIP.
WORK ON THAT NAME LATER.
I CAN'T WAIT TO TRY SOME.
YEAH, EAT UP.
あむ
AMU (GULP)

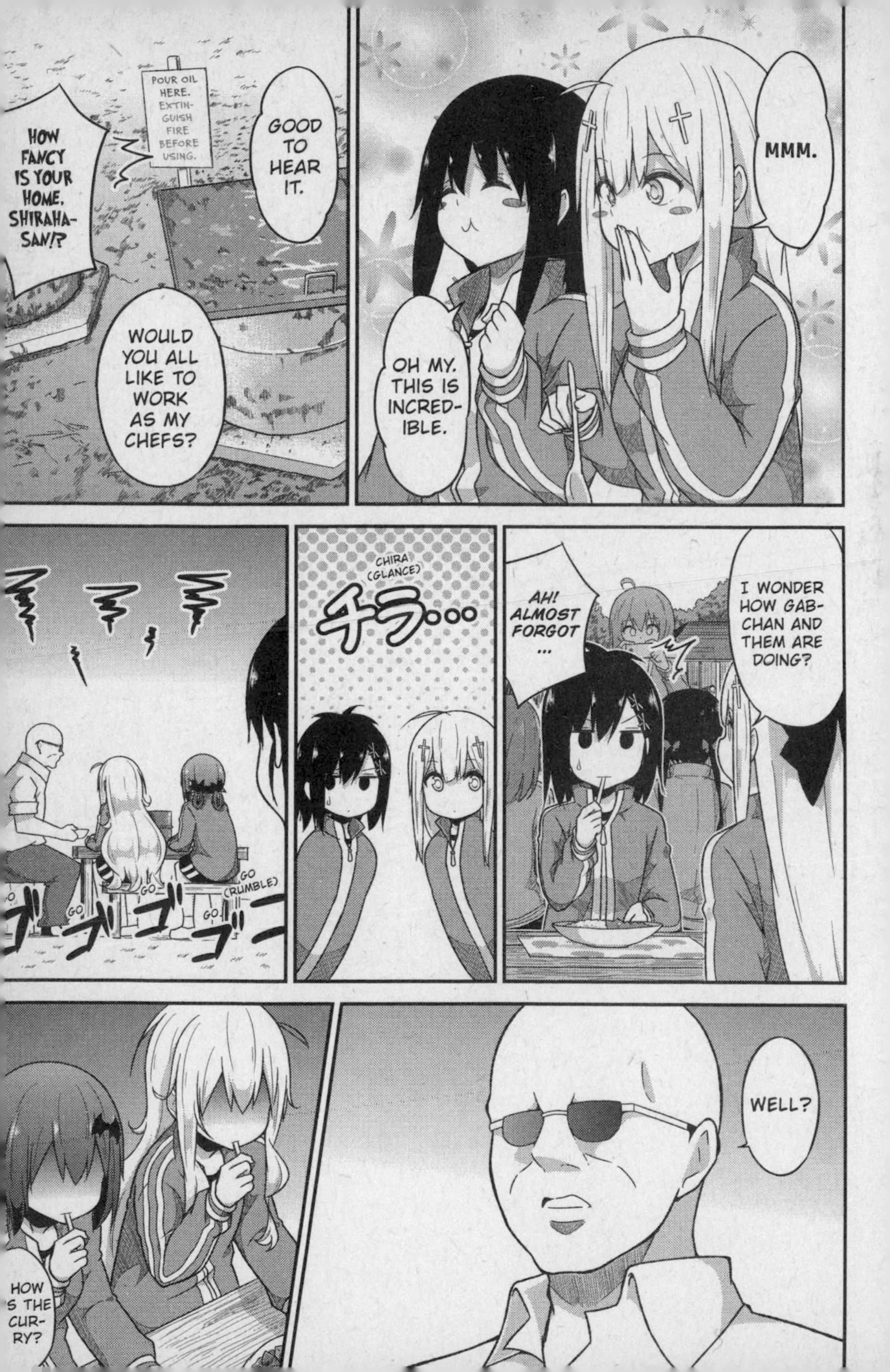
MMM.
OH MY. THIS IS INCRED-IBLE.
GOOD TO HEAR IT.
POUR OIL HERE. EXTIN-GUISH FIRE BEFORE USING.
HOW FANCY IS YOUR HOME, SHIRAHA-SAN!?
WOULD YOU ALL LIKE TO WORK AS MY CHEFS?
I WONDER HOW GAB-CHAN AND THEM ARE DOING?
AH! ALMOST FORGOT ...
CHIRA (GLANCE)
チラ・・・
GO GO (RUMBLE)
GO GO GO
ゴゴゴゴ
WELL?
HOW S THE CUR-RY?

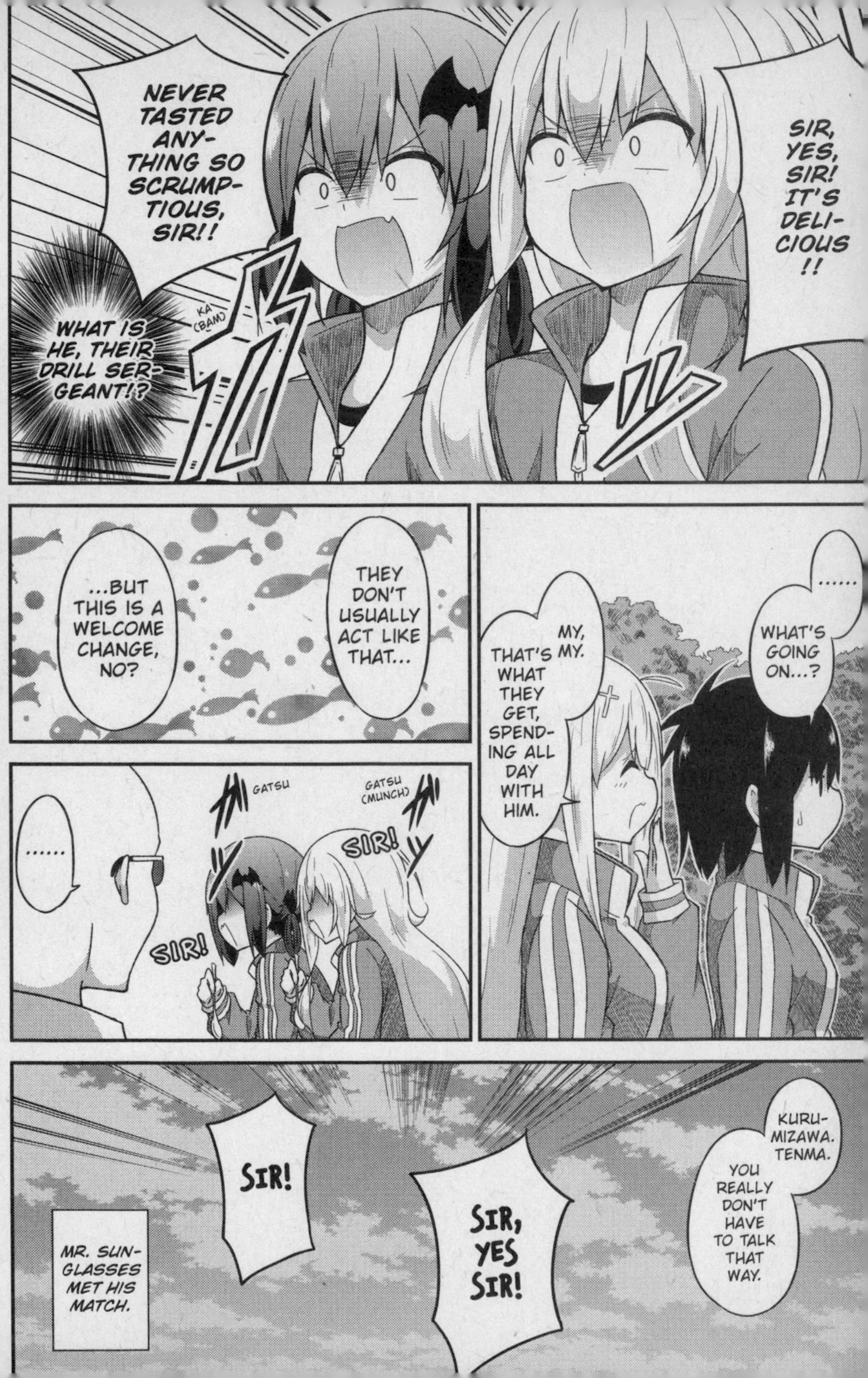
SIR, YES, SIR! IT'S DELICIOUS!!
NEVER TASTED ANYTHING SO SCRUMPTIOUS, SIR!!
KA (BAM)
WHAT IS HE, THEIR DRILL SERGEANT!?
......
WHAT'S GOING ON...?
MY, MY. THAT'S WHAT THEY GET, SPENDING ALL DAY WITH HIM.
THEY DON'T USUALLY ACT LIKE THAT...
...BUT THIS IS A WELCOME CHANGE, NO?
GATSU (MUNCH)
SIR!
GATSU
SIR!
......
KURUMIZAWA. TENMA.
YOU REALLY DON'T HAVE TO TALK THAT WAY.
SIR, YES SIR!
SIR!
MR. SUNGLASSES MET HIS MATCH.

COLONEL SUNGLASSES

Gabriel DropOut

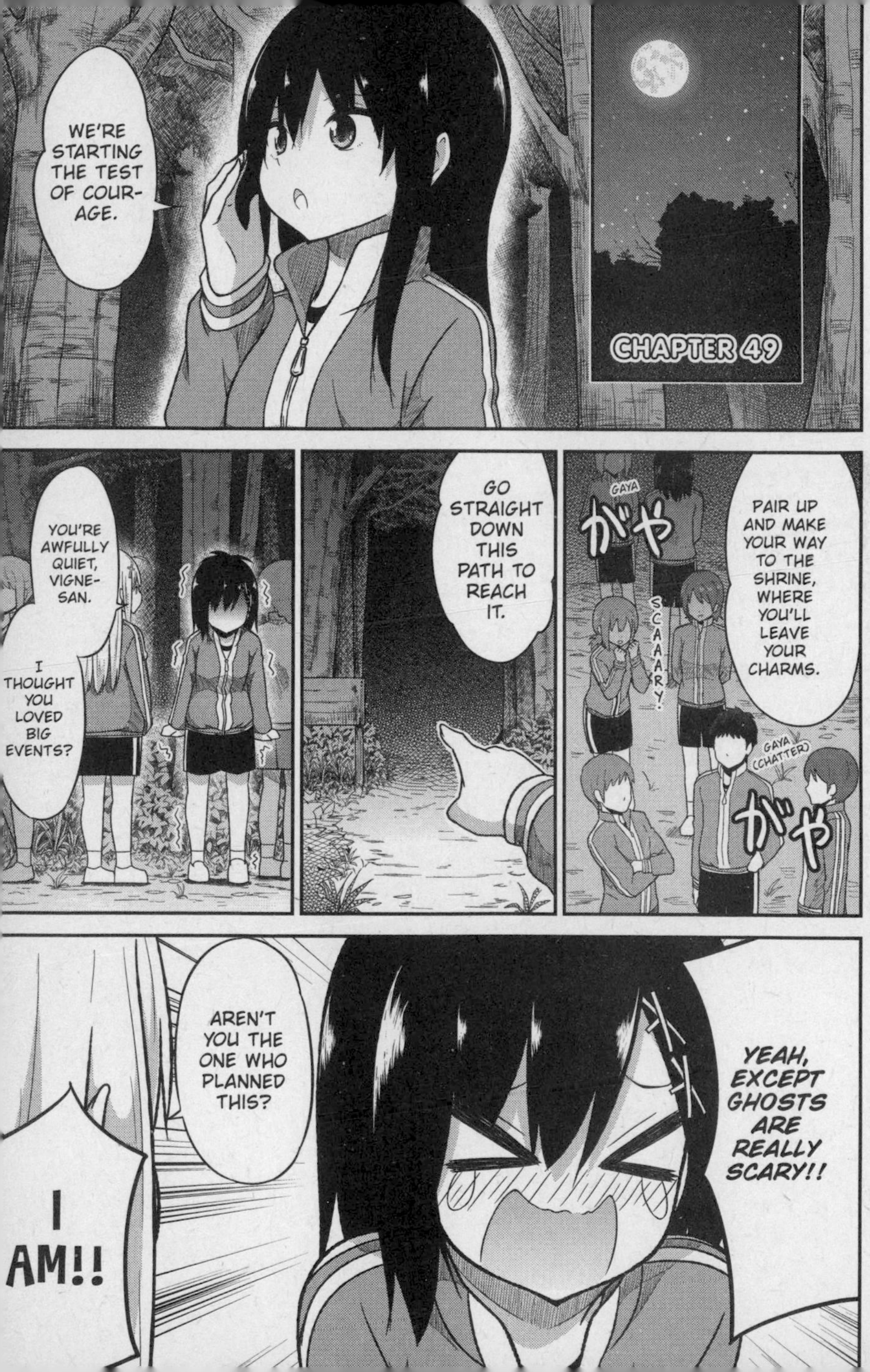
CHAPTER 49
WE'RE STARTING THE TEST OF COURAGE.
GAYA
がや
PAIR UP AND MAKE YOUR WAY TO THE SHRINE, WHERE YOU'LL LEAVE YOUR CHARMS.
SCAAAARY.
GAYA (CHATTER)
がや
GO STRAIGHT DOWN THIS PATH TO REACH IT.
YOU'RE AWFULLY QUIET, VIGNE-SAN.
I THOUGHT YOU LOVED BIG EVENTS?
YEAH, EXCEPT GHOSTS ARE REALLY SCARY!!
AREN'T YOU THE ONE WHO PLANNED THIS?
I AM!!

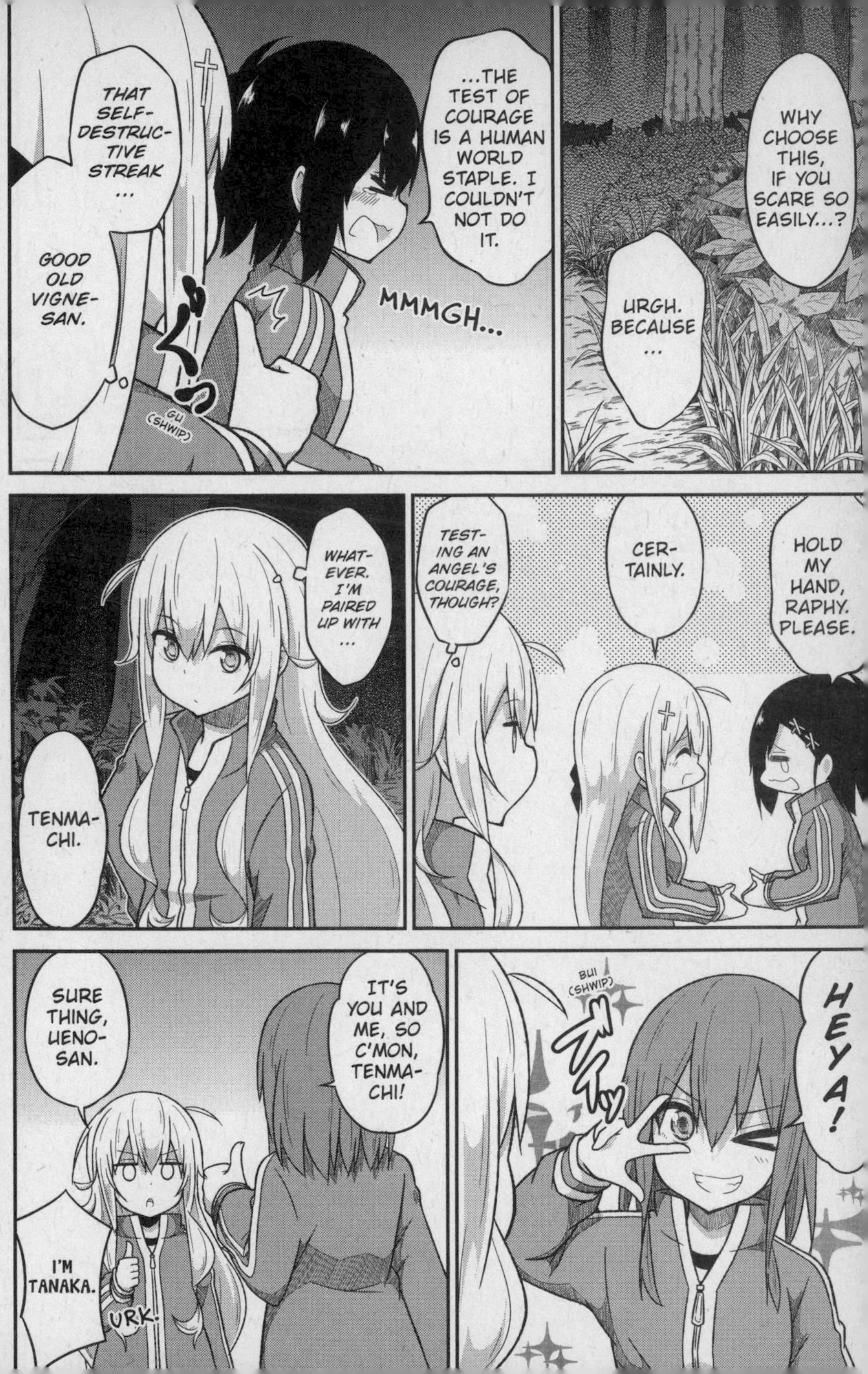
WHY CHOOSE THIS, IF YOU SCARE SO EASILY...?
URGH. BECAUSE ...
...THE TEST OF COURAGE IS A HUMAN WORLD STAPLE. I COULDN'T NOT DO IT.
MMMGH...
THAT SELF-DESTRUCTIVE STREAK ...
GOOD OLD VIGNE-SAN.
GU (SHWIP)
HOLD MY HAND, RAPHY. PLEASE.
CERTAINLY.
TESTING AN ANGEL'S COURAGE, THOUGH?
WHATEVER. I'M PAIRED UP WITH ...
TENMACHI.
HEYA!
BUI (SHWIP)
IT'S YOU AND ME, SO C'MON, TENMACHI!
SURE THING, UENO-SAN.
I'M TANAKA.
URK.

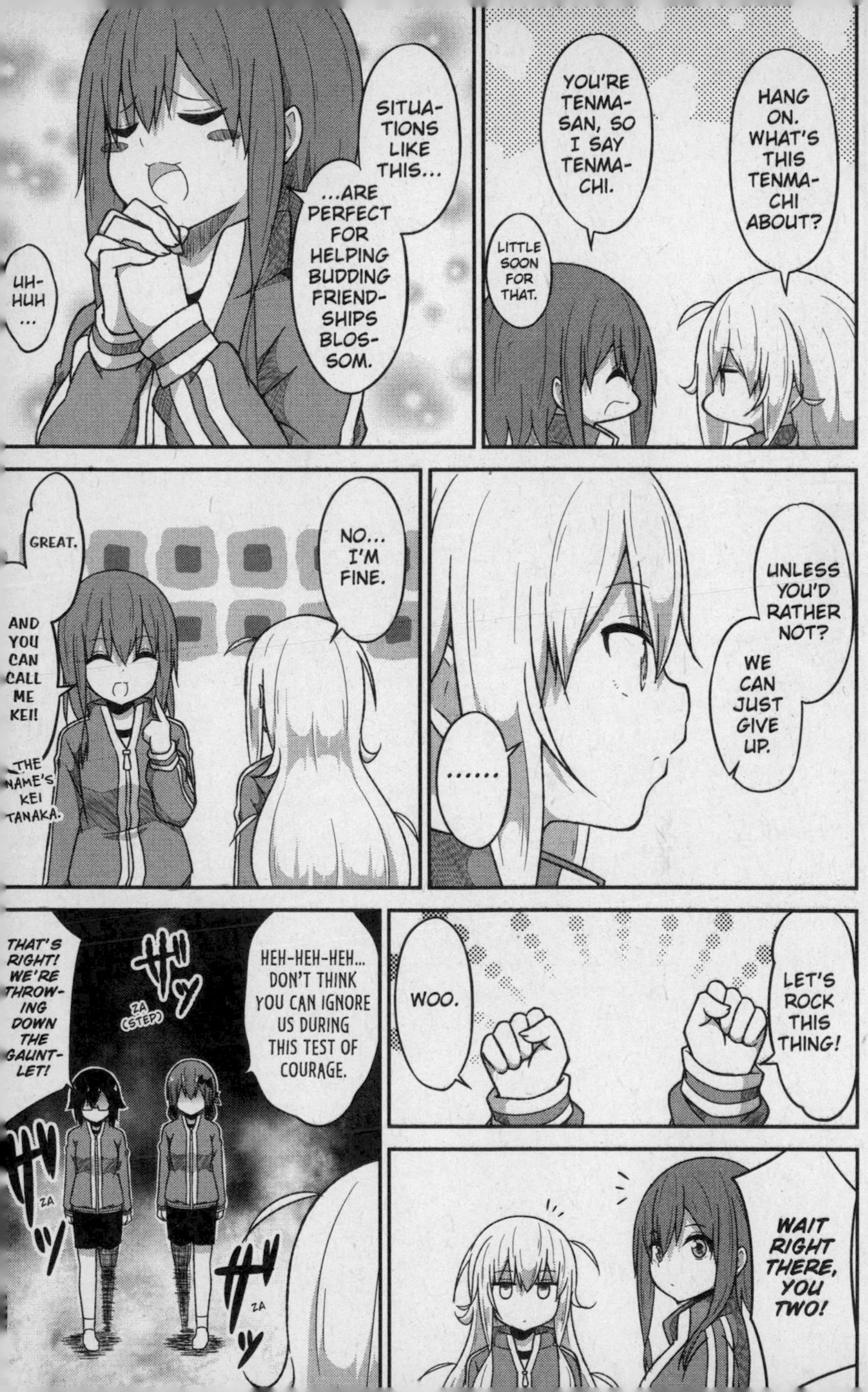
HANG ON. WHAT'S THIS TENMA-CHI ABOUT?
YOU'RE TENMA-SAN, SO I SAY TENMA-CHI.
LITTLE SOON FOR THAT.
SITUATIONS LIKE THIS...
...ARE PERFECT FOR HELPING BUDDING FRIENDSHIPS BLOSSOM.
UH-HUH...
UNLESS YOU'D RATHER NOT?
WE CAN JUST GIVE UP.
......
NO... I'M FINE.
GREAT.
THE NAME'S KEI TANAKA.
AND YOU CAN CALL ME KEI!
LET'S ROCK THIS THING!
WOO.
WAIT RIGHT THERE, YOU TWO!
HEH-HEH-HEH... DON'T THINK YOU CAN IGNORE US DURING THIS TEST OF COURAGE.
ZA (STEP)
THAT'S RIGHT! WE'RE THROWING DOWN THE GAUNTLET!
ZA
ZA

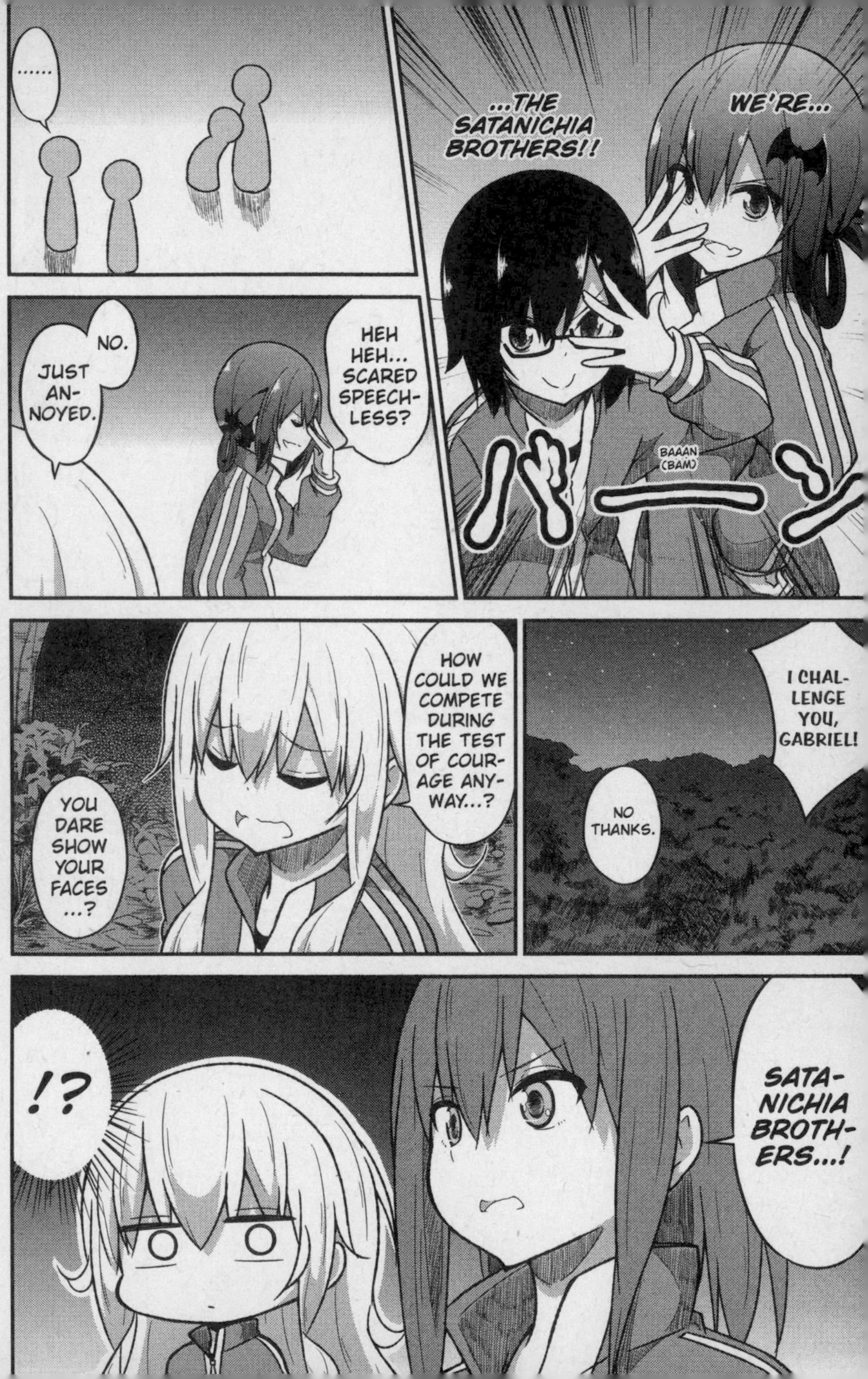
WE'RE...
...THE SATANICHIA BROTHERS!!
BAAAN (BAM)
......
HEH HEH... SCARED SPEECH-LESS?
NO. JUST AN-NOYED.
I CHAL-LENGE YOU, GABRIEL!
NO THANKS.
HOW COULD WE COMPETE DURING THE TEST OF COUR-AGE ANY-WAY...?
YOU DARE SHOW YOUR FACES ...?
SATA-NICHIA BROTH-ERS...!
!?

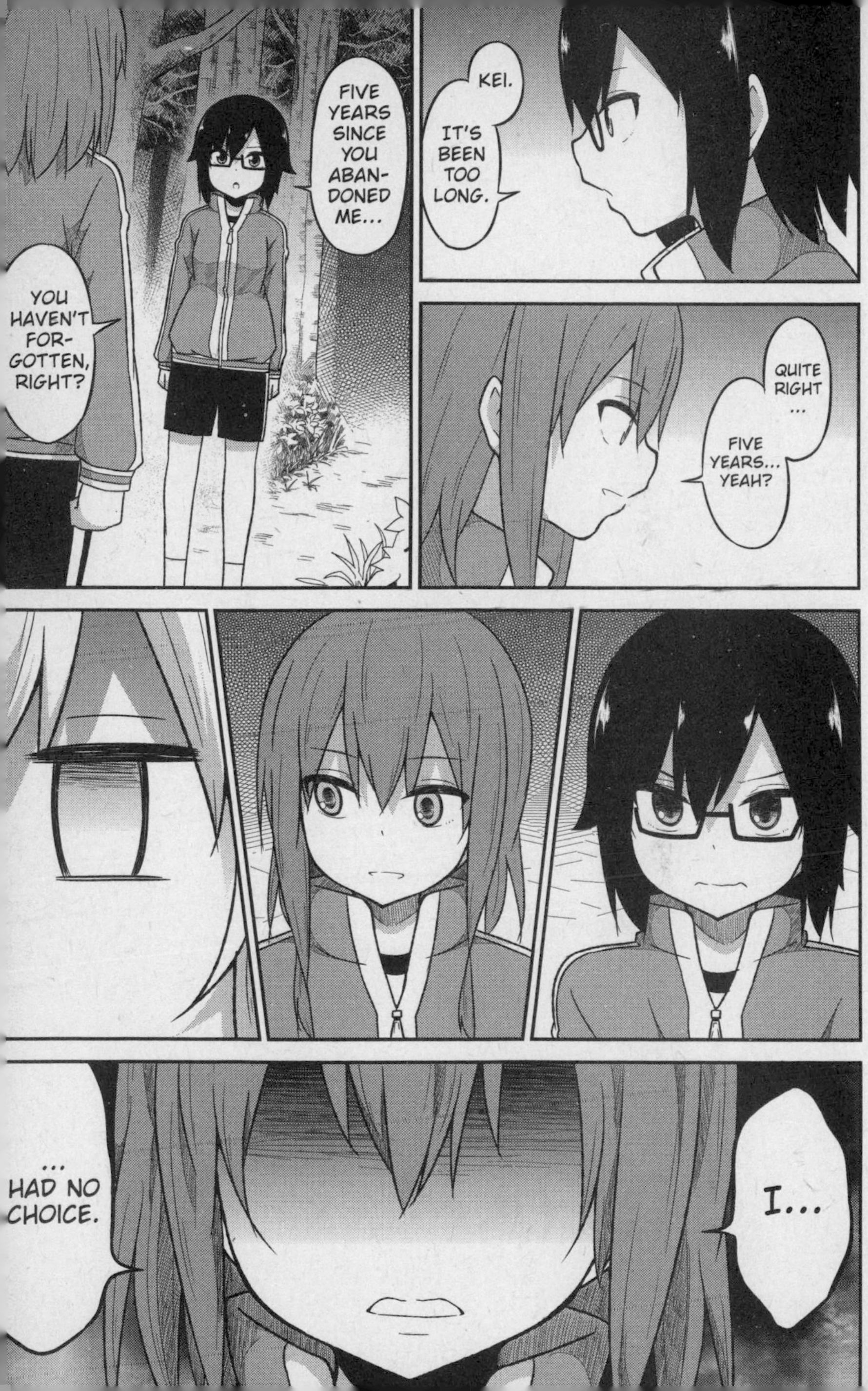
KEI.
IT'S BEEN TOO LONG.
QUITE RIGHT...
FIVE YEARS... YEAH?
FIVE YEARS SINCE YOU ABANDONED ME...
YOU HAVEN'T FORGOTTEN, RIGHT?
I...
...HAD NO CHOICE.

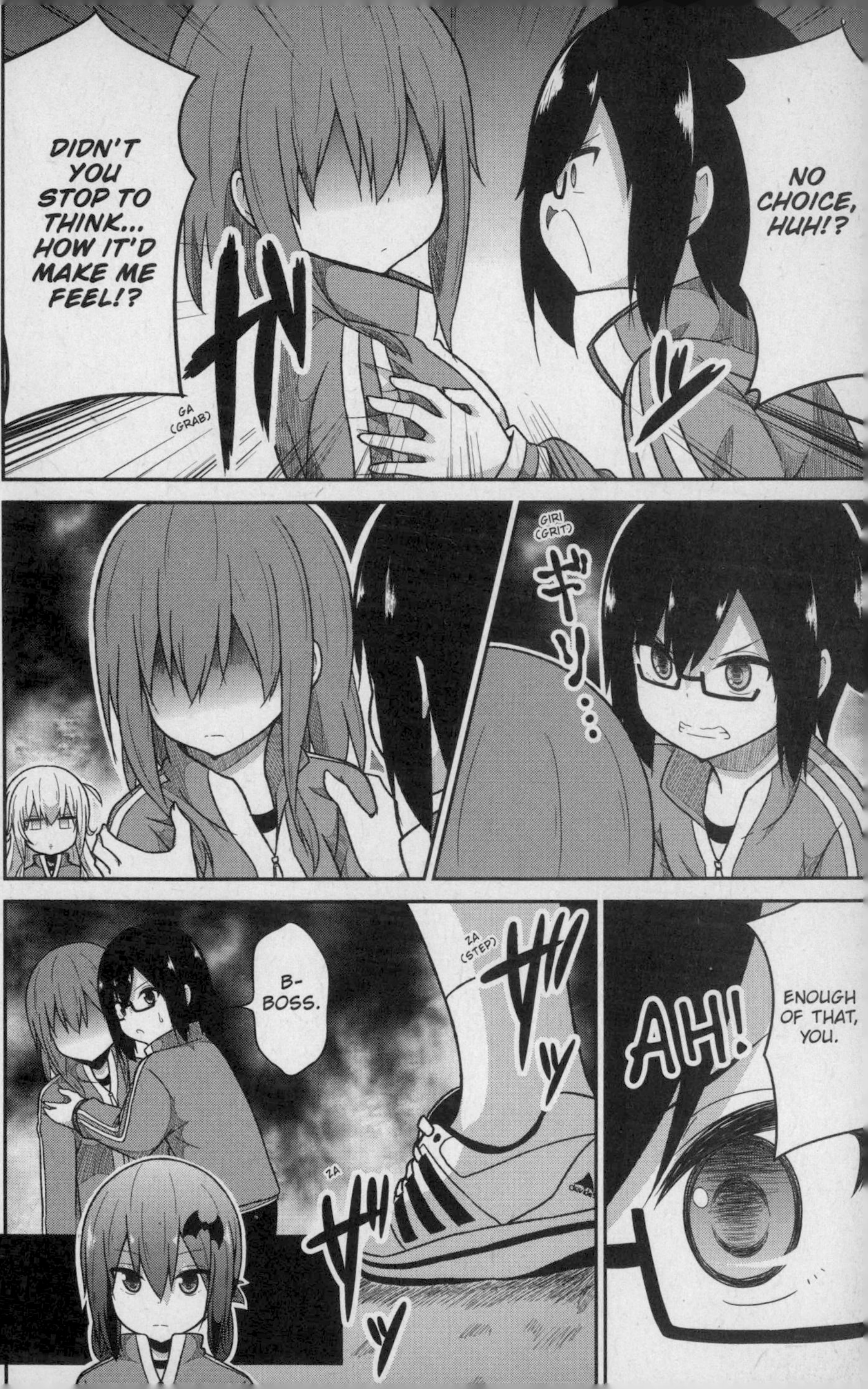
NO CHOICE, HUH!?
DIDN'T YOU STOP TO THINK... HOW IT'D MAKE ME FEEL!?
GA (GRAB)
GIRI (GRIT)
AH!
ENOUGH OF THAT, YOU.
ZA (STEP)
ZA
B- BOSS.

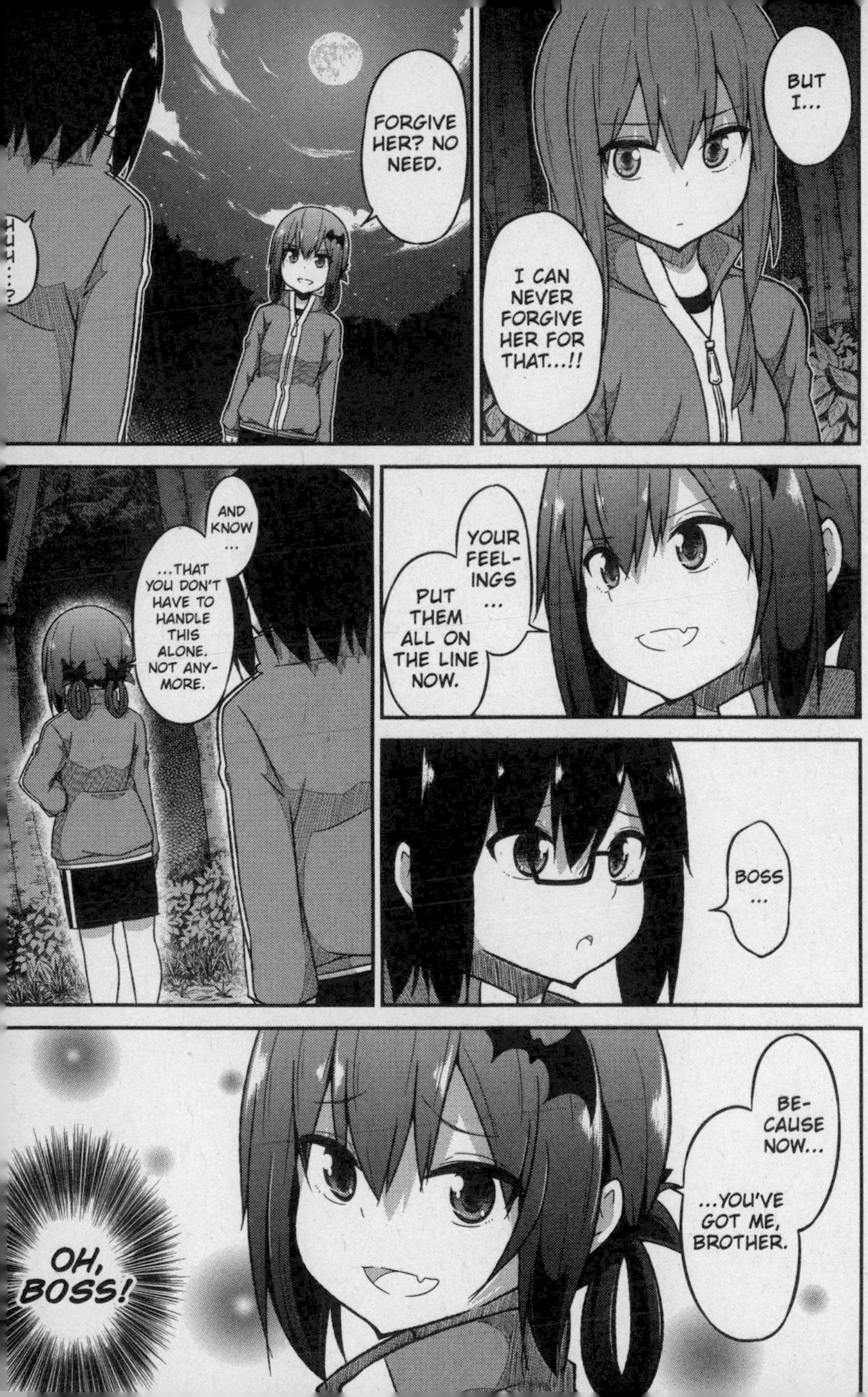
BUT I...
I CAN NEVER FORGIVE HER FOR THAT...!!
FORGIVE HER? NO NEED.
YOUR FEELINGS...
PUT THEM ALL ON THE LINE NOW.
BOSS...
AND KNOW...
...THAT YOU DON'T HAVE TO HANDLE THIS ALONE. NOT ANYMORE.
BECAUSE NOW...
...YOU'VE GOT ME, BROTHER.
OH, BOSS!

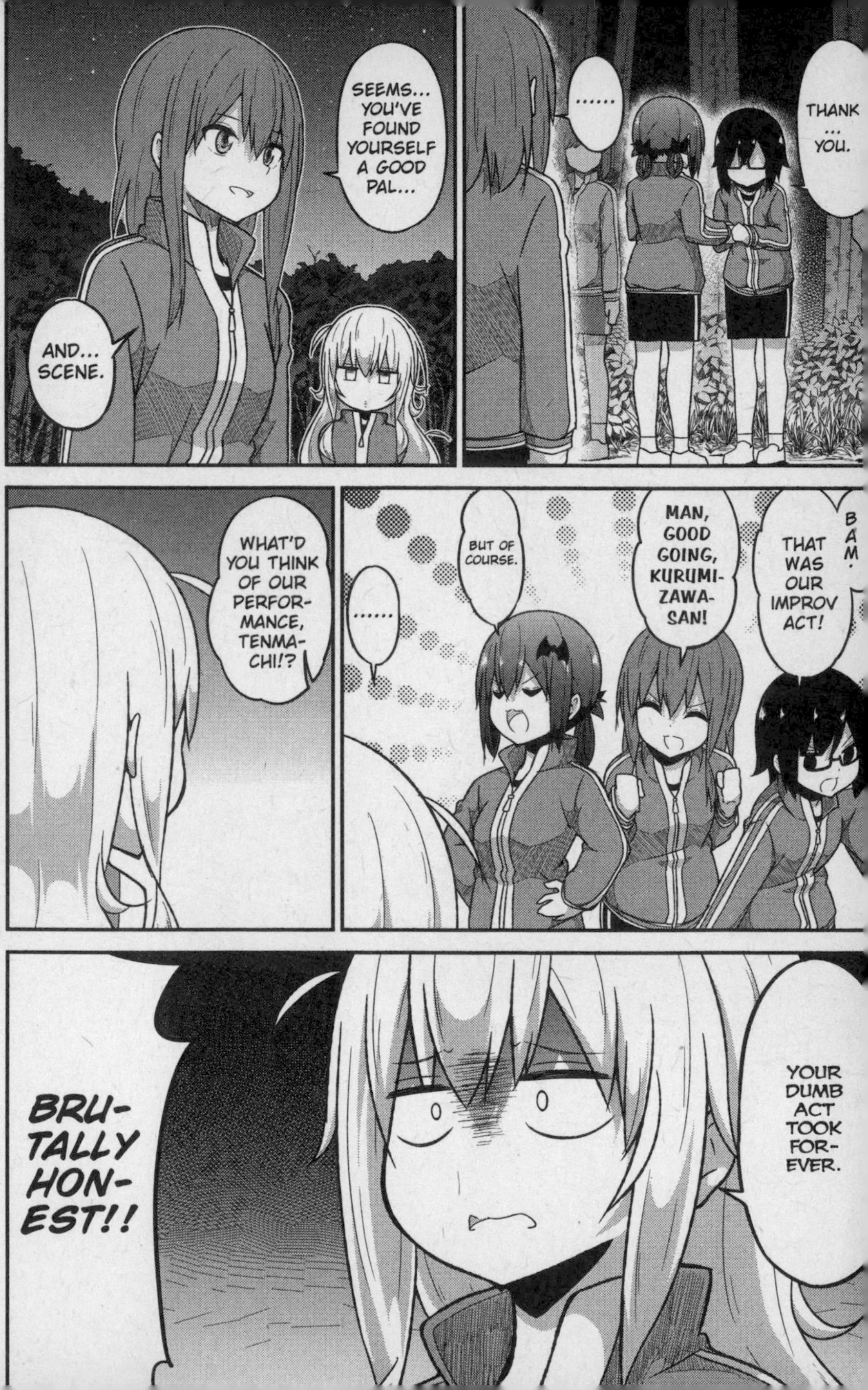
THANK ... YOU.
......
SEEMS... YOU'VE FOUND YOURSELF A GOOD PAL...
AND... SCENE.
BAM!
THAT WAS OUR IMPROV ACT!
MAN, GOOD GOING, KURUMIZAWA-SAN!
BUT OF COURSE.
......
WHAT'D YOU THINK OF OUR PERFORMANCE, TENMACHI!?
YOUR DUMB ACT TOOK FOREVER.
BRUTALLY HONEST!!

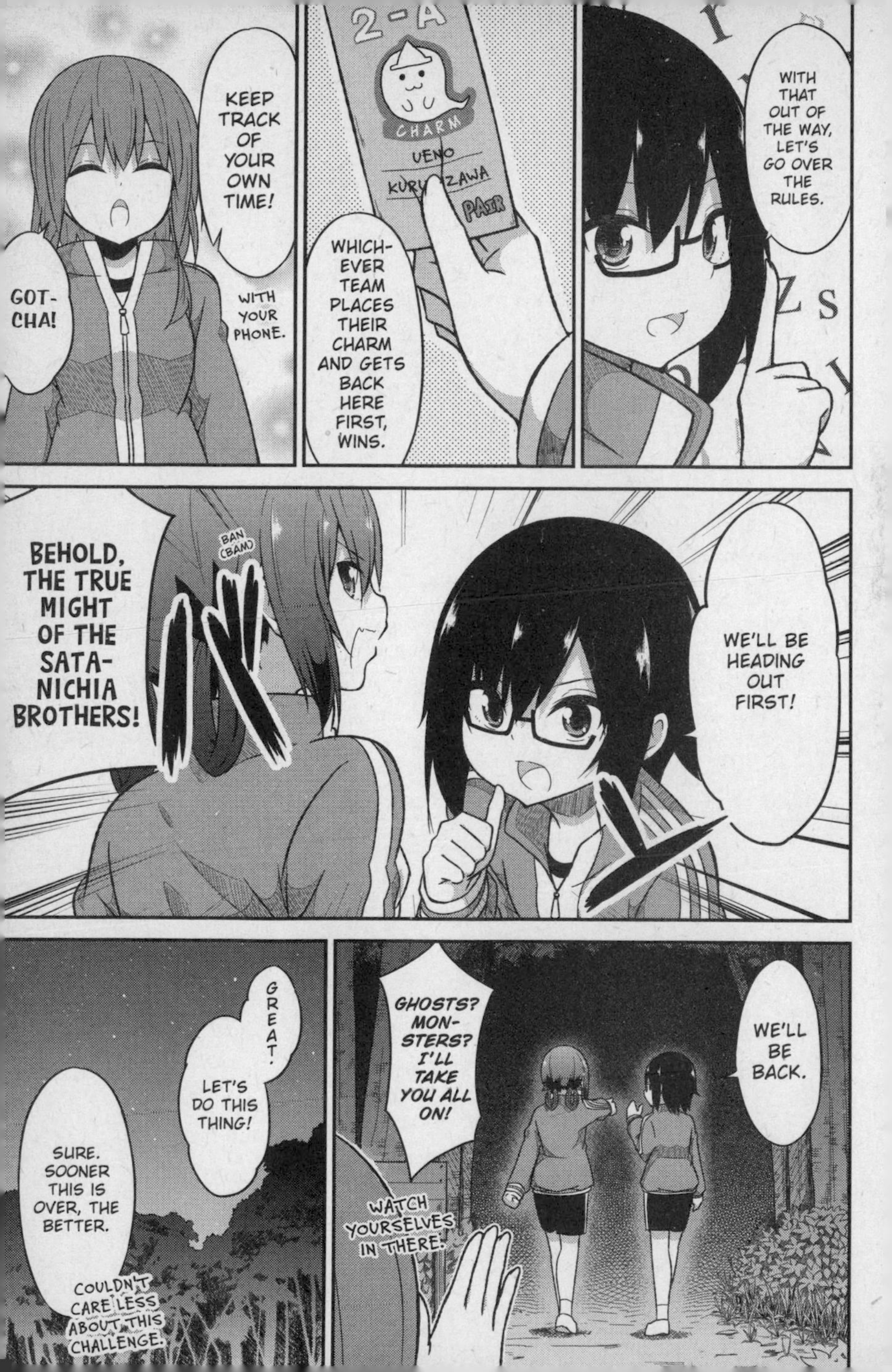
WITH THAT OUT OF THE WAY, LET'S GO OVER THE RULES.
2-A
CHARM
UENO
PAIR
WHICH-EVER TEAM PLACES THEIR CHARM AND GETS BACK HERE FIRST, WINS.
KEEP TRACK OF YOUR OWN TIME!
WITH YOUR PHONE.
GOT-CHA!
WE'LL BE HEADING OUT FIRST!
BAN (BAM)
BEHOLD, THE TRUE MIGHT OF THE SATA-NICHIA BROTHERS!
WE'LL BE BACK.
GHOSTS? MON-STERS? I'LL TAKE YOU ALL ON!
WATCH YOURSELVES IN THERE.
GREAT.
LET'S DO THIS THING!
SURE. SOONER THIS IS OVER, THE BETTER.
COULDN'T CARE LESS ABOUT THIS CHALLENGE.

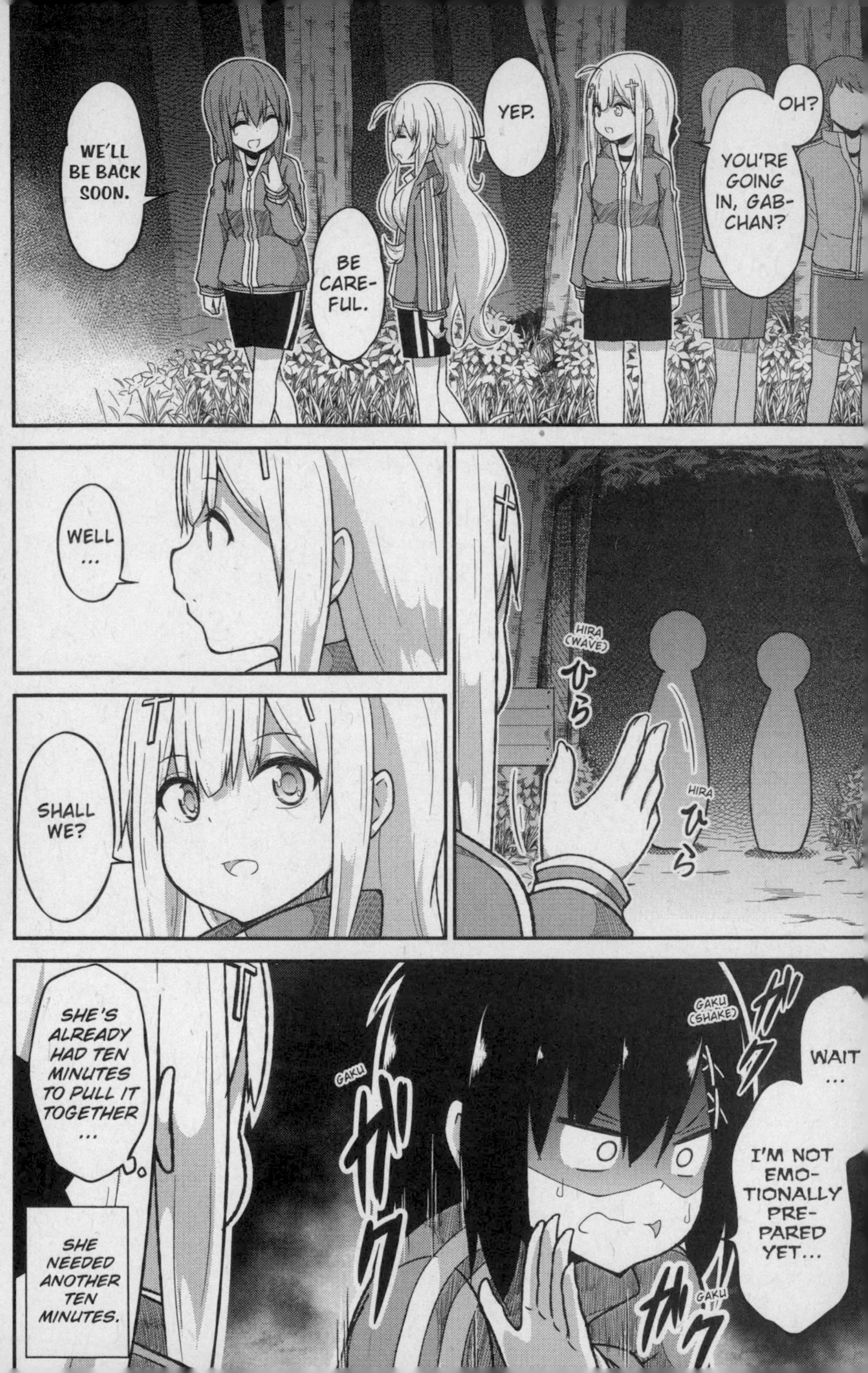
OH?
YOU'RE GOING IN, GAB-CHAN?
YEP.
WE'LL BE BACK SOON.
BE CAREFUL.
HIRA (WAVE)
ひら
HIRA
ひら
WELL ...
SHALL WE?
GAKU (SHAKE)
WAIT ...
I'M NOT EMOTIONALLY PREPARED YET...
GAKU
GAKU
SHE'S ALREADY HAD TEN MINUTES TO PULL IT TOGETHER ...
SHE NEEDED ANOTHER TEN MINUTES.

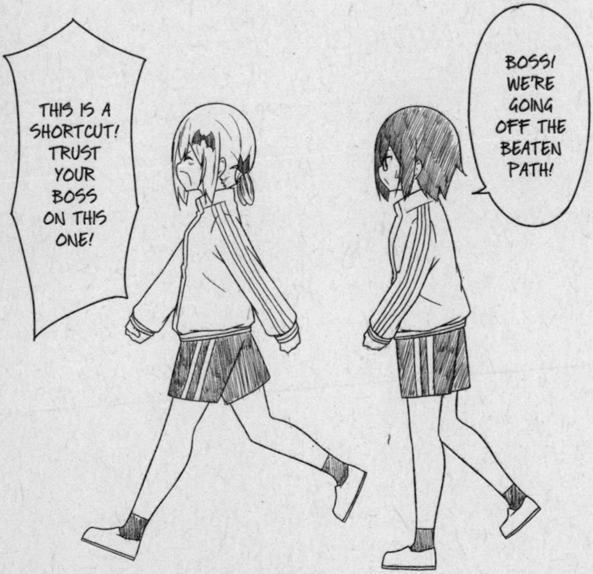
BOSS! WE'RE GOING OFF THE BEATEN PATH!
THIS IS A SHORTCUT! TRUST YOUR BOSS ON THIS ONE!

Gabriel Dropout

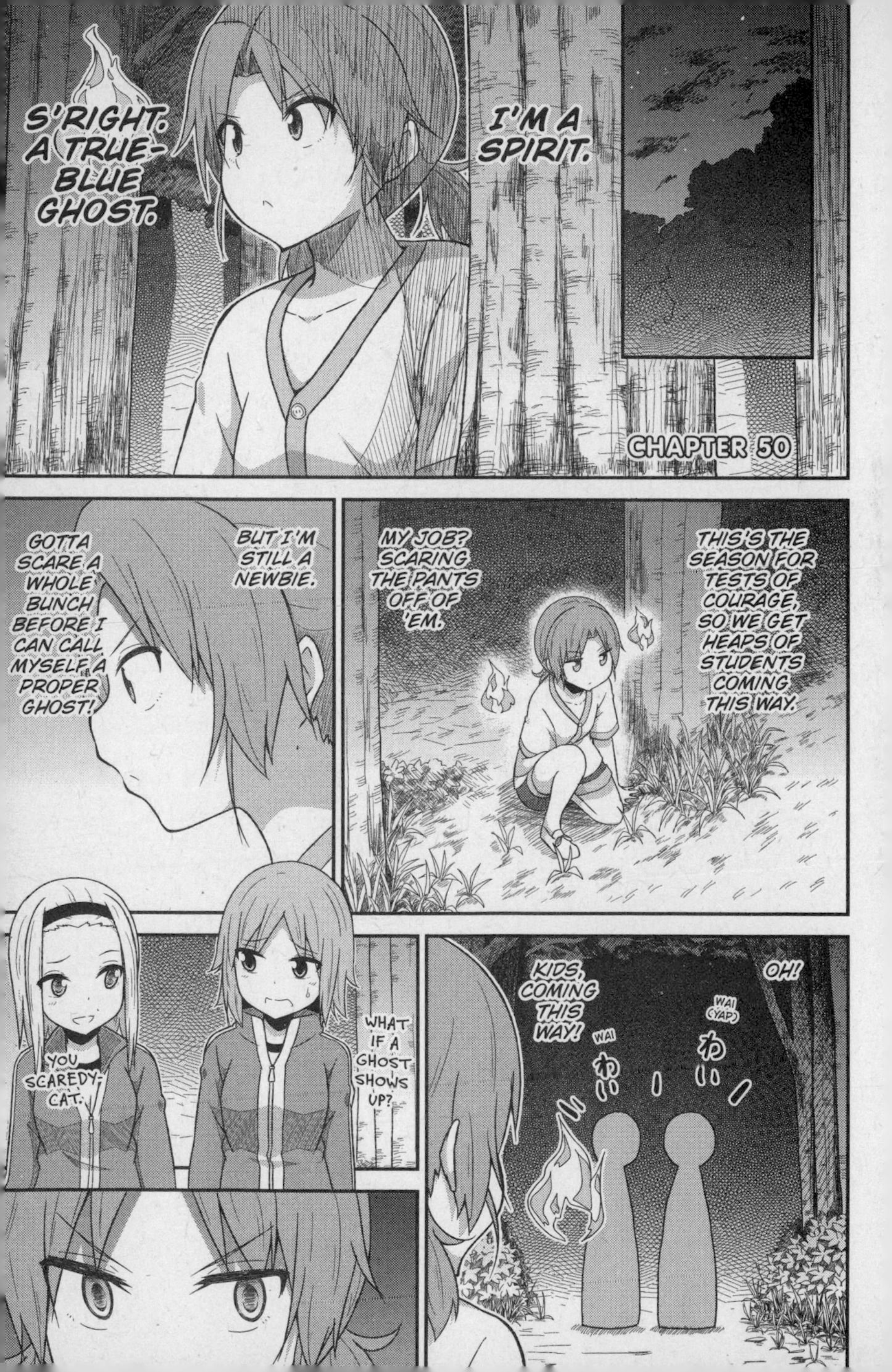
I'M A SPIRIT.
S'RIGHT. A TRUE-BLUE GHOST.
CHAPTER 50
THIS'S THE SEASON FOR TESTS OF COURAGE, SO WE GET HEAPS OF STUDENTS COMING THIS WAY.
MY JOB? SCARING THE PANTS OFF OF 'EM.
BUT I'M STILL A NEWBIE.
GOTTA SCARE A WHOLE BUNCH BEFORE I CAN CALL MYSELF A PROPER GHOST!
OH!
WAI (YAP)
わい
KIDS, COMING THIS WAY!
WAI
わい
WHAT IF A GHOST SHOWS UP?
YOU SCAREDY-CAT.

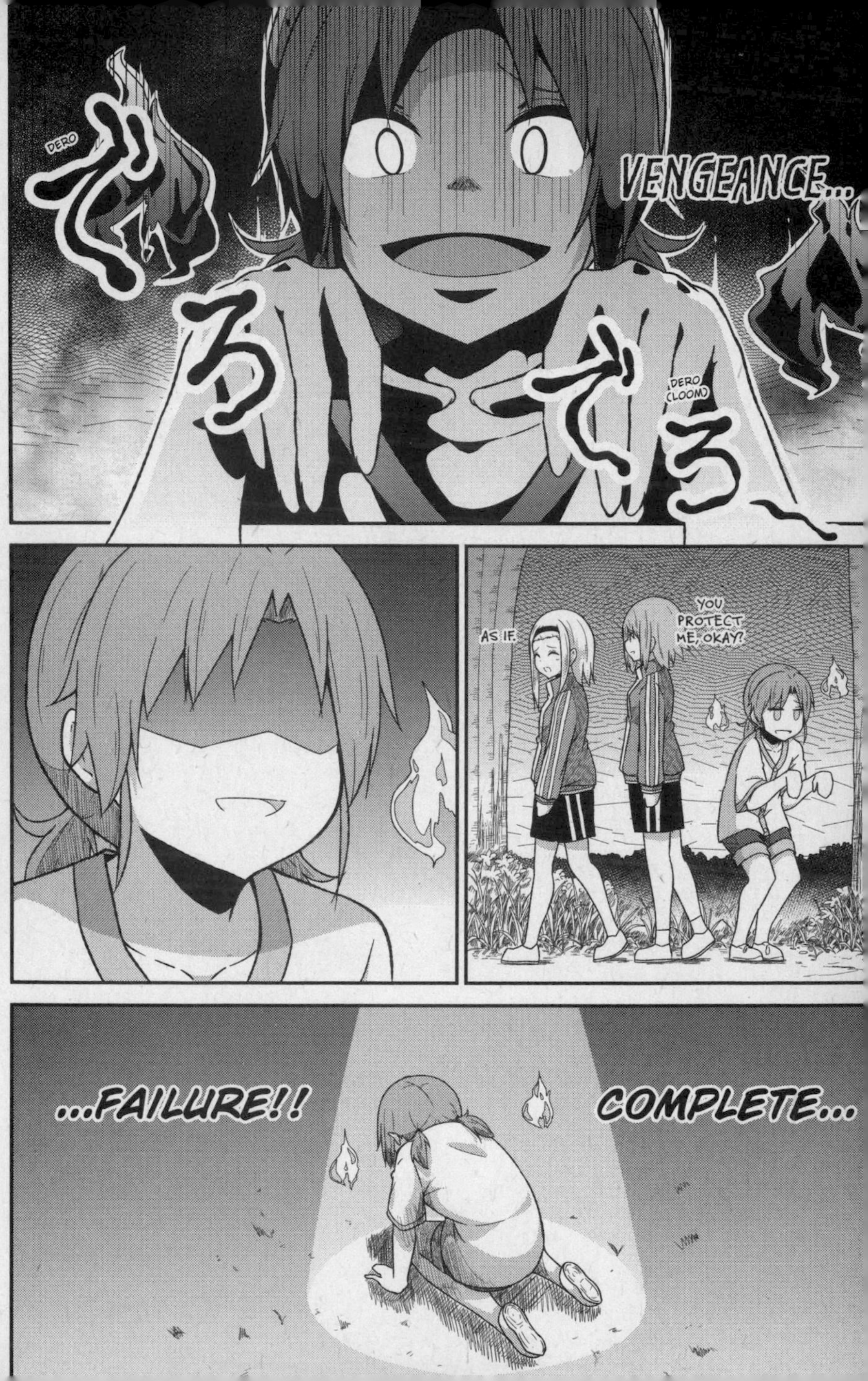
VENGEANCE...
でろ~
DERO (LOOM)
でろ
DERO
YOU PROTECT ME, OKAY?
AS IF.
COMPLETE...
...FAILURE!!

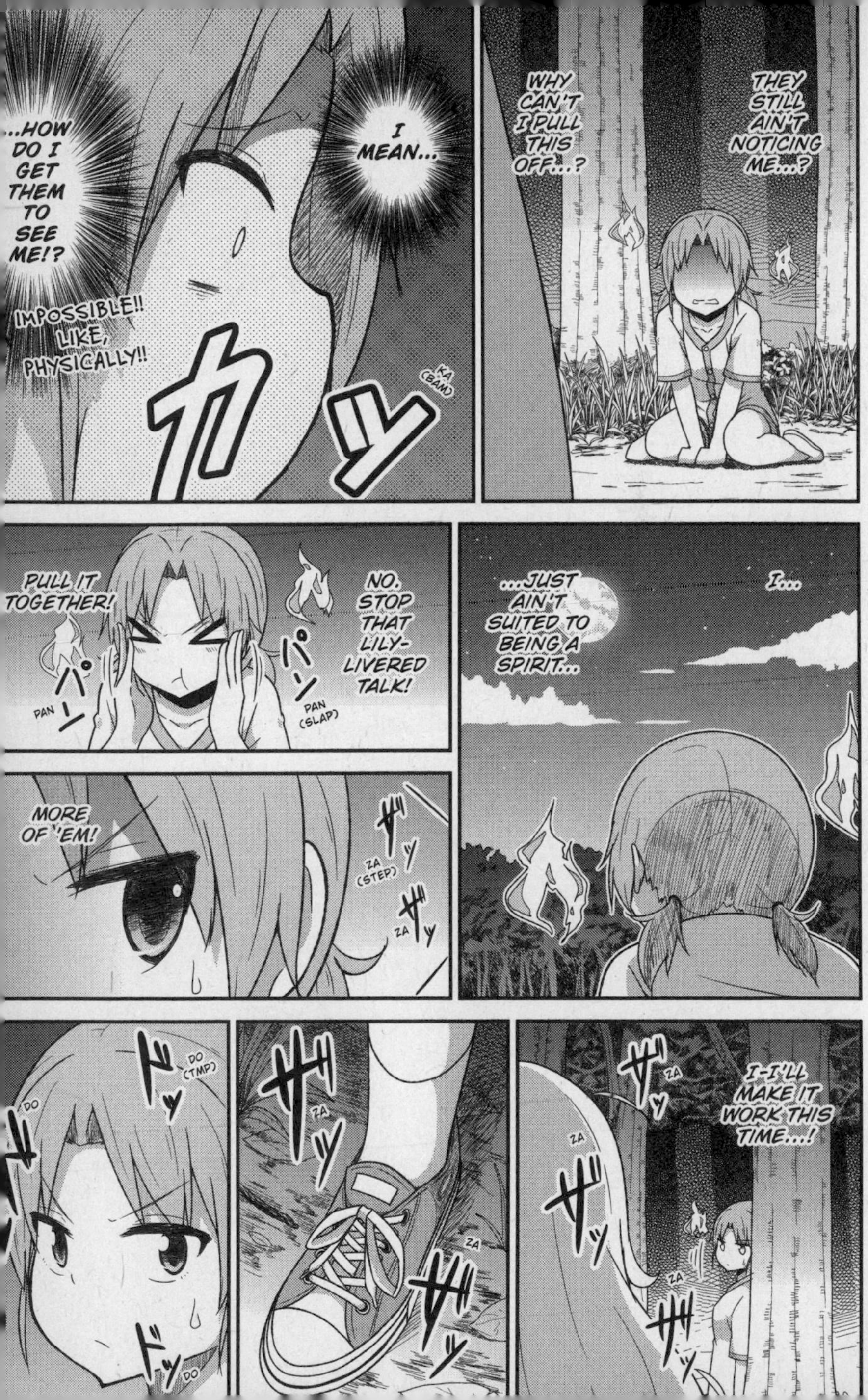
THEY STILL AIN'T NOTICING ME...?
WHY CAN'T I PULL THIS OFF...?
I MEAN...
...HOW DO I GET THEM TO SEE ME!?
IMPOSSIBLE!! LIKE, PHYSICALLY!!
カッ
KA (BAM)
I...
...JUST AIN'T SUITED TO BEING A SPIRIT...
NO. STOP THAT LILY-LIVERED TALK!
パン
PAN (SLAP)
PULL IT TOGETHER!
パン
PAN
ザッ
ZA (STEP)
ザッ
ZA
MORE OF 'EM!
I-I'LL MAKE IT WORK THIS TIME...!
ザッ
ZA
ザッ
ZA
ザッ
ZA
ザッ
ZA
ザッ
ZA
ドッ
DO (TMP)
ドッ
DO
ドッ
DO

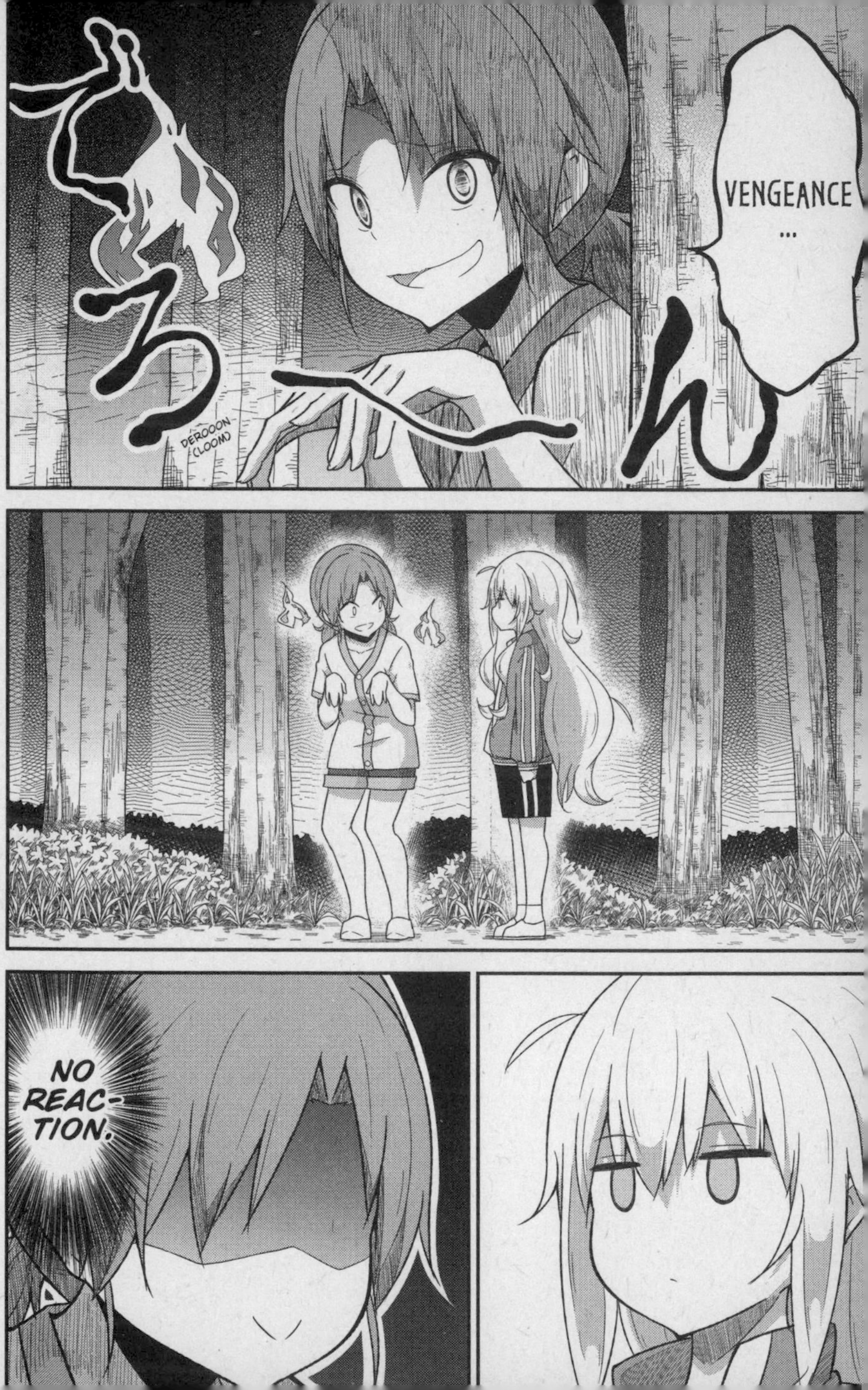
VENGEANCE ...
どろ～ん
DEROOON (LOOM)
NO REACTION.

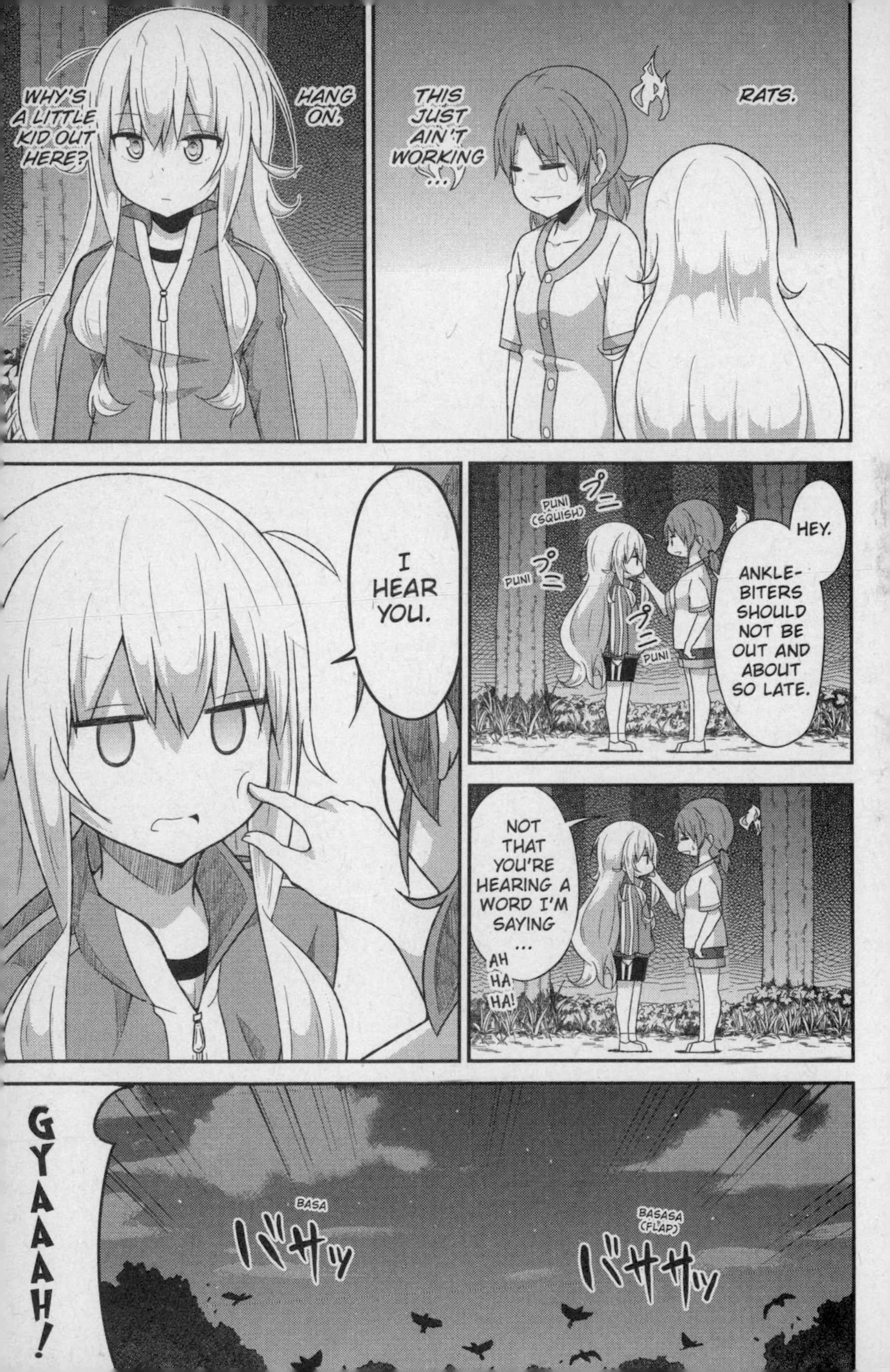

RATS.
THIS JUST AIN'T WORKING ...
HANG ON.
WHY'S A LITTLE KID OUT HERE?
HEY.
ANKLE-BITERS SHOULD NOT BE OUT AND ABOUT SO LATE.
プニ
PUNI (SQUISH)
プニ
PUNI
プニ
PUNI
NOT THAT YOU'RE HEARING A WORD I'M SAYING ...
AH HA HA!
I HEAR YOU.
バサササッ
BASASA (FLAP)
バサッ
BASA
GYAAAH!

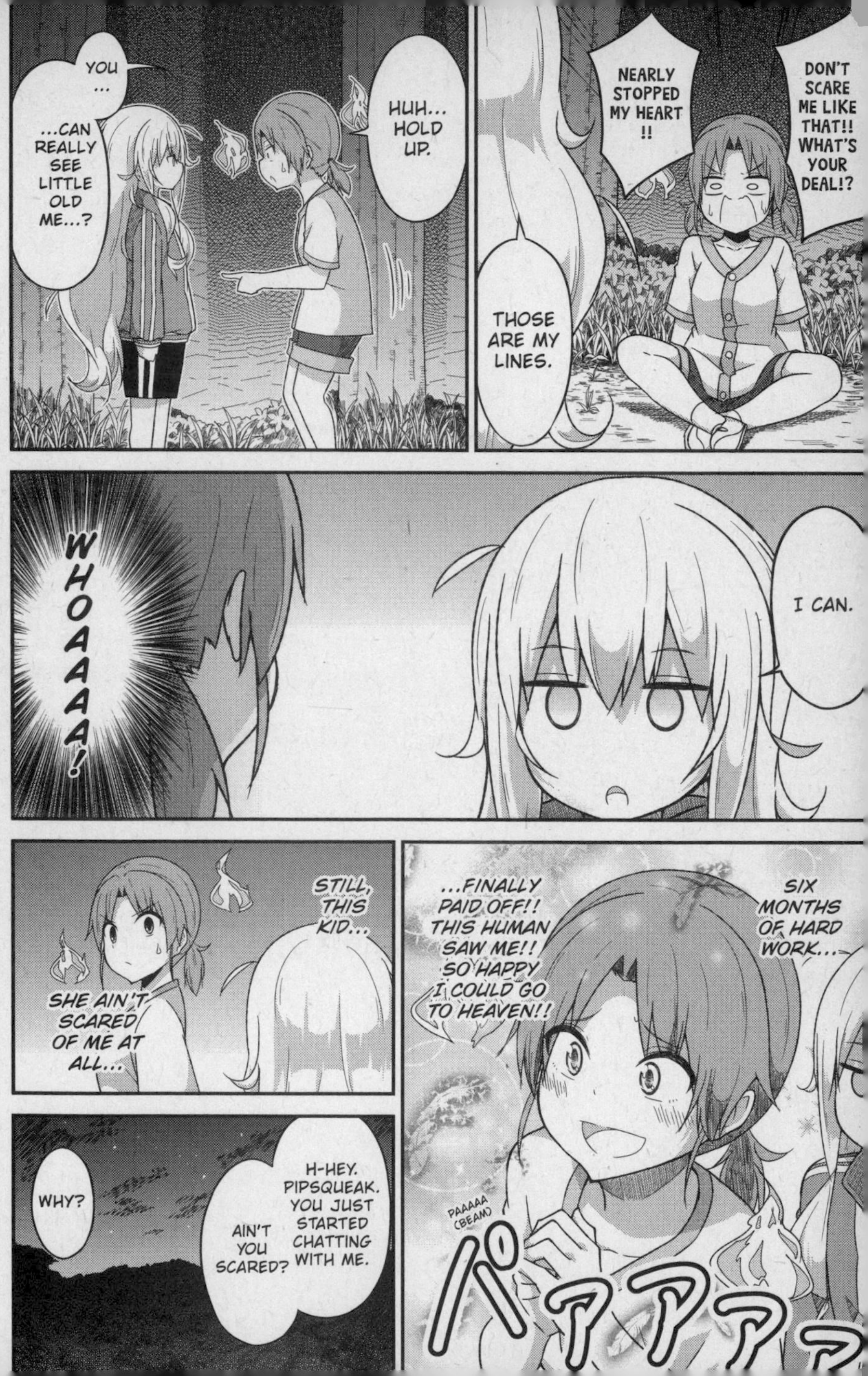
DON'T SCARE ME LIKE THAT!! WHAT'S YOUR DEAL!?
NEARLY STOPPED MY HEART !!
THOSE ARE MY LINES.
HUH... HOLD UP.
YOU ...
...CAN REALLY SEE LITTLE OLD ME...?
I CAN.
WHOAAAAA!
SIX MONTHS OF HARD WORK...
...FINALLY PAID OFF!! THIS HUMAN SAW ME!! SO HAPPY I COULD GO TO HEAVEN!!
PAAAAA (BEAM)
STILL, THIS KID...
SHE AIN'T SCARED OF ME AT ALL...
H-HEY. PIPSQUEAK. YOU JUST STARTED CHATTING WITH ME.
AIN'T YOU SCARED?
WHY?

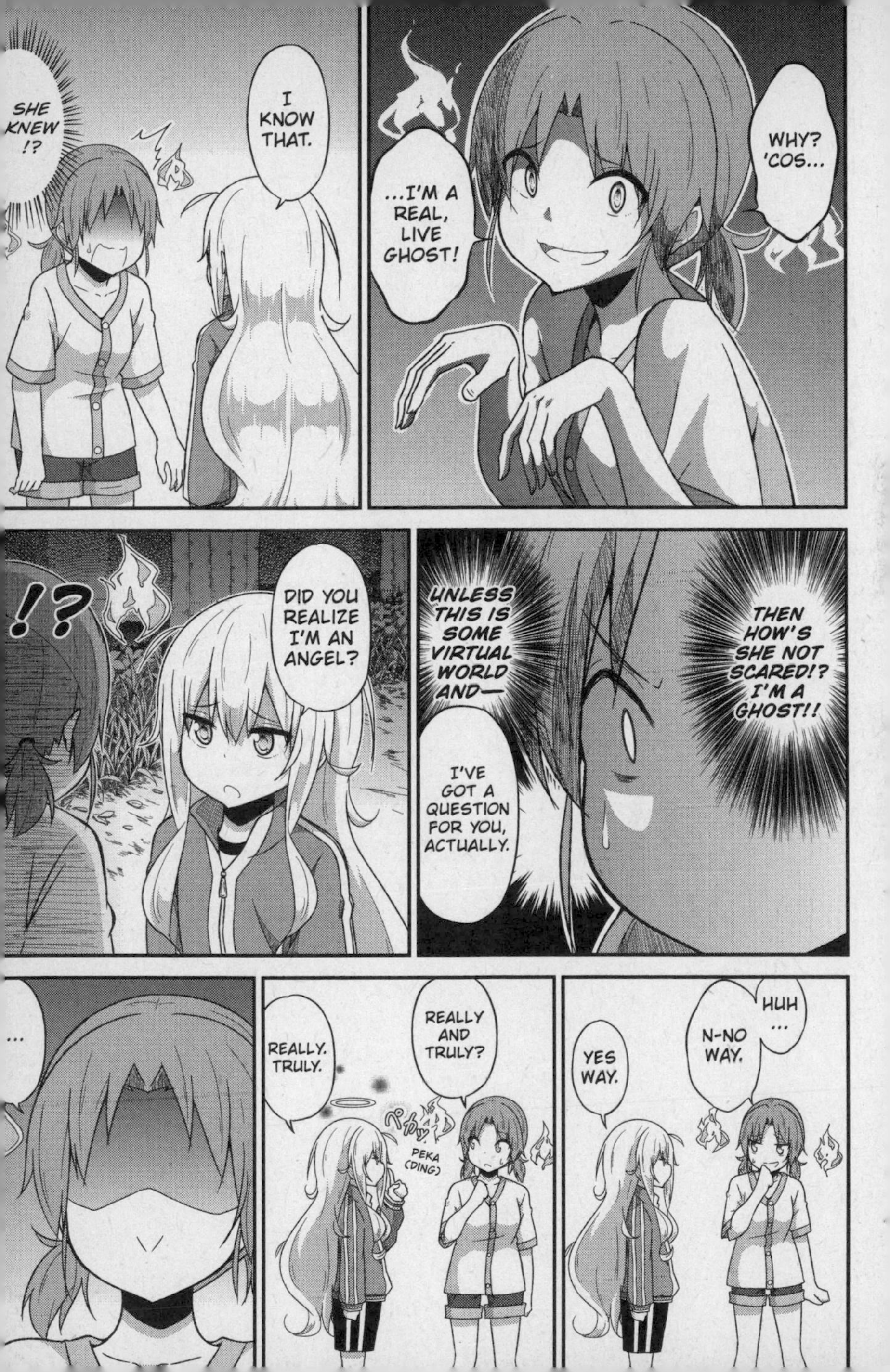
WHY? 'COS...
...I'M A REAL, LIVE GHOST!
I KNOW THAT.
SHE KNEW!?
THEN HOW'S SHE NOT SCARED!? I'M A GHOST!!
UNLESS THIS IS SOME VIRTUAL WORLD AND—
I'VE GOT A QUESTION FOR YOU, ACTUALLY.
DID YOU REALIZE I'M AN ANGEL?
!?
HUH...
N-NO WAY.
YES WAY.
REALLY AND TRULY?
REALLY. TRULY.
PEKA (DING)
...

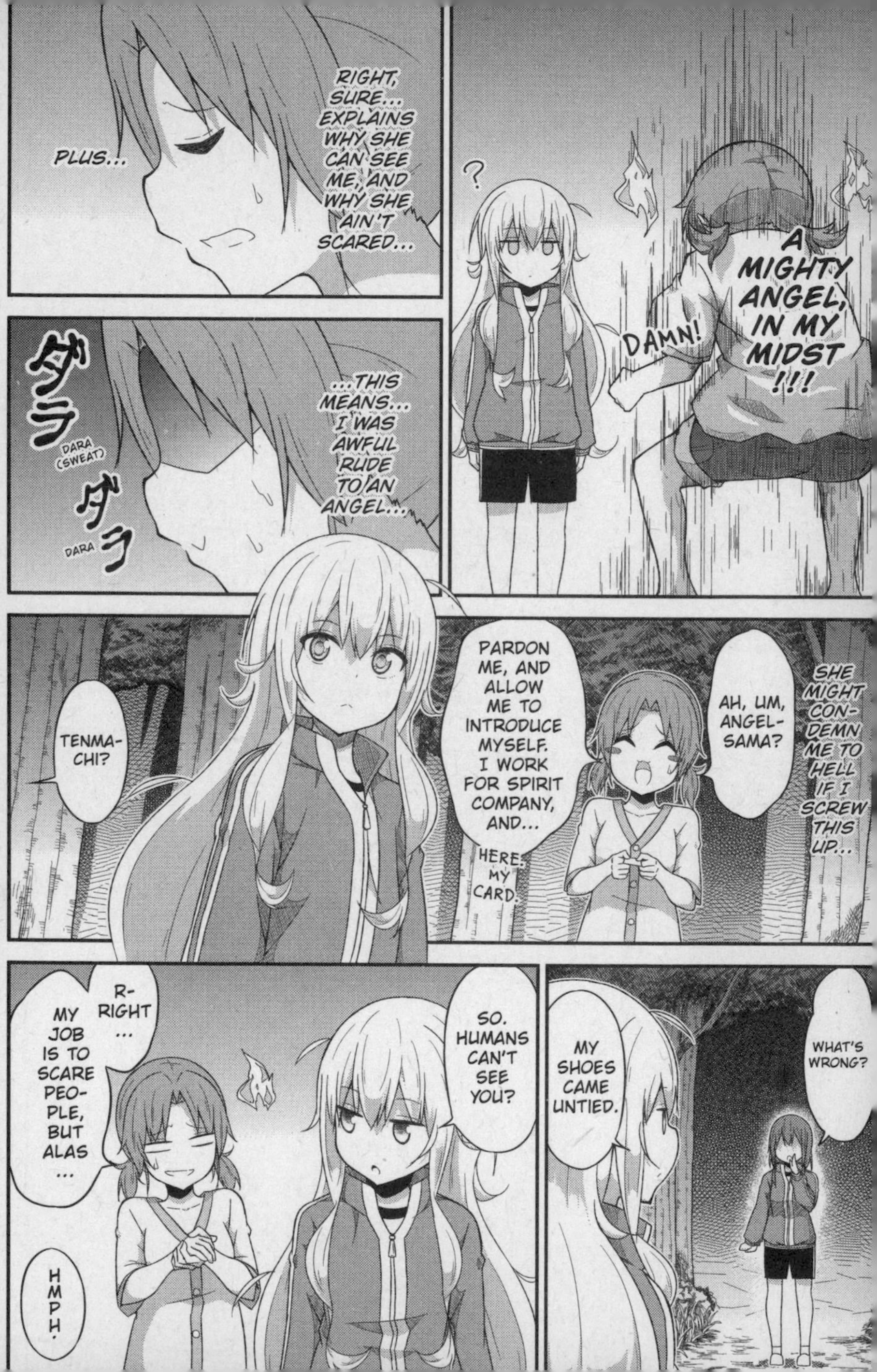
?
A MIGHTY ANGEL, IN MY MIDST!!!
DAMN!
RIGHT, SURE... EXPLAINS WHY SHE CAN SEE ME, AND WHY SHE AIN'T SCARED...
PLUS...
...THIS MEANS... I WAS AWFUL RUDE TO AN ANGEL...
ダラ DARA (SWEAT)
ダラ DARA
SHE MIGHT CON-DEMN ME TO HELL IF I SCREW THIS UP...
AH, UM, ANGEL-SAMA?
PARDON ME, AND ALLOW ME TO INTRODUCE MYSELF. I WORK FOR SPIRIT COMPANY, AND...
HERE. MY CARD.
TENMA-CHI?
WHAT'S WRONG?
MY SHOES CAME UNTIED.
SO. HUMANS CAN'T SEE YOU?
R-RIGHT...
MY JOB IS TO SCARE PEO-PLE, BUT ALAS...
HMPH.

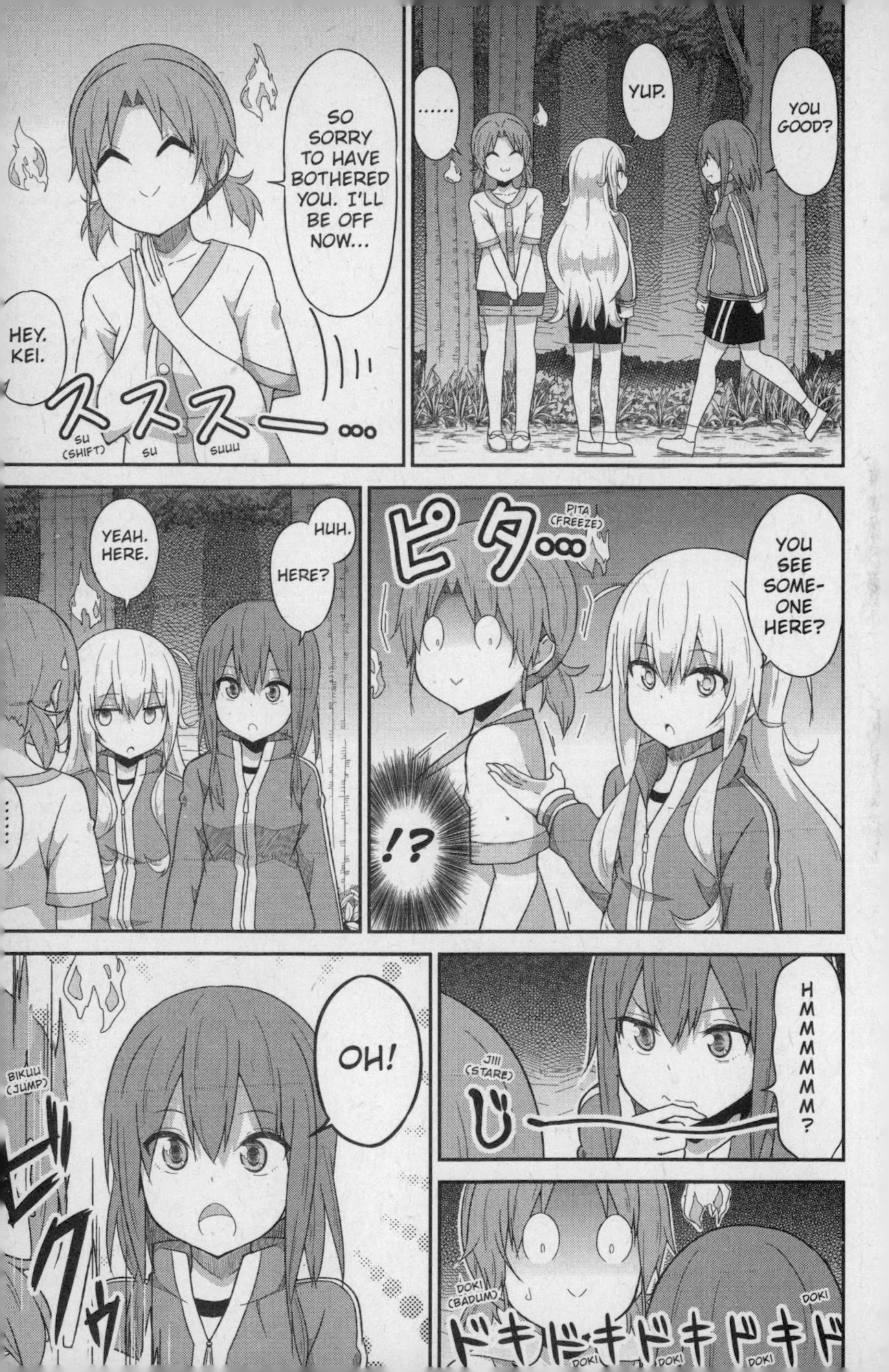
YOU GOOD?
YUP.
......
SO SORRY TO HAVE BOTHERED YOU. I'LL BE OFF NOW...
スススー…
SU (SHIFT) SU SUUU
HEY. KEI.
ピタ…
PITA (FREEZE)
YOU SEE SOME-ONE HERE?
!?
HUH. HERE?
YEAH. HERE.
......
HMMMMMMM?
JIII (STARE)
じー
ドキドキドキドキ
DOKI (BADUM) DOKI DOKI DOKI DOKI
OH!
BIKUU (JUMP)
ビクゥ

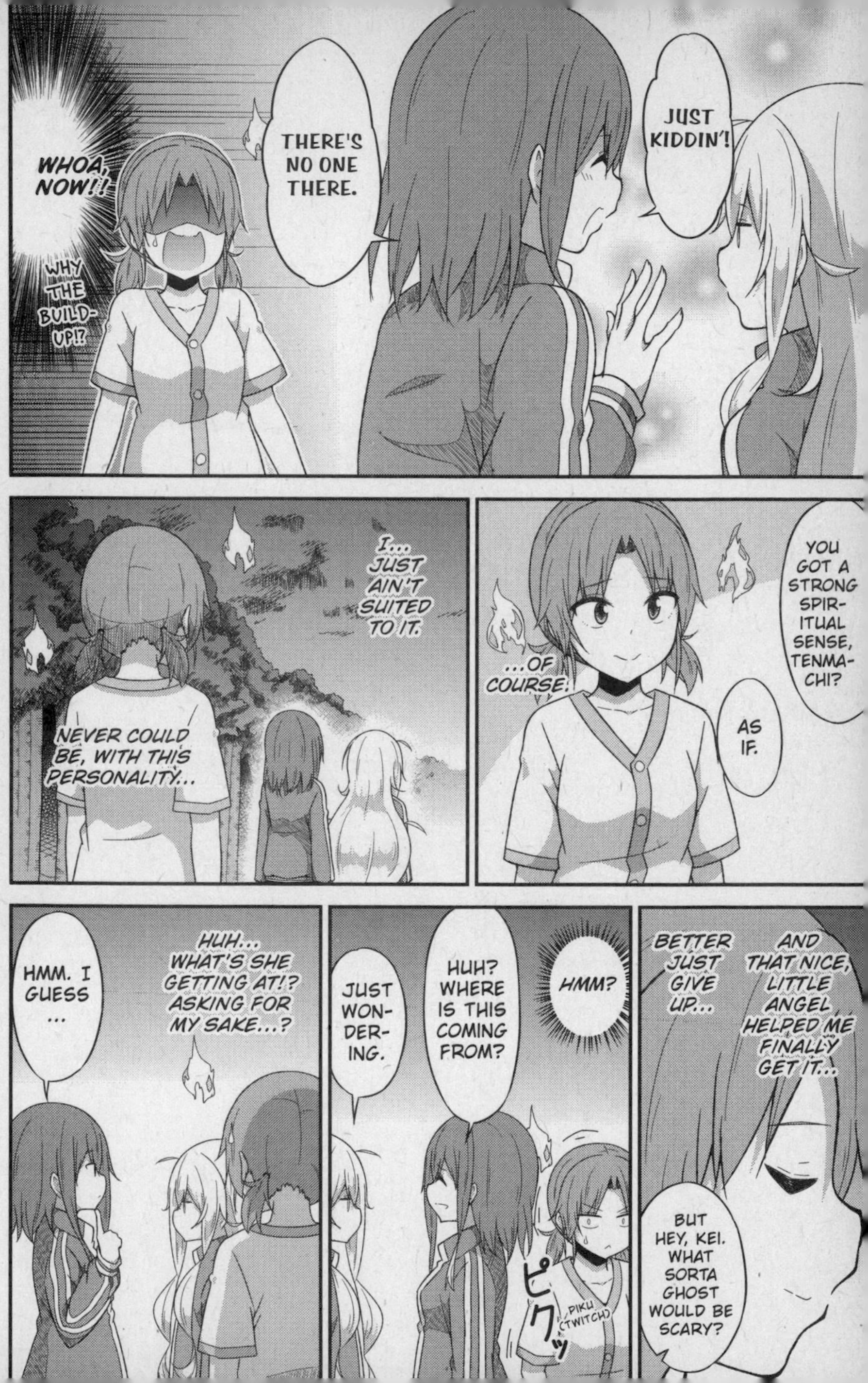
JUST KIDDIN'!
THERE'S NO ONE THERE.
WHOA, NOW!!
WHY THE BUILD-UP!?
YOU GOT A STRONG SPIRITUAL SENSE, TENMACHI?
AS IF.
...OF COURSE.
I... JUST AIN'T SUITED TO IT.
NEVER COULD BE, WITH THIS PERSONALITY...
AND THAT NICE, LITTLE ANGEL HELPED ME FINALLY GET IT...
BETTER JUST GIVE UP...
BUT HEY, KEI. WHAT SORTA GHOST WOULD BE SCARY?
HMM?
HUH? WHERE IS THIS COMING FROM?
JUST WONDERING.
ピクッ
PIKU (TWITCH)
HUH... WHAT'S SHE GETTING AT!? ASKING FOR MY SAKE...?
HMM. I GUESS ...

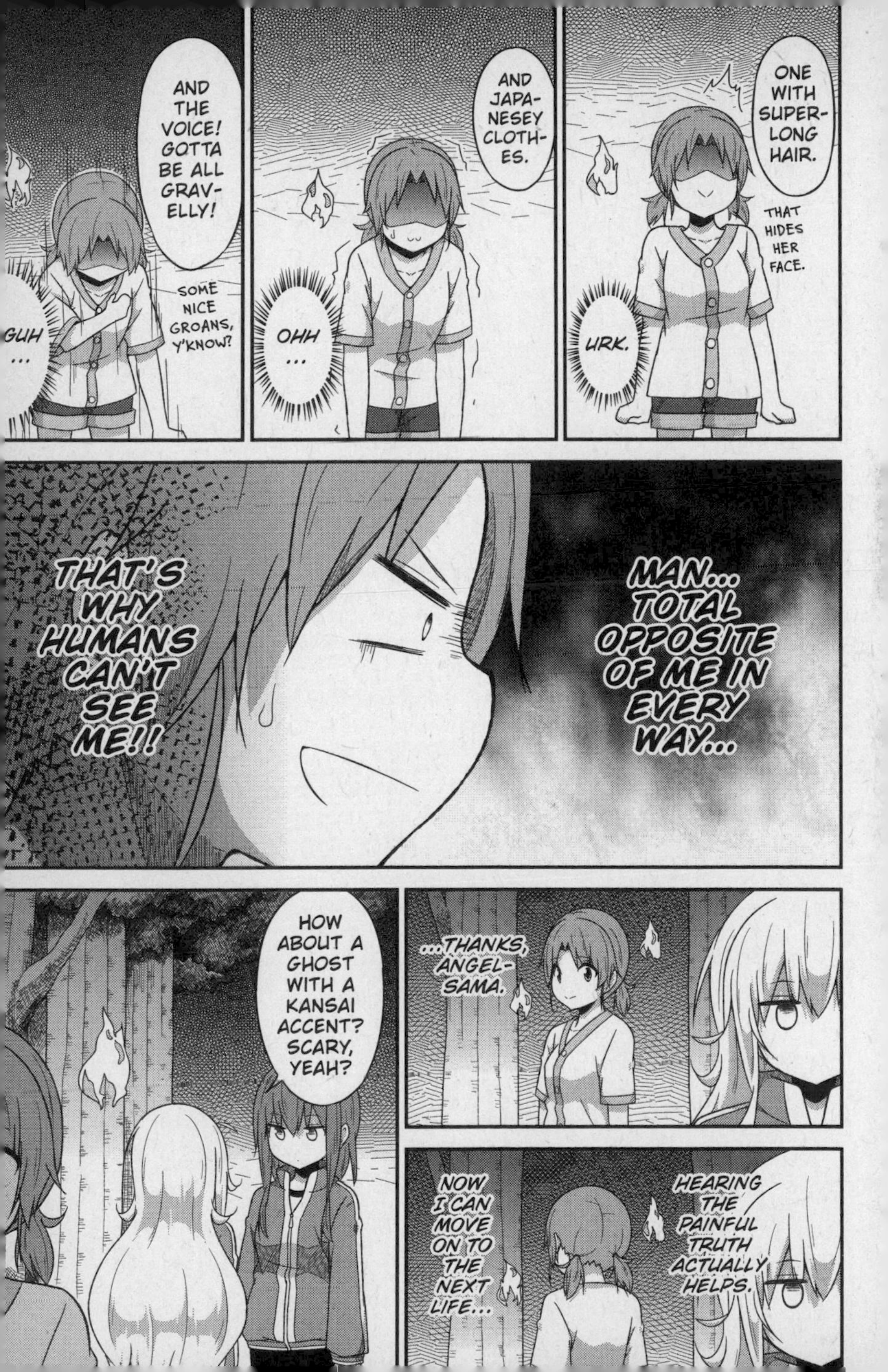
ONE WITH SUPER-LONG HAIR.
THAT HIDES HER FACE.
URK.
AND JAPANESEY CLOTHES.
OHH...
AND THE VOICE! GOTTA BE ALL GRAVELLY!
SOME NICE GROANS, Y'KNOW?
GUH...
MAN... TOTAL OPPOSITE OF ME IN EVERY WAY...
THAT'S WHY HUMANS CAN'T SEE ME!!
...THANKS, ANGEL-SAMA.
HEARING THE PAINFUL TRUTH ACTUALLY HELPS.
NOW I CAN MOVE ON TO THE NEXT LIFE...
HOW ABOUT A GHOST WITH A KANSAI ACCENT? SCARY, YEAH?

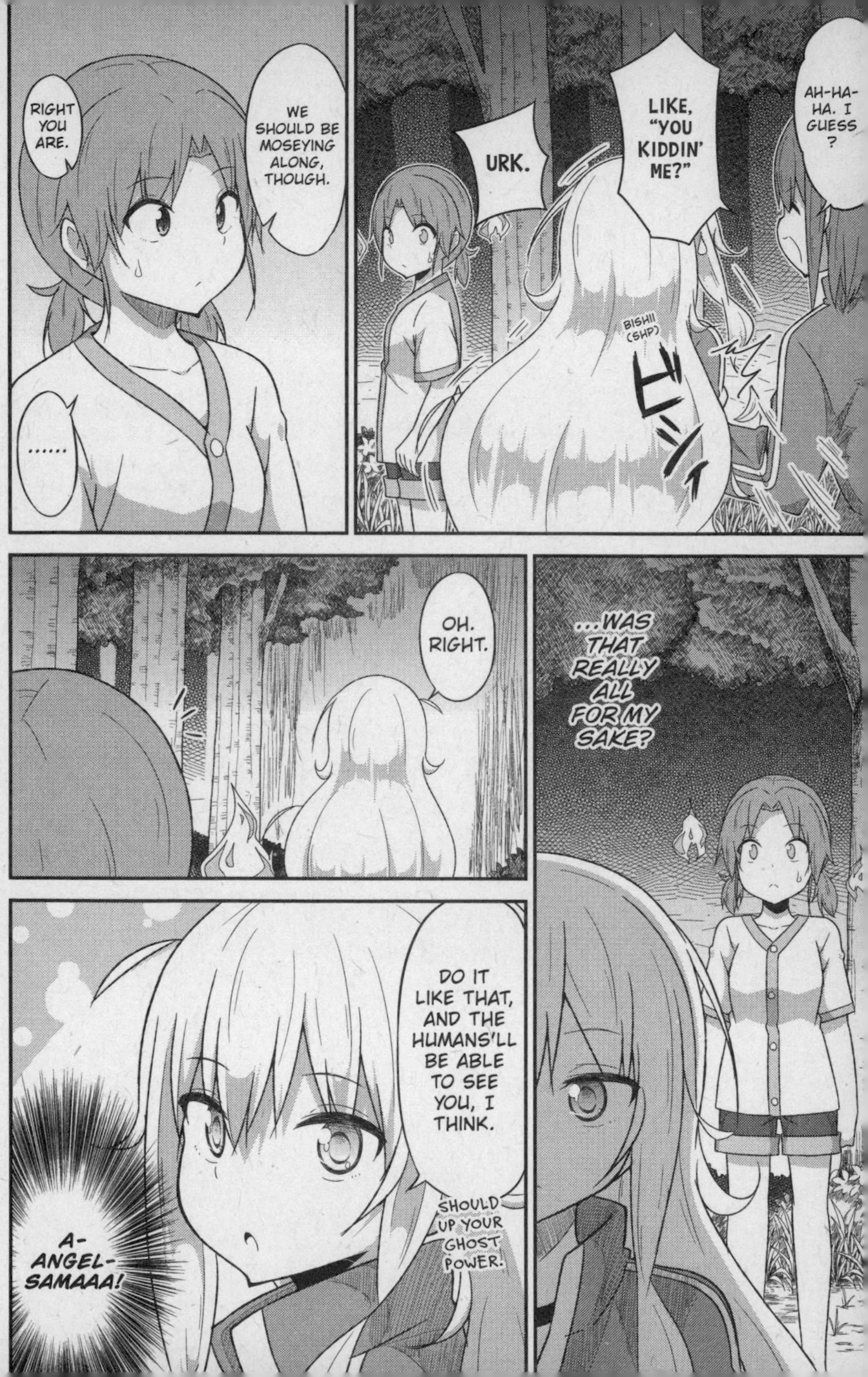
AH-HA-HA. I GUESS?
LIKE, "YOU KIDDIN' ME?"
URK.
BISHII (SHP)
WE SHOULD BE MOSEYING ALONG, THOUGH.
RIGHT YOU ARE.
......
...WAS THAT REALLY ALL FOR MY SAKE?
OH. RIGHT.
DO IT LIKE THAT, AND THE HUMANS'LL BE ABLE TO SEE YOU, I THINK.
SHOULD UP YOUR GHOST POWER.
A-ANGEL-SAMAAA!

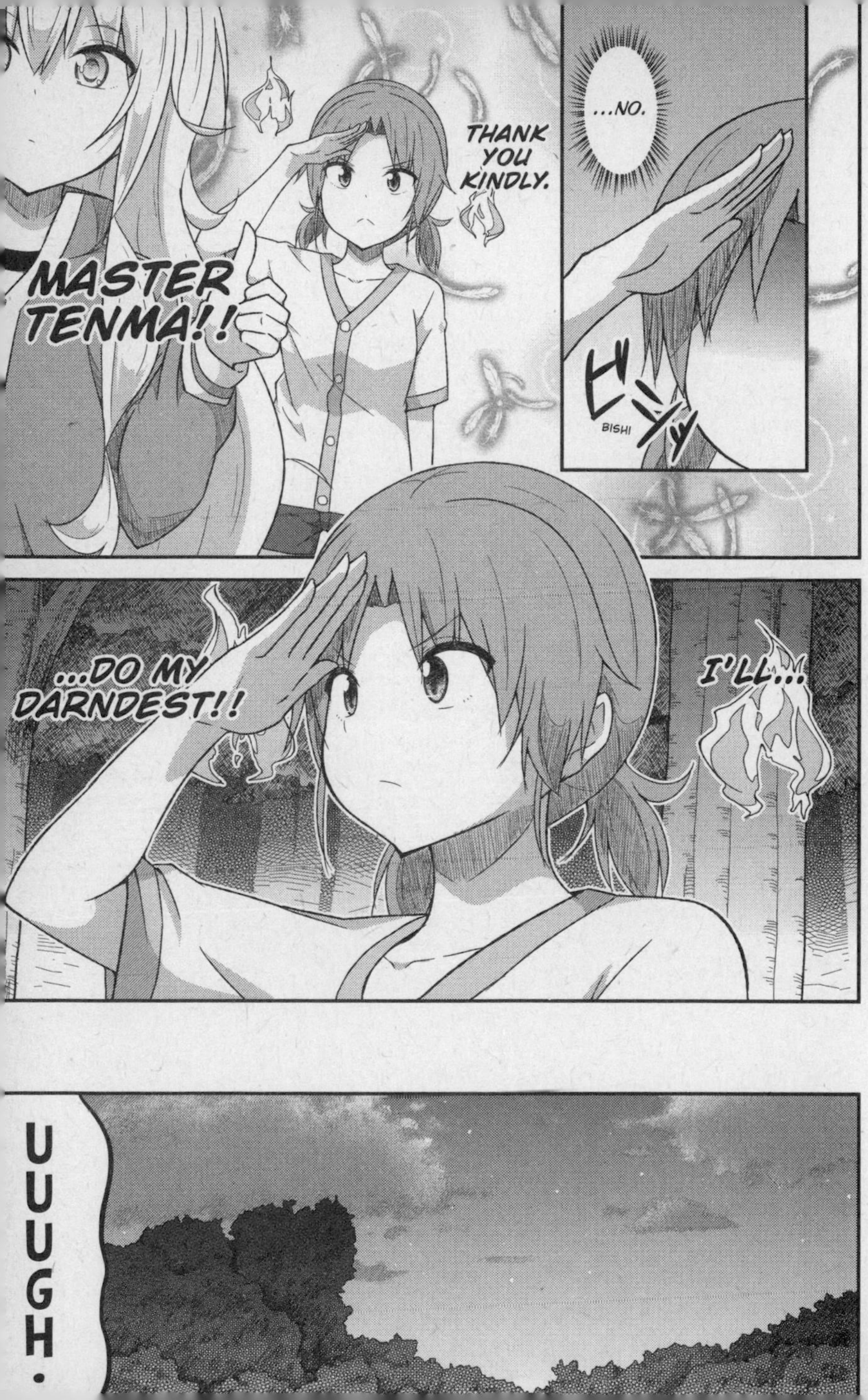
…NO.
ビシッ
BISHI
THANK YOU KINDLY.
MASTER TENMA!!
I'LL…
…DO MY DARNDEST!!
UUUGH.

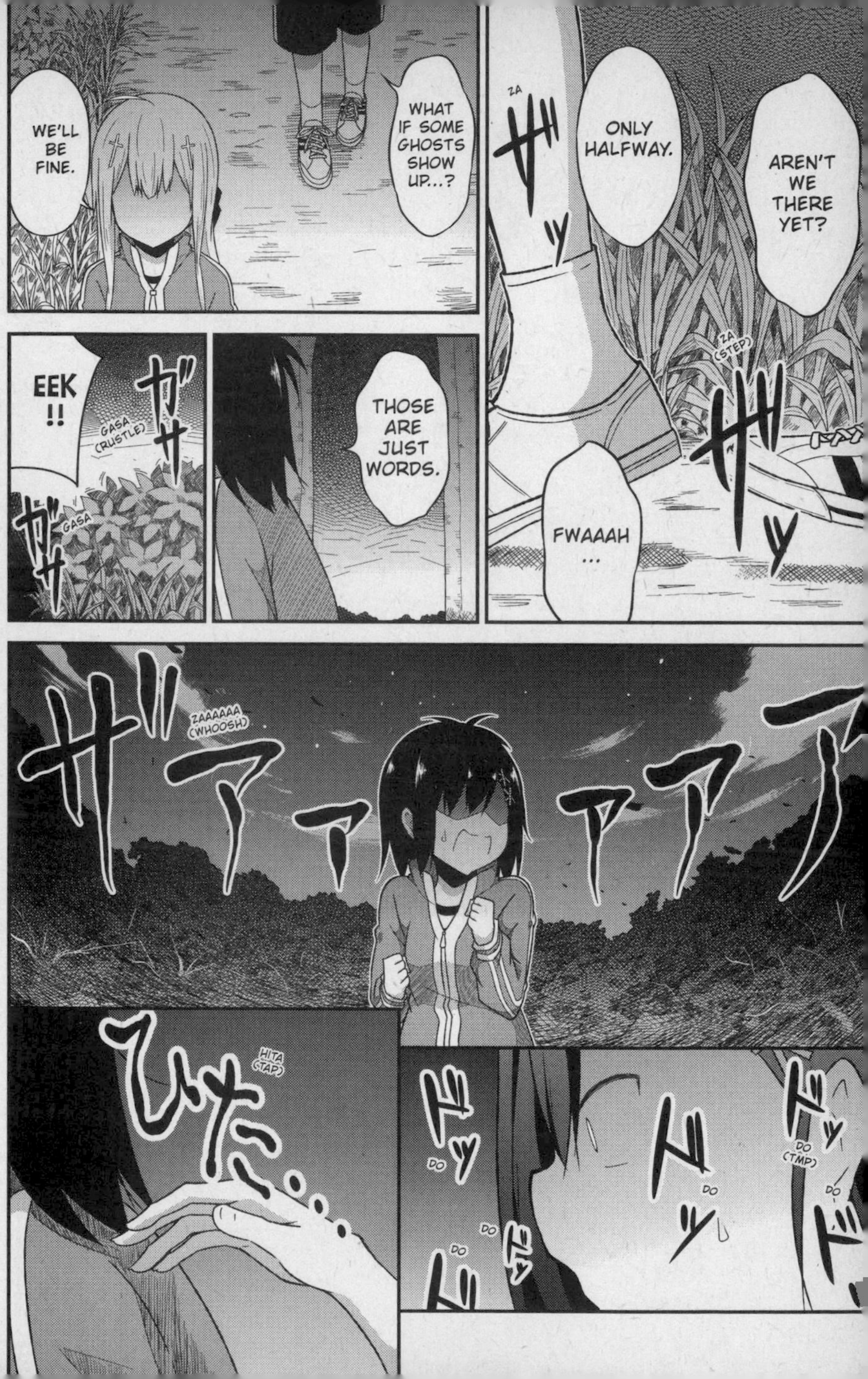
AREN'T WE THERE YET?
ONLY HALFWAY.
ZA
ZA (STEP)
FWAAAH...
WHAT IF SOME GHOSTS SHOW UP...?
WE'LL BE FINE.
THOSE ARE JUST WORDS.
EEK!!
GASA (RUSTLE)
GASA
ZAAAAAA (WHOOSH)
DO (TMP)
DO
DO
DO
DO
DO
HITA (TAP)

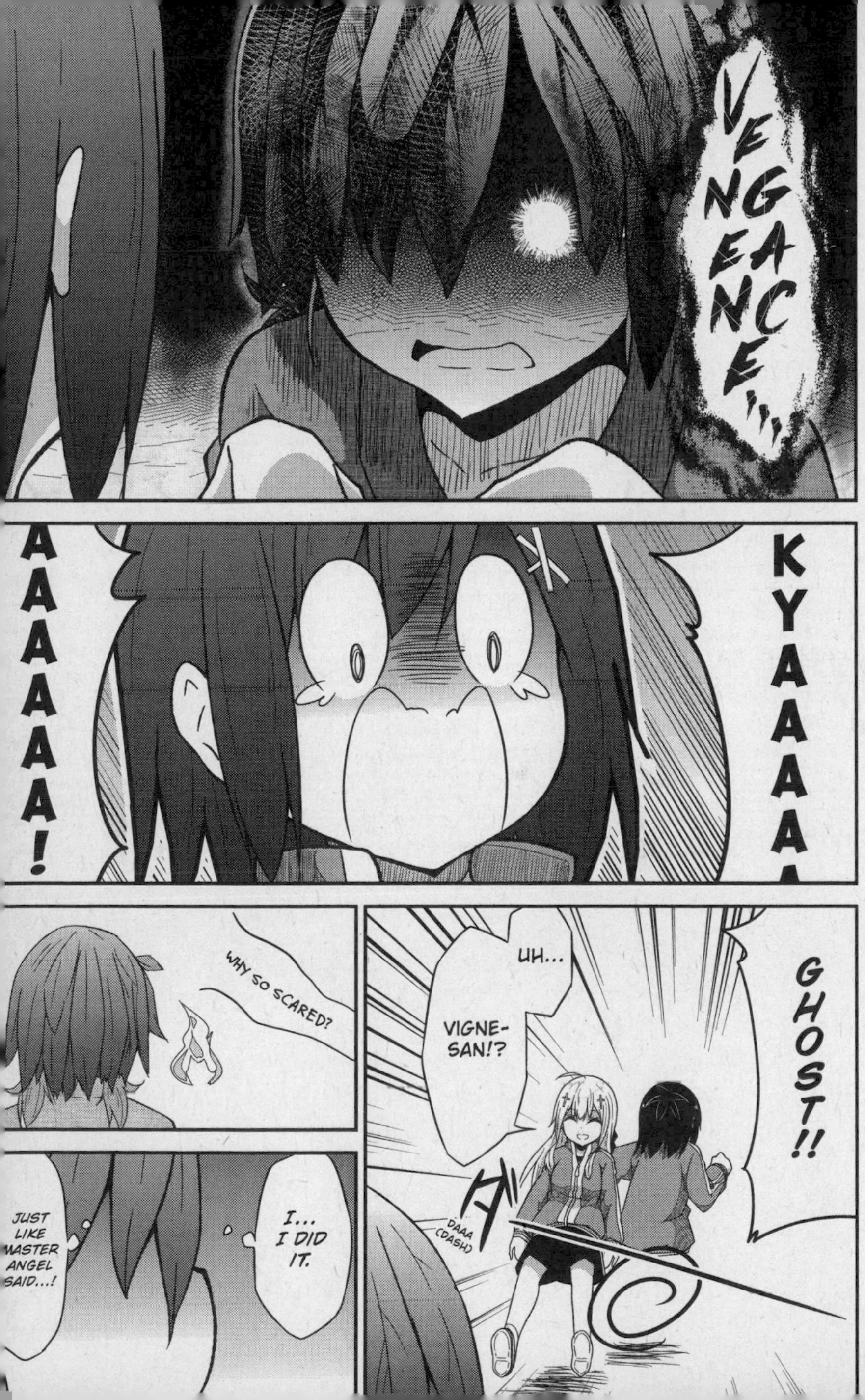
VENGEANCE...
KYAAAAA
AAAAAAA!
GHOST!!
UH...
VIGNE-SAN!?
DAAA (DASH)
WHY SO SCARED?
I... I DID IT.
JUST LIKE MASTER ANGEL SAID...!

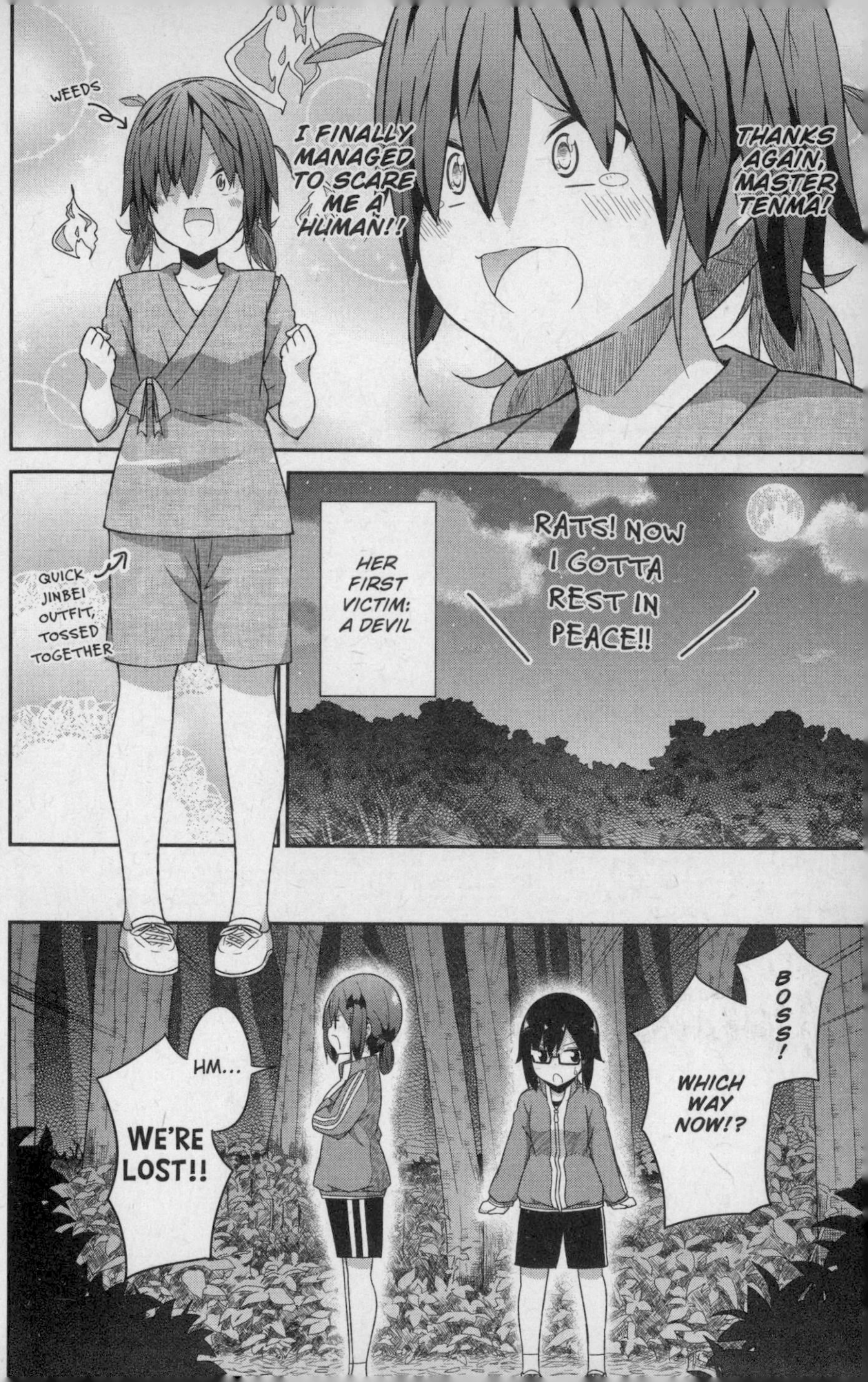
THANKS AGAIN, MASTER TENMA!
I FINALLY MANAGED TO SCARE ME A HUMAN!!
WEEDS
RATS! NOW I GOTTA REST IN PEACE!!
HER FIRST VICTIM: A DEVIL
QUICK JINBEI OUTFIT, TOSSED TOGETHER
BOSS! WHICH WAY NOW!?
HM... WE'RE LOST!!

Spirit Company Limited

Supplier: **Miho Shiraishi**

000-1227 Akenodai Ward, 000-4 YuYu Building 4F
TEL. 0009-12-12
miho-s@yureic.ano

Gabriel Dropout

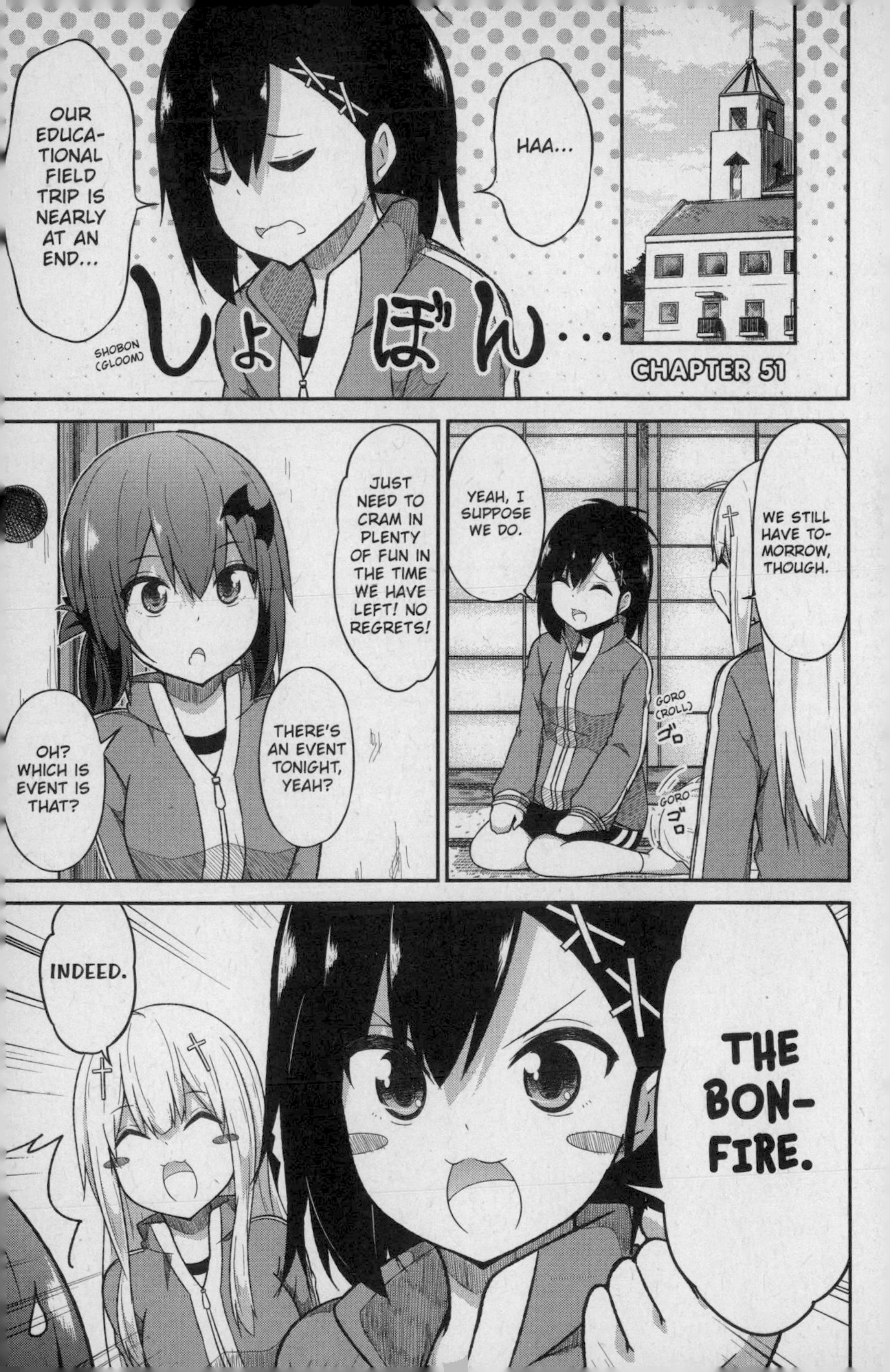
CHAPTER 51
HAA...
OUR EDUCATIONAL FIELD TRIP IS NEARLY AT AN END...
しょぼん…
SHOBON (GLOOM)
WE STILL HAVE TOMORROW, THOUGH.
YEAH, I SUPPOSE WE DO.
GORO (ROLL) ゴロ
GORO ゴロ
JUST NEED TO CRAM IN PLENTY OF FUN IN THE TIME WE HAVE LEFT! NO REGRETS!
THERE'S AN EVENT TONIGHT, YEAH?
OH? WHICH IS EVENT IS THAT?
THE BONFIRE.
INDEED.

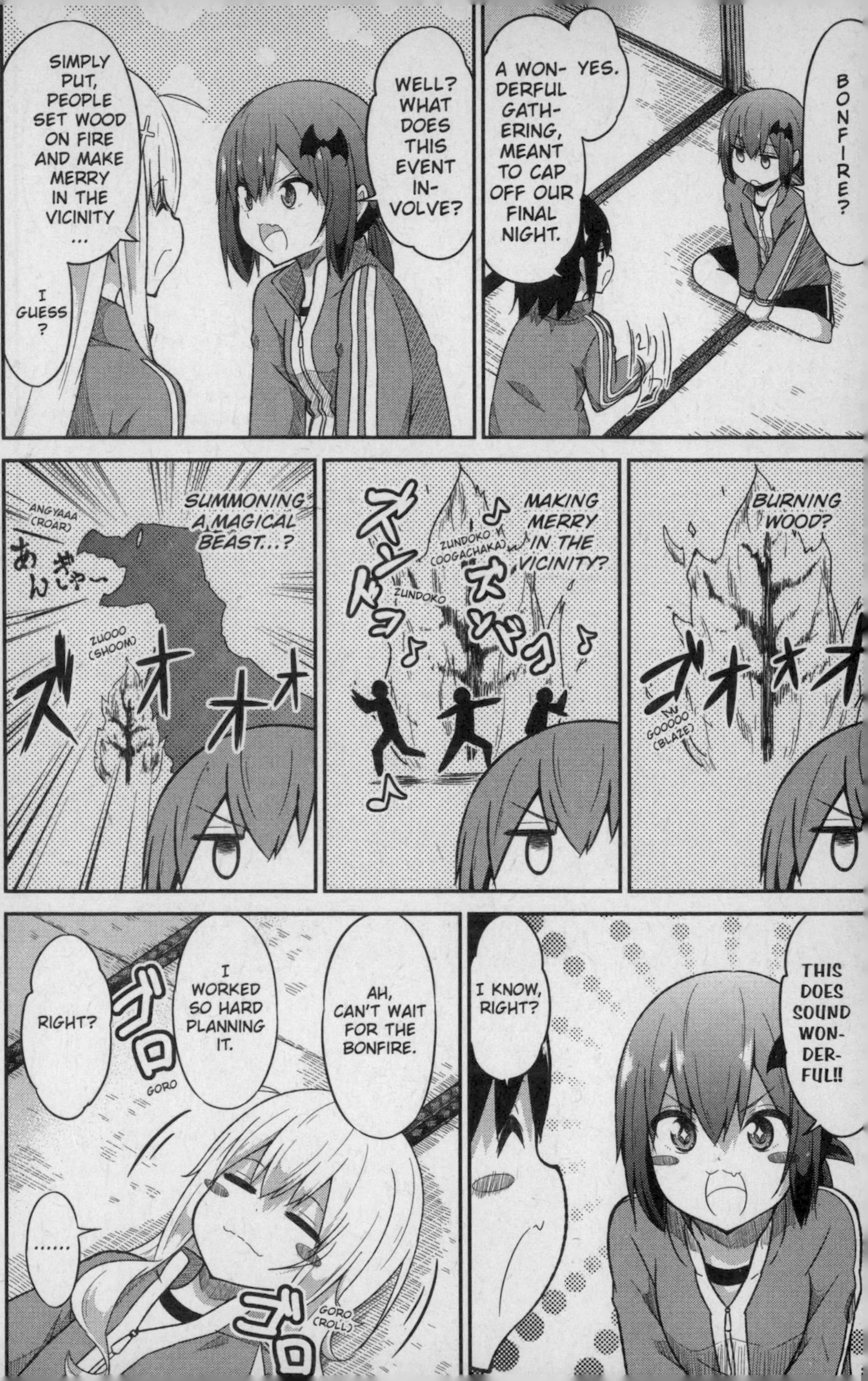
BONFIRE?
YES.
A WONDERFUL GATHERING, MEANT TO CAP OFF OUR FINAL NIGHT.
WELL? WHAT DOES THIS EVENT INVOLVE?
SIMPLY PUT, PEOPLE SET WOOD ON FIRE AND MAKE MERRY IN THE VICINITY...
I GUESS?
BURNING WOOD?
GOOOOO (BLAZE)
MAKING MERRY IN THE VICINITY?
ZUNDOKO (OOGACHAKA)
ZUNDOKO
SUMMONING A MAGICAL BEAST...?
ANGYAAA (ROAR)
ZUOOO (SHOOM)
THIS DOES SOUND WONDERFUL!!
I KNOW, RIGHT?
AH, CAN'T WAIT FOR THE BONFIRE.
I WORKED SO HARD PLANNING IT.
RIGHT?
......
GORO
GORO (ROLL)

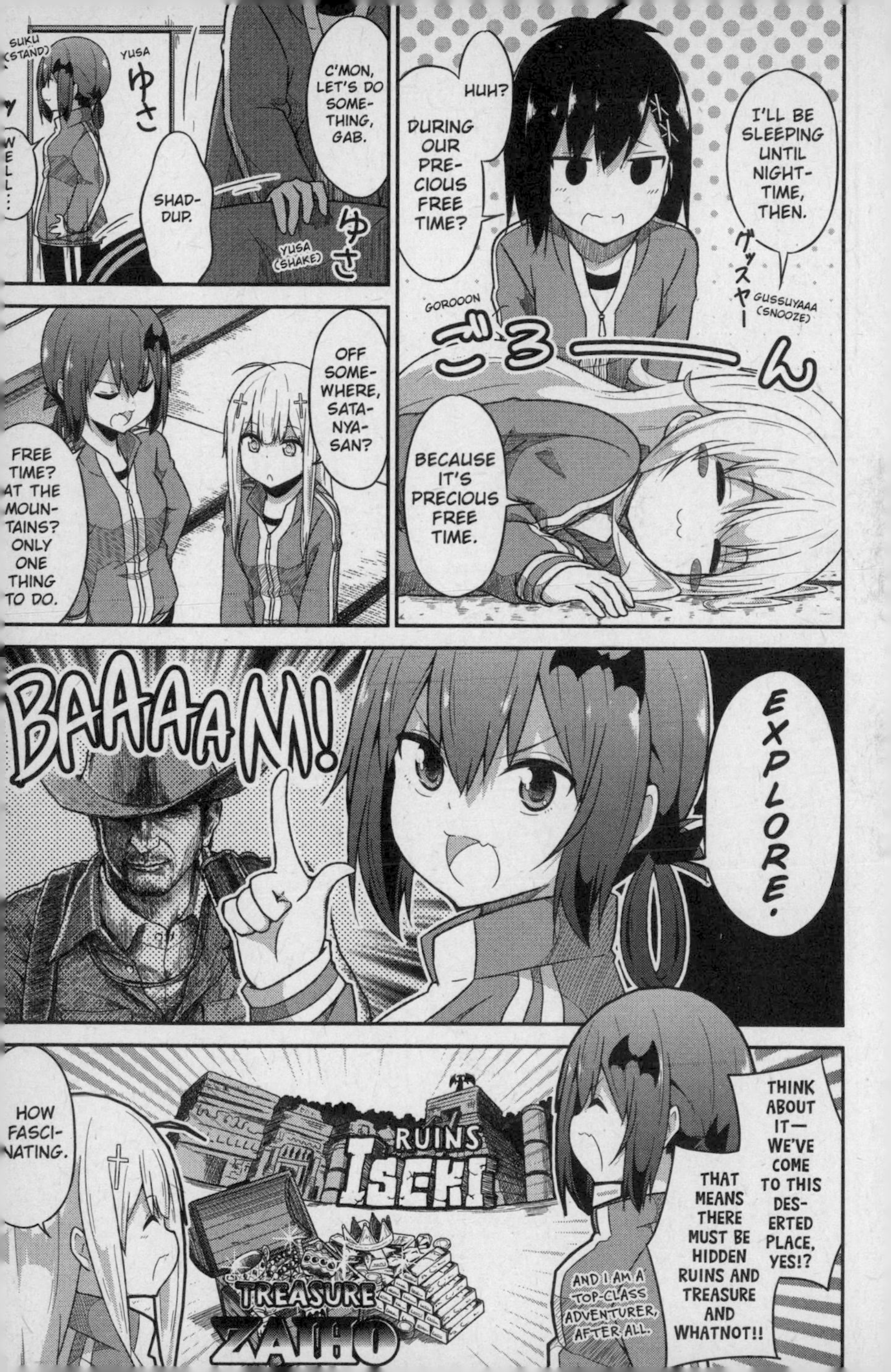
I'LL BE SLEEPING UNTIL NIGHTTIME, THEN.
ヴッスヤー
GUSSUYAAA (SNOOZE)
HUH? DURING OUR PRECIOUS FREE TIME?
ごろーーん
GOROOON
BECAUSE IT'S PRECIOUS FREE TIME.
C'MON, LET'S DO SOMETHING, GAB.
ゆさ
YUSA (SHAKE)
SHADDUP.
ゆさ
YUSA
SUKU (STAND)
WELL...
OFF SOMEWHERE, SATANYA-SAN?
FREE TIME? AT THE MOUNTAINS? ONLY ONE THING TO DO.
EXPLORE.
BAAAAM!
THINK ABOUT IT—WE'VE COME TO THIS DESERTED PLACE, YES!?
THAT MEANS THERE MUST BE HIDDEN RUINS AND TREASURE AND WHATNOT!!
AND I AM A TOP-CLASS ADVENTURER, AFTER ALL.
RUINS
ISEKI
TREASURE
ZAIHO
HOW FASCINATING.

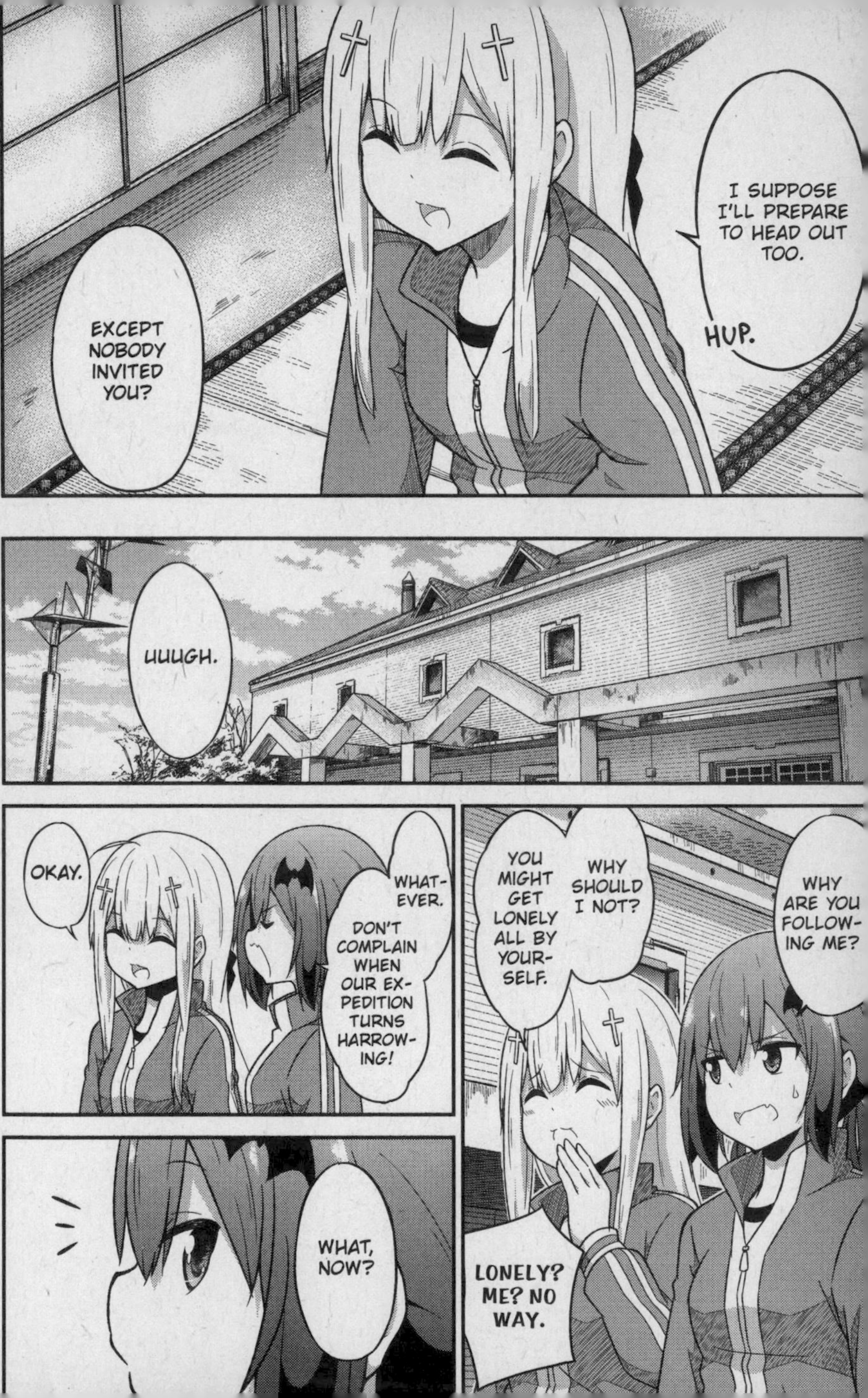
I SUPPOSE I'LL PREPARE TO HEAD OUT TOO.
HUP.
EXCEPT NOBODY INVITED YOU?
UUUGH.
WHY ARE YOU FOLLOW-ING ME?
WHY SHOULD I NOT?
YOU MIGHT GET LONELY ALL BY YOUR-SELF.
LONELY? ME? NO WAY.
WHAT-EVER.
DON'T COMPLAIN WHEN OUR EX-PEDITION TURNS HARROW-ING!
OKAY.
WHAT, NOW?

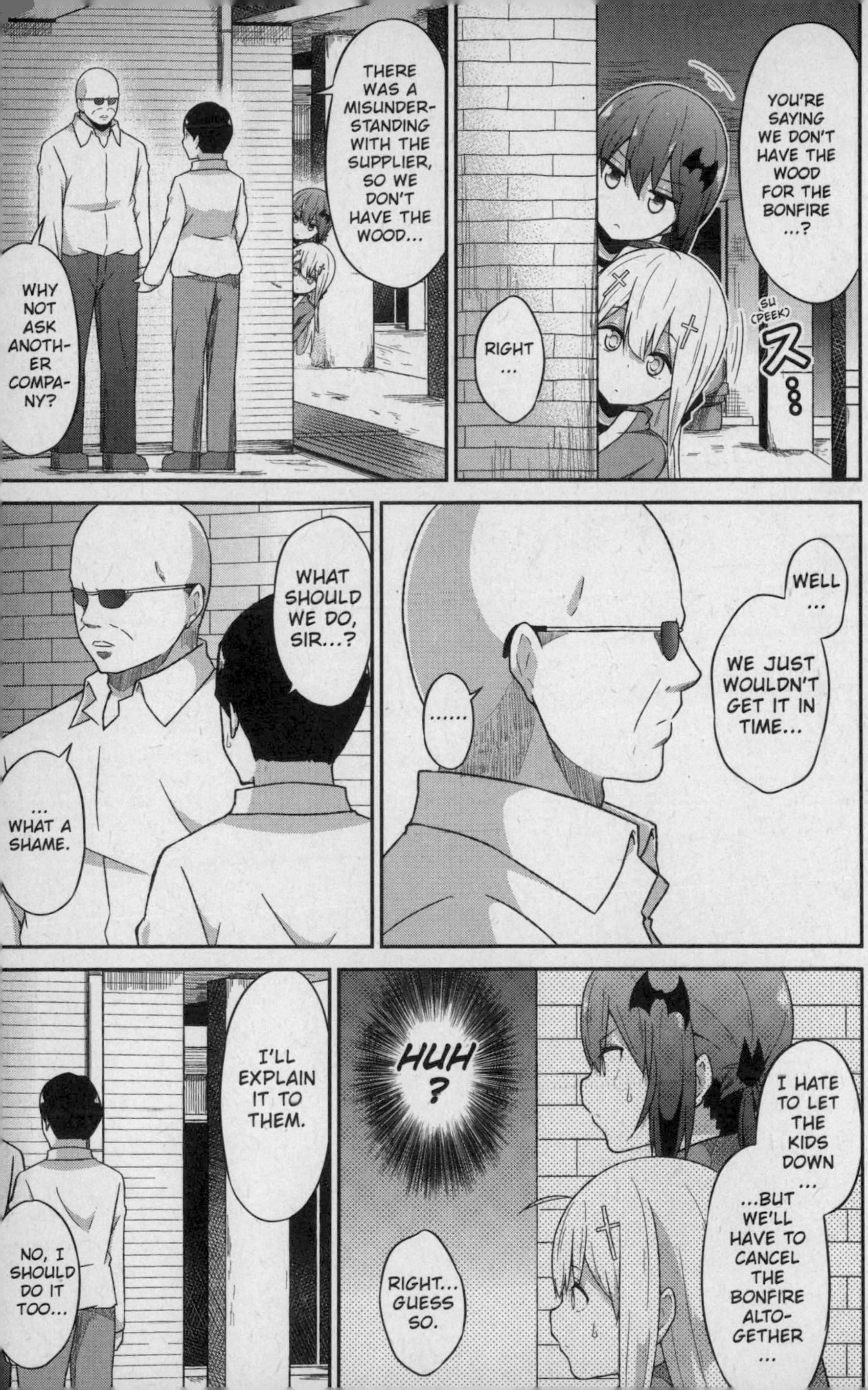
YOU'RE SAYING WE DON'T HAVE THE WOOD FOR THE BONFIRE ...?
SU (PEEK)
ス
RIGHT ...
THERE WAS A MISUNDERSTANDING WITH THE SUPPLIER, SO WE DON'T HAVE THE WOOD...
WHY NOT ASK ANOTHER COMPANY?
WELL ...
WE JUST WOULDN'T GET IT IN TIME...
......
WHAT SHOULD WE DO, SIR...?
... WHAT A SHAME.
I HATE TO LET THE KIDS DOWN ...
...BUT WE'LL HAVE TO CANCEL THE BONFIRE ALTOGETHER ...
RIGHT... GUESS SO.
HUH ?
I'LL EXPLAIN IT TO THEM.
NO, I SHOULD DO IT TOO...

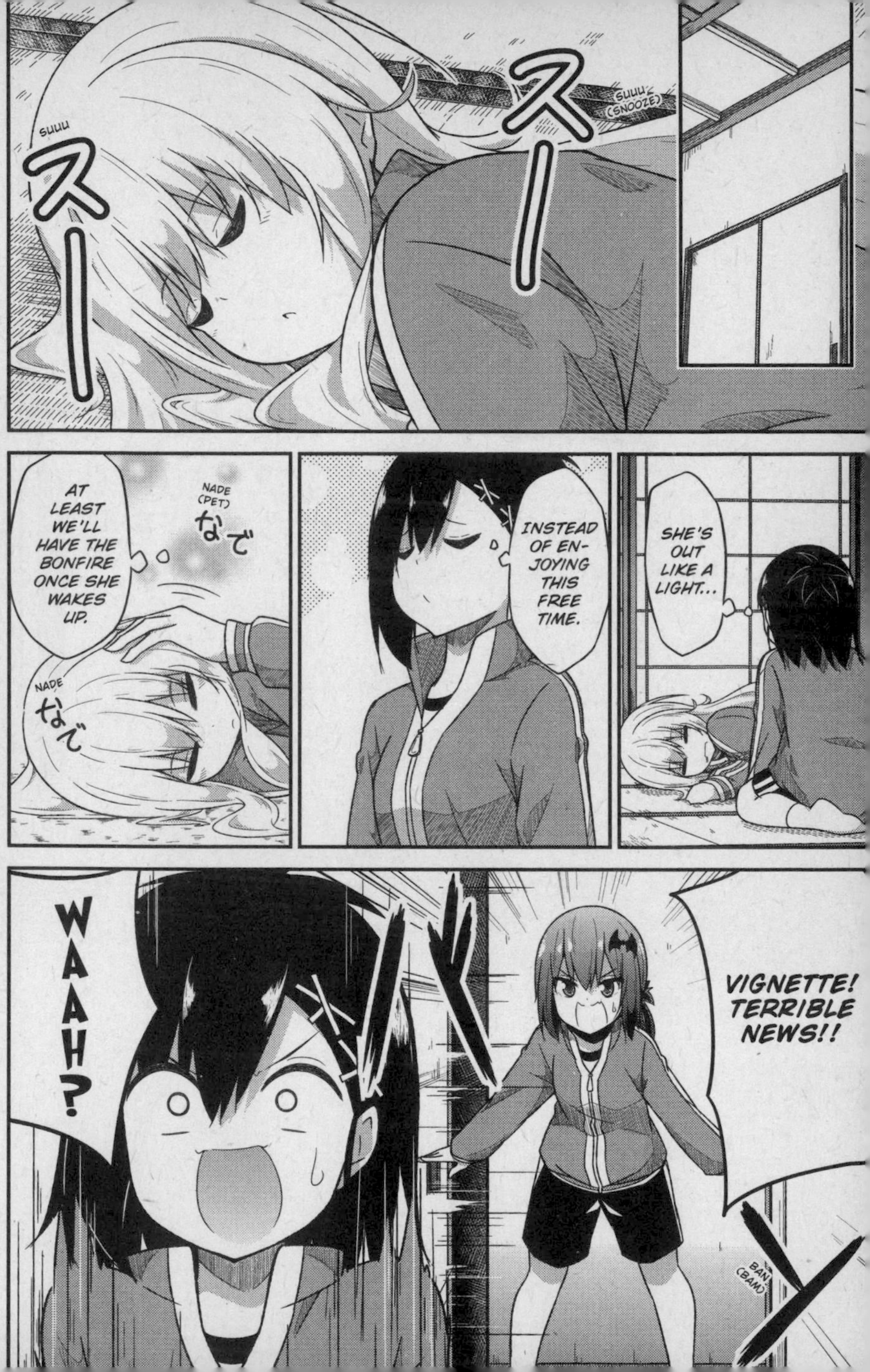

SUUU (SNOOZE)
スー
SUUU
スー
SHE'S OUT LIKE A LIGHT...
INSTEAD OF EN-JOYING THIS FREE TIME.
NADE (PET)
なで
AT LEAST WE'LL HAVE THE BONFIRE ONCE SHE WAKES UP.
NADE
なで
VIGNETTE! TERRIBLE NEWS!!
BAN (BAM)
WAAH?

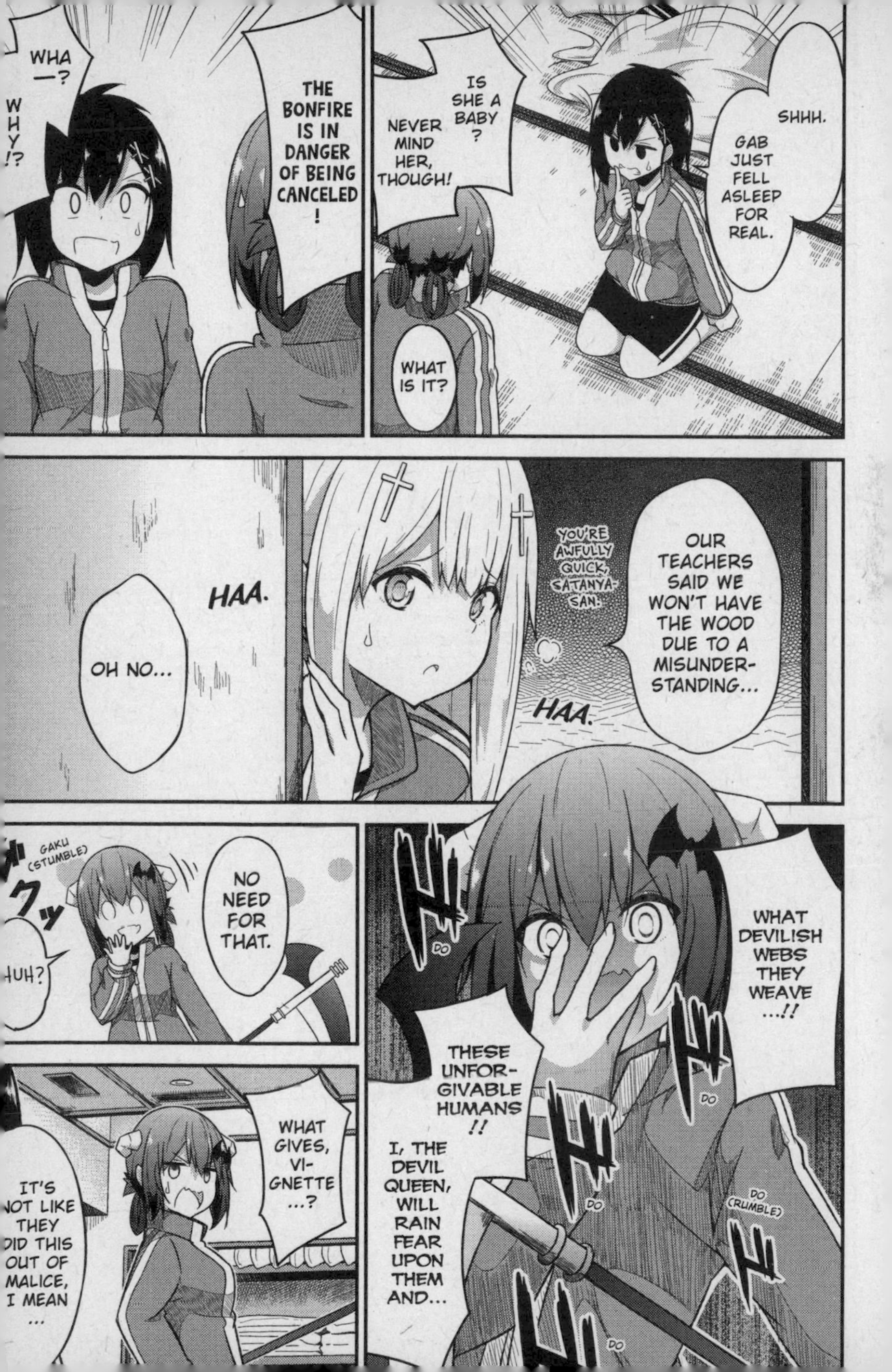
SHHH.
GAB JUST FELL ASLEEP FOR REAL.
IS SHE A BABY?
NEVER MIND HER, THOUGH!
WHAT IS IT?
THE BONFIRE IS IN DANGER OF BEING CANCELED!
WHA—?
WHY!?
OUR TEACHERS SAID WE WON'T HAVE THE WOOD DUE TO A MISUNDERSTANDING...
YOU'RE AWFULLY QUICK, SATANYA-SAN.
HAA.
HAA.
OH NO...
WHAT DEVILISH WEBS THEY WEAVE...!!
DO
THESE UNFORGIVABLE HUMANS!!
DO
I, THE DEVIL QUEEN, WILL RAIN FEAR UPON THEM AND...
DO
DO (RUMBLE)
DO
NO NEED FOR THAT.
GAKU (STUMBLE)
HUH?
WHAT GIVES, VIGNETTE...?
IT'S NOT LIKE THEY DID THIS OUT OF MALICE, I MEAN...

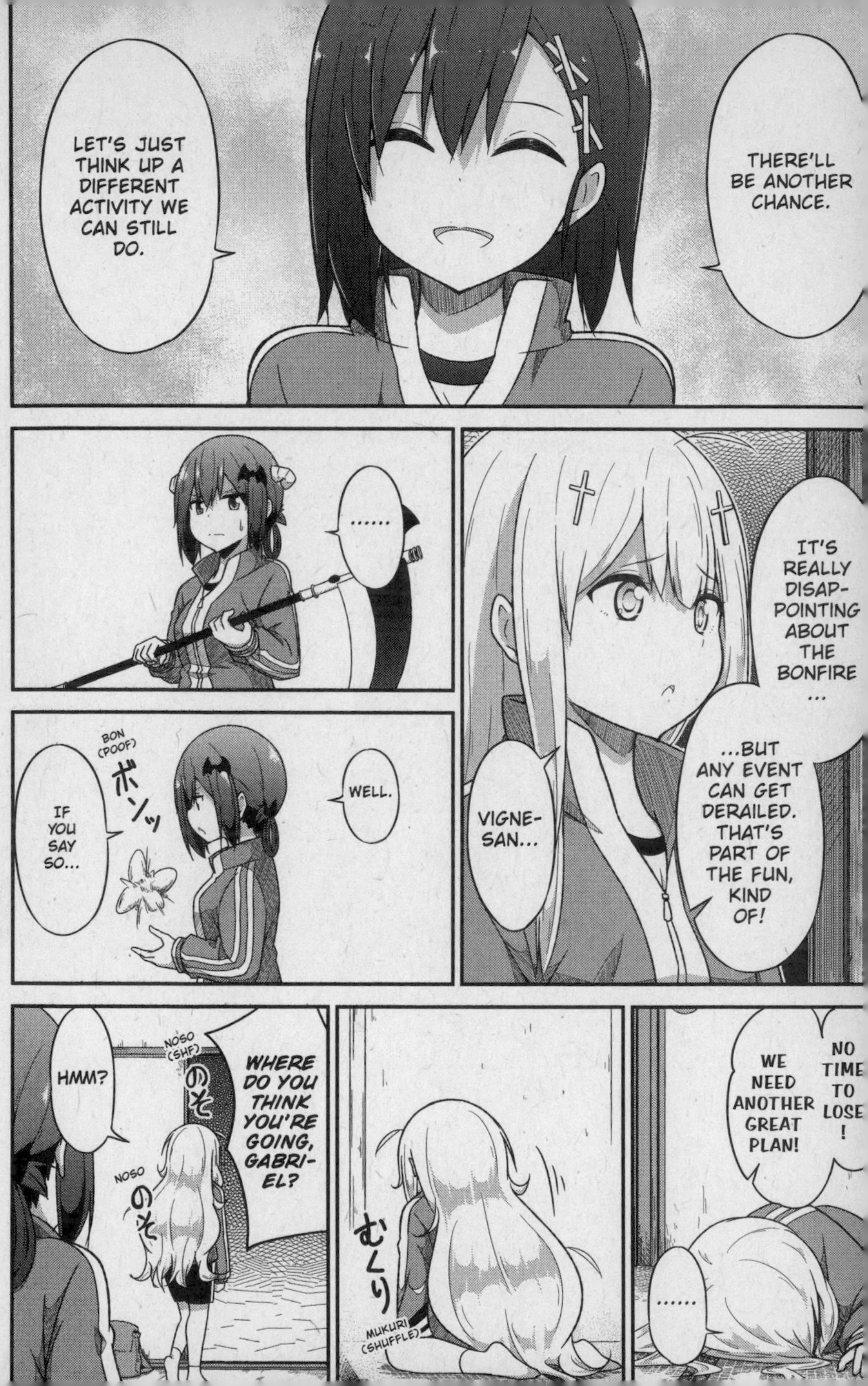
THERE'LL BE ANOTHER CHANCE.
LET'S JUST THINK UP A DIFFERENT ACTIVITY WE CAN STILL DO.
IT'S REALLY DISAPPOINTING ABOUT THE BONFIRE...
...BUT ANY EVENT CAN GET DERAILED. THAT'S PART OF THE FUN, KIND OF!
VIGNE-SAN...
......
WELL.
ボンッ
BON (POOF)
IF YOU SAY SO...
NO TIME TO LOSE!
WE NEED ANOTHER GREAT PLAN!
......
むくり
MUKURI (SHUFFLE)
WHERE DO YOU THINK YOU'RE GOING, GABRIEL?
のそ
NOSO (SHF)
HMM?
のそ
NOSO

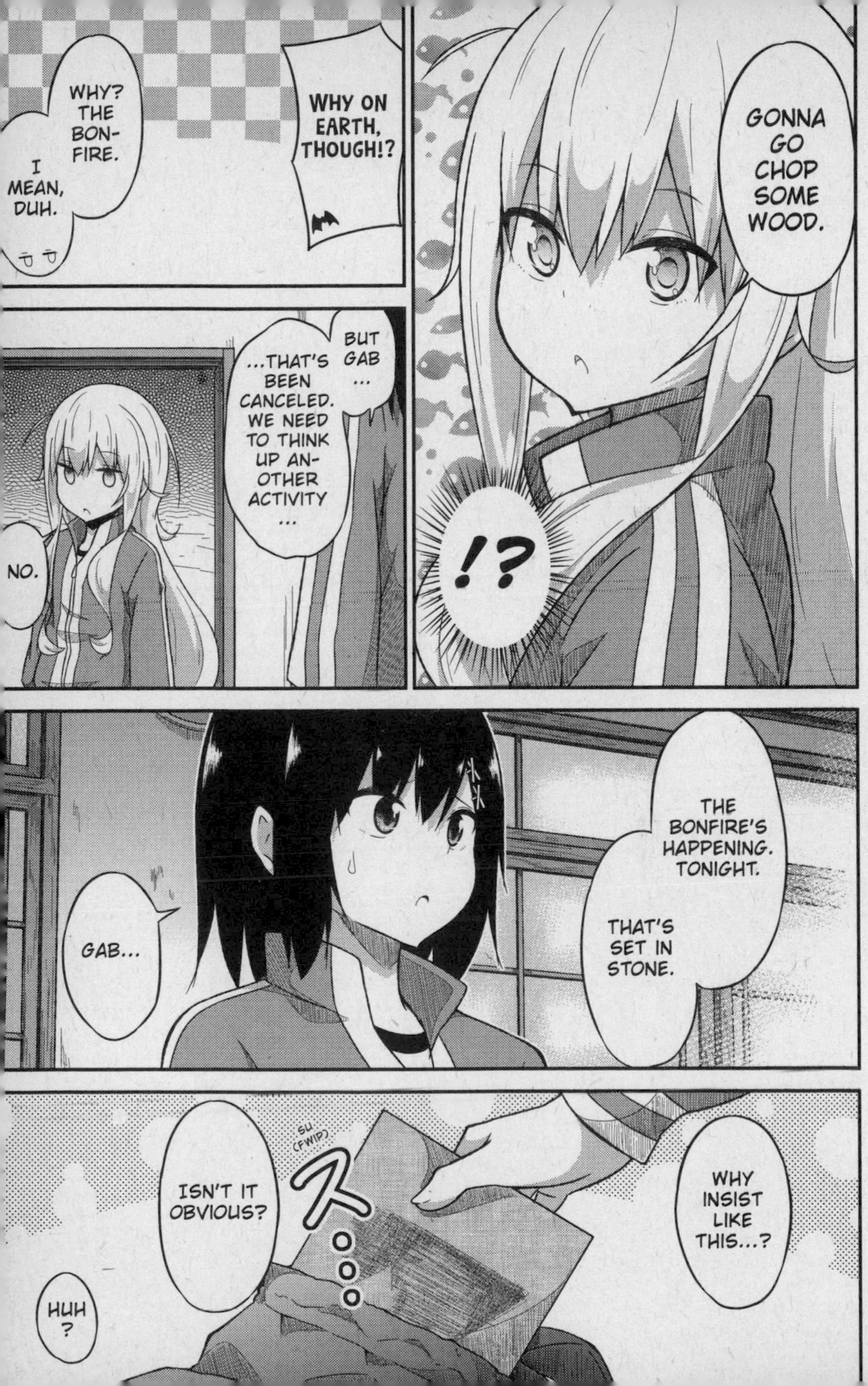
GONNA GO CHOP SOME WOOD.
!?
WHY ON EARTH, THOUGH!?
WHY? THE BON-FIRE.
I MEAN, DUH.
BUT GAB ...
...THAT'S BEEN CANCELED. WE NEED TO THINK UP AN-OTHER ACTIVITY ...
NO.
THE BONFIRE'S HAPPENING. TONIGHT.
THAT'S SET IN STONE.
GAB...
WHY INSIST LIKE THIS...?
SU (FWIP)
ISN'T IT OBVIOUS?
HUH ?

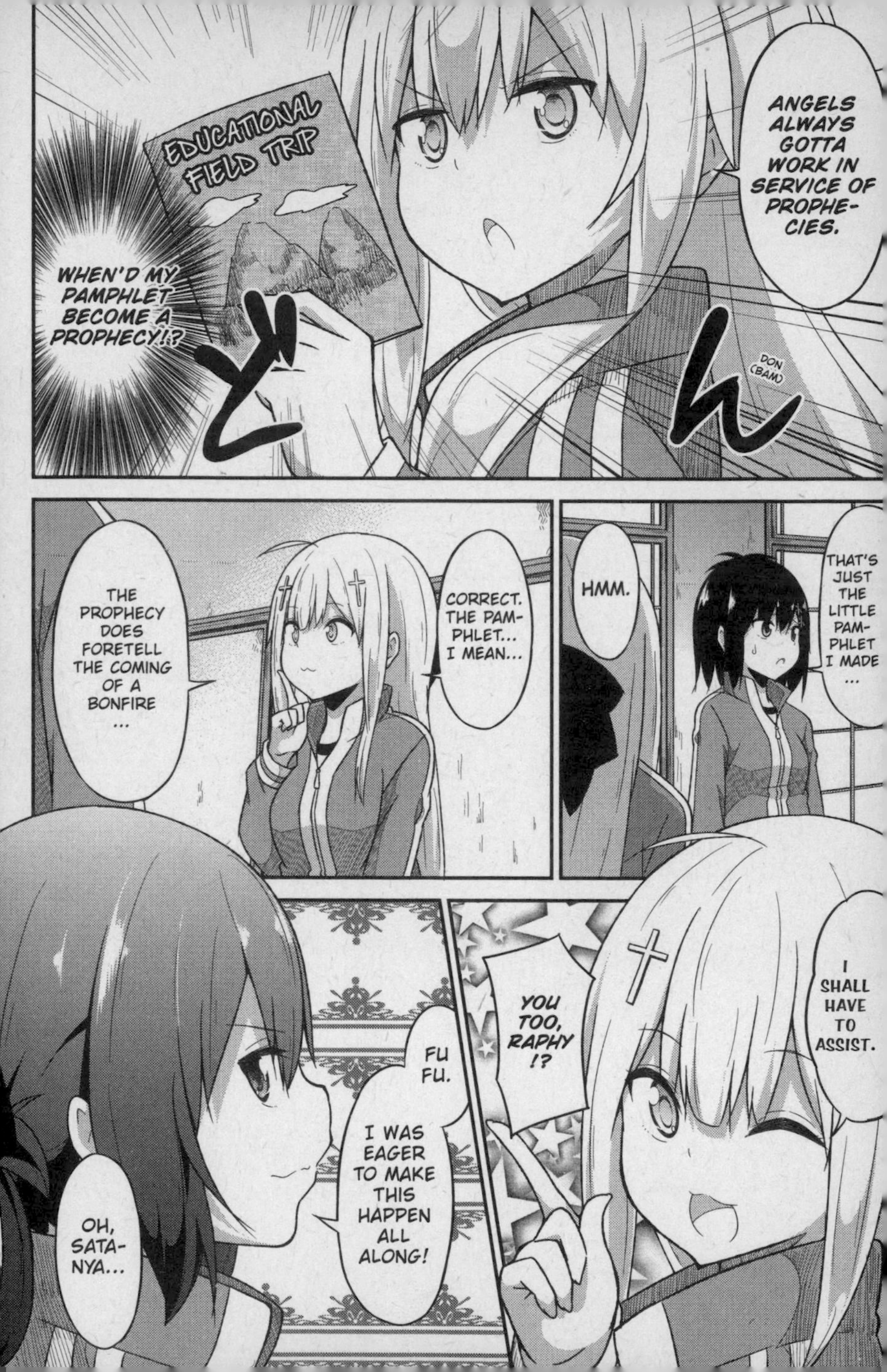
ANGELS ALWAYS GOTTA WORK IN SERVICE OF PROPHECIES.
どん
DON (BAM)
EDUCATIONAL FIELD TRIP
WHEN'D MY PAMPHLET BECOME A PROPHECY!?
THAT'S JUST THE LITTLE PAMPHLET I MADE...
HMM.
CORRECT. THE PAMPHLET... I MEAN...
THE PROPHECY DOES FORETELL THE COMING OF A BONFIRE...
I SHALL HAVE TO ASSIST.
YOU TOO, RAPHY!?
FU FU.
I WAS EAGER TO MAKE THIS HAPPEN ALL ALONG!
OH, SATANYA...

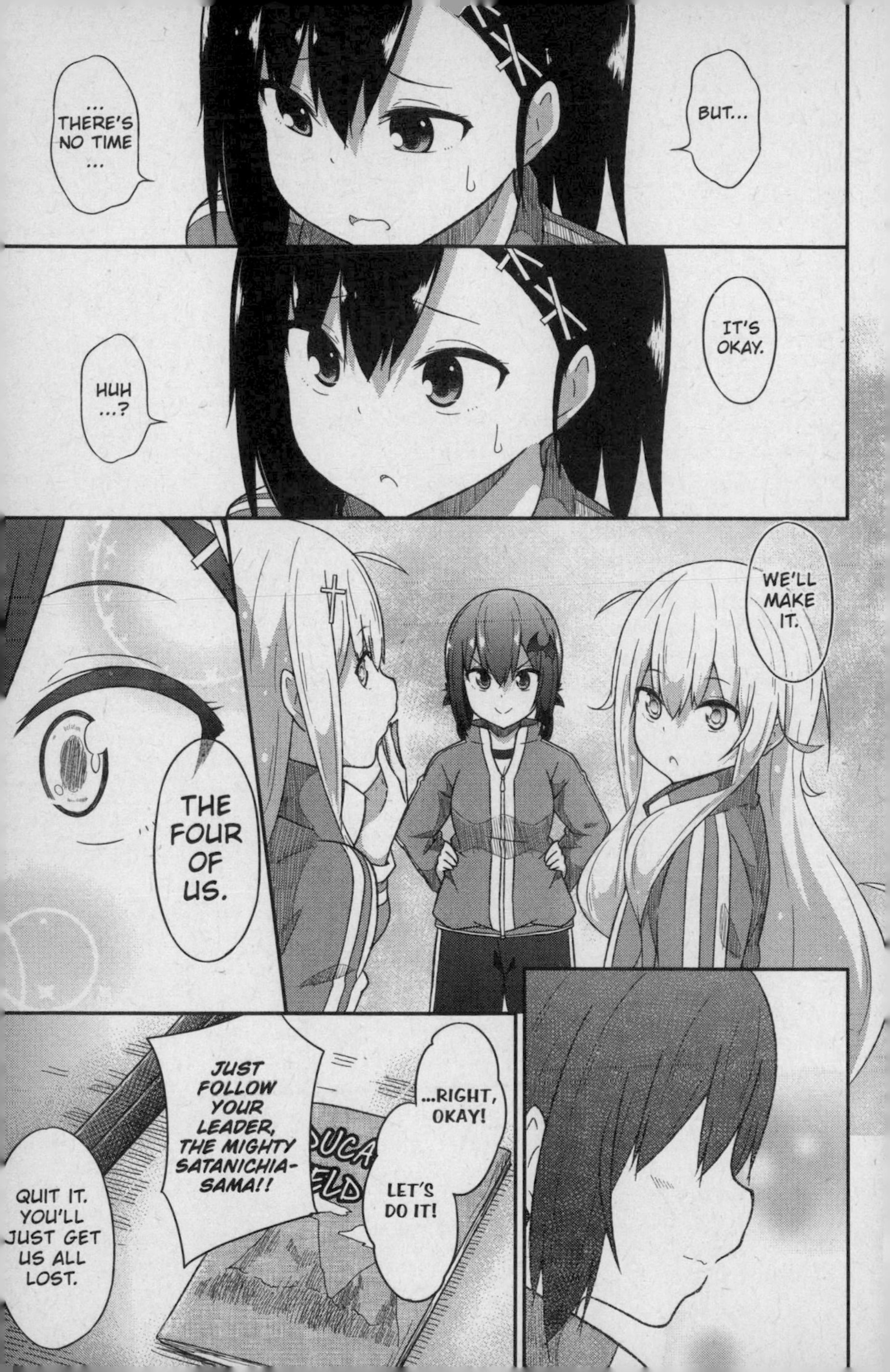
BUT...
... THERE'S NO TIME ...
IT'S OKAY.
HUH ...?
WE'LL MAKE IT.
THE FOUR OF US.
...RIGHT, OKAY!
LET'S DO IT!
JUST FOLLOW YOUR LEADER, THE MIGHTY SATANICHIA-SAMA!!
QUIT IT. YOU'LL JUST GET US ALL LOST.

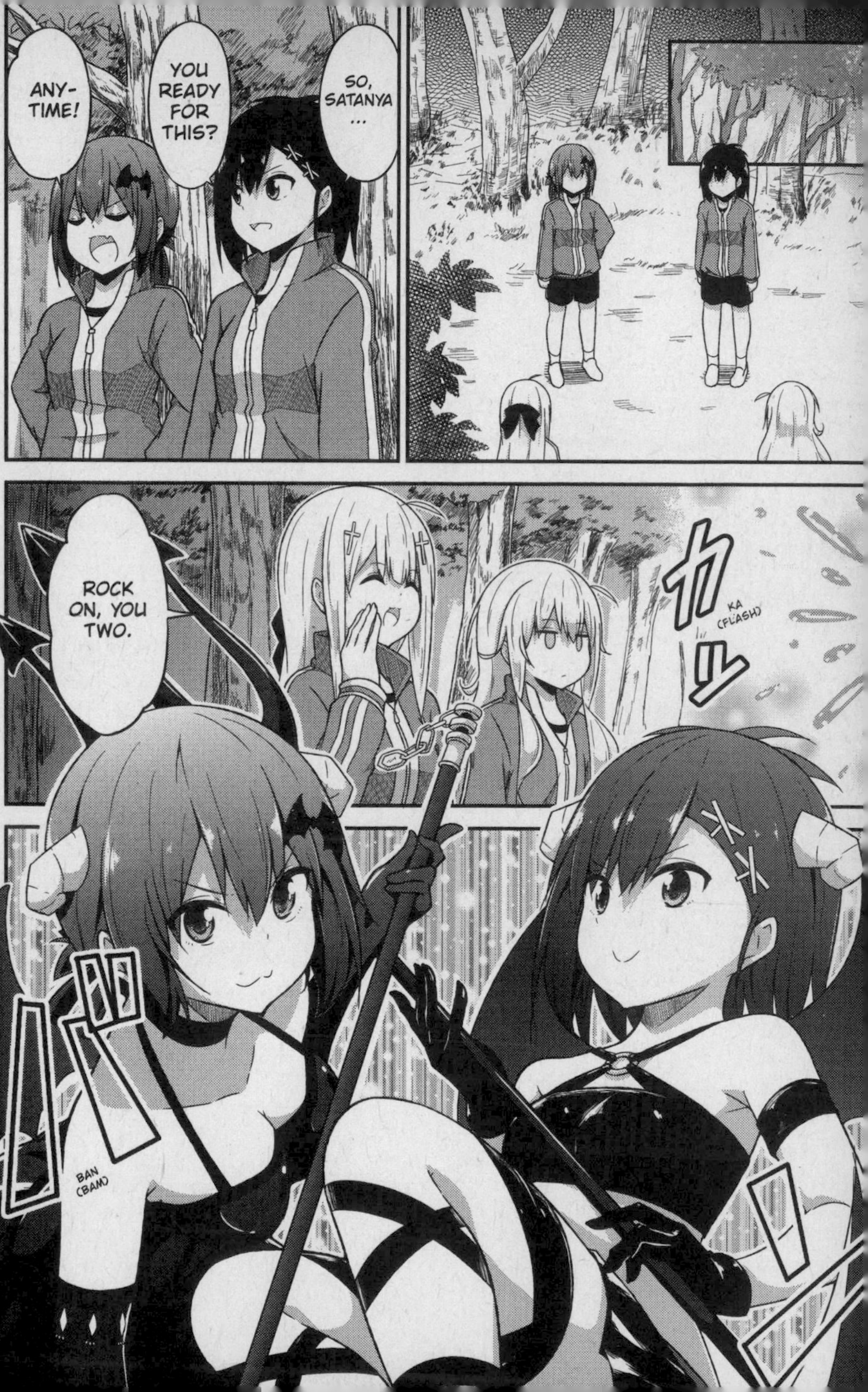
SO, SATANYA ...
YOU READY FOR THIS?
ANY-TIME!
カッ
KA (FLASH)
ROCK ON, YOU TWO.
BAN (BAM)

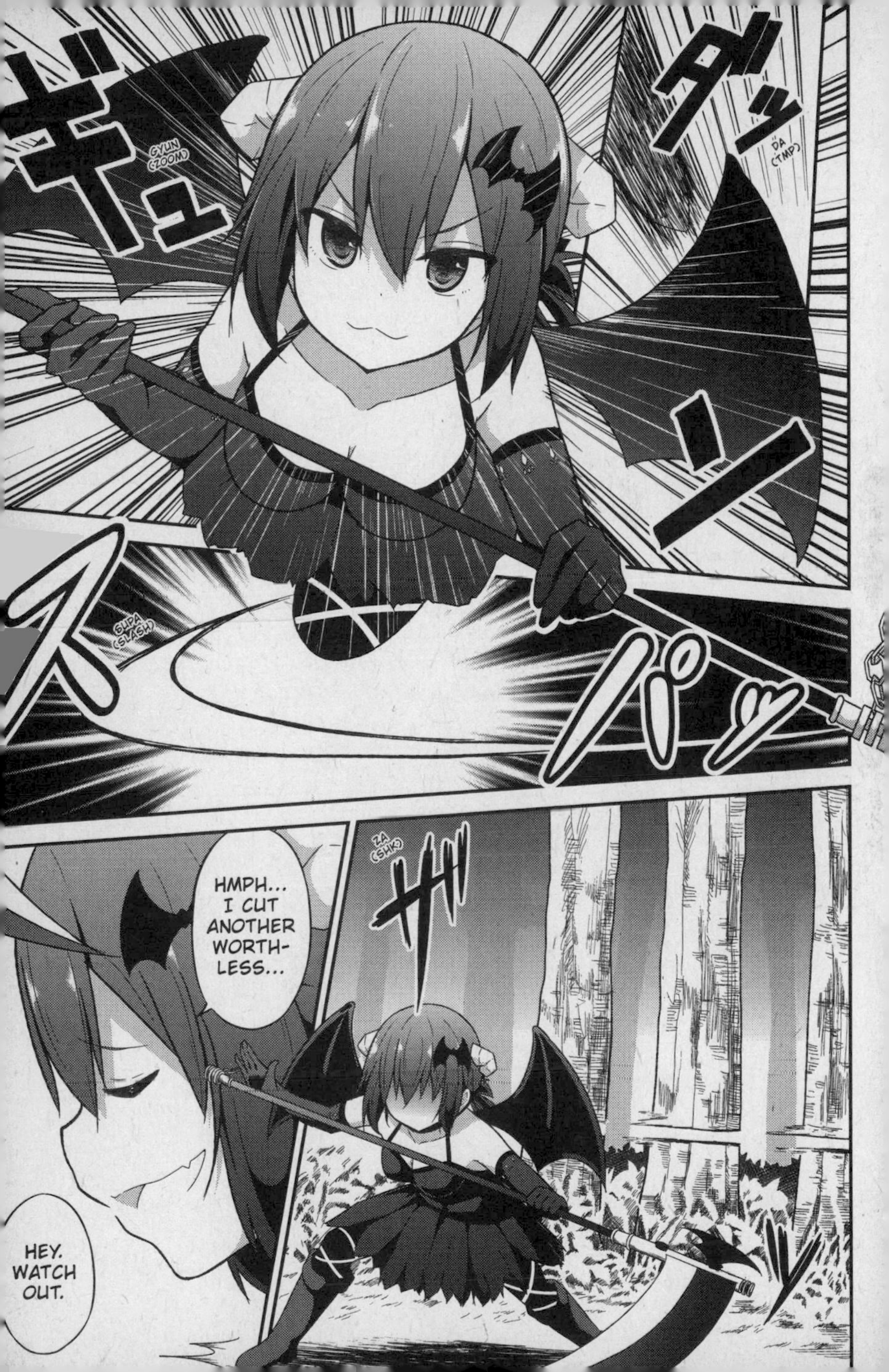
ダッ
DA (TMP)
ギュン
GYUN (ZOOM)
ズパッ
ZUPA (SLASH)
ザッ
ZA (SHK)
HMPH... I CUT ANOTHER WORTH-LESS...
HEY. WATCH OUT.

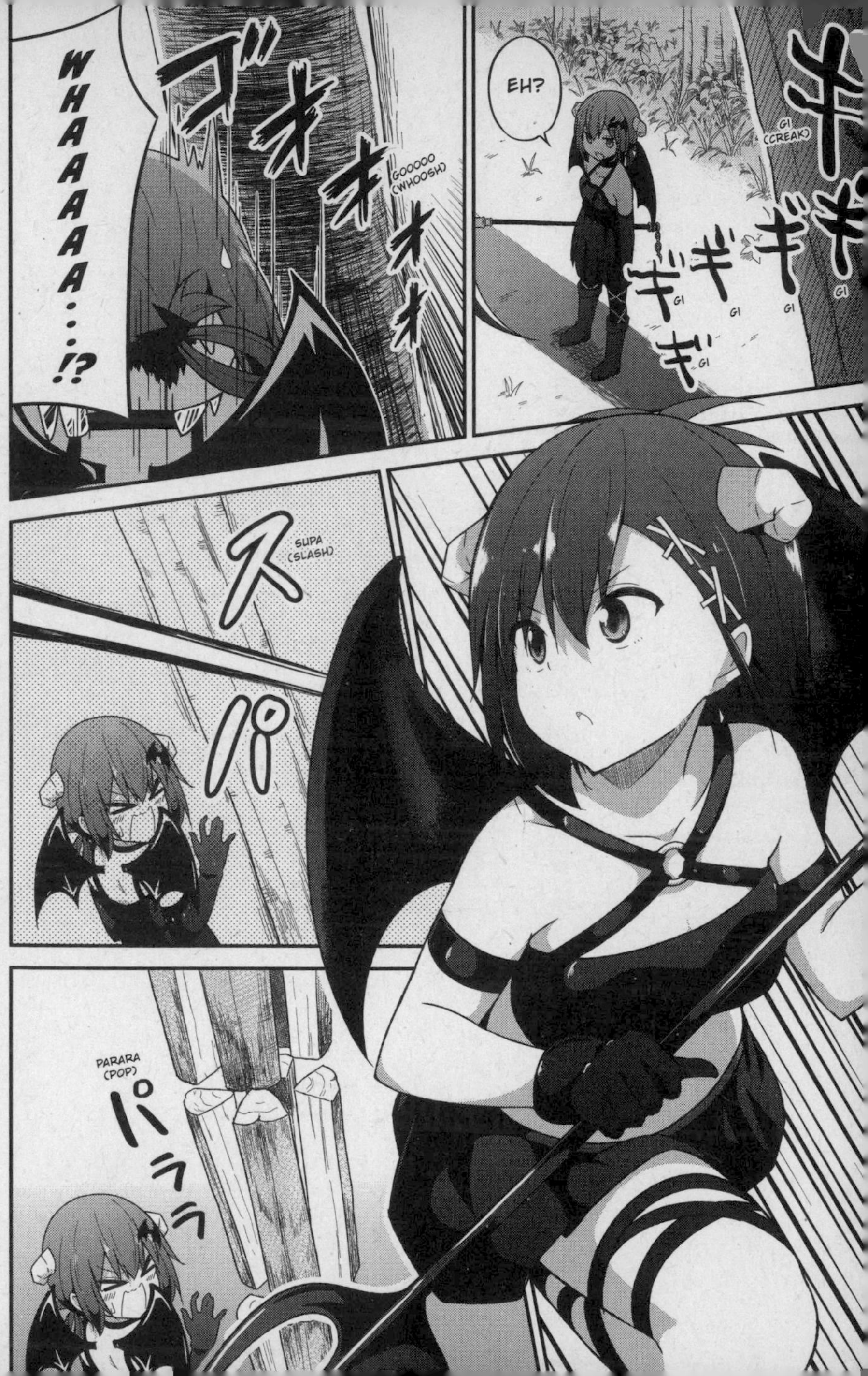
EH?
GI (CREAK)
GI
GI
GI
GI
GI
GOOOOO (WHOOSH)
WHAAAAAA...!?
SUPA (SLASH)
PARARA (POP)

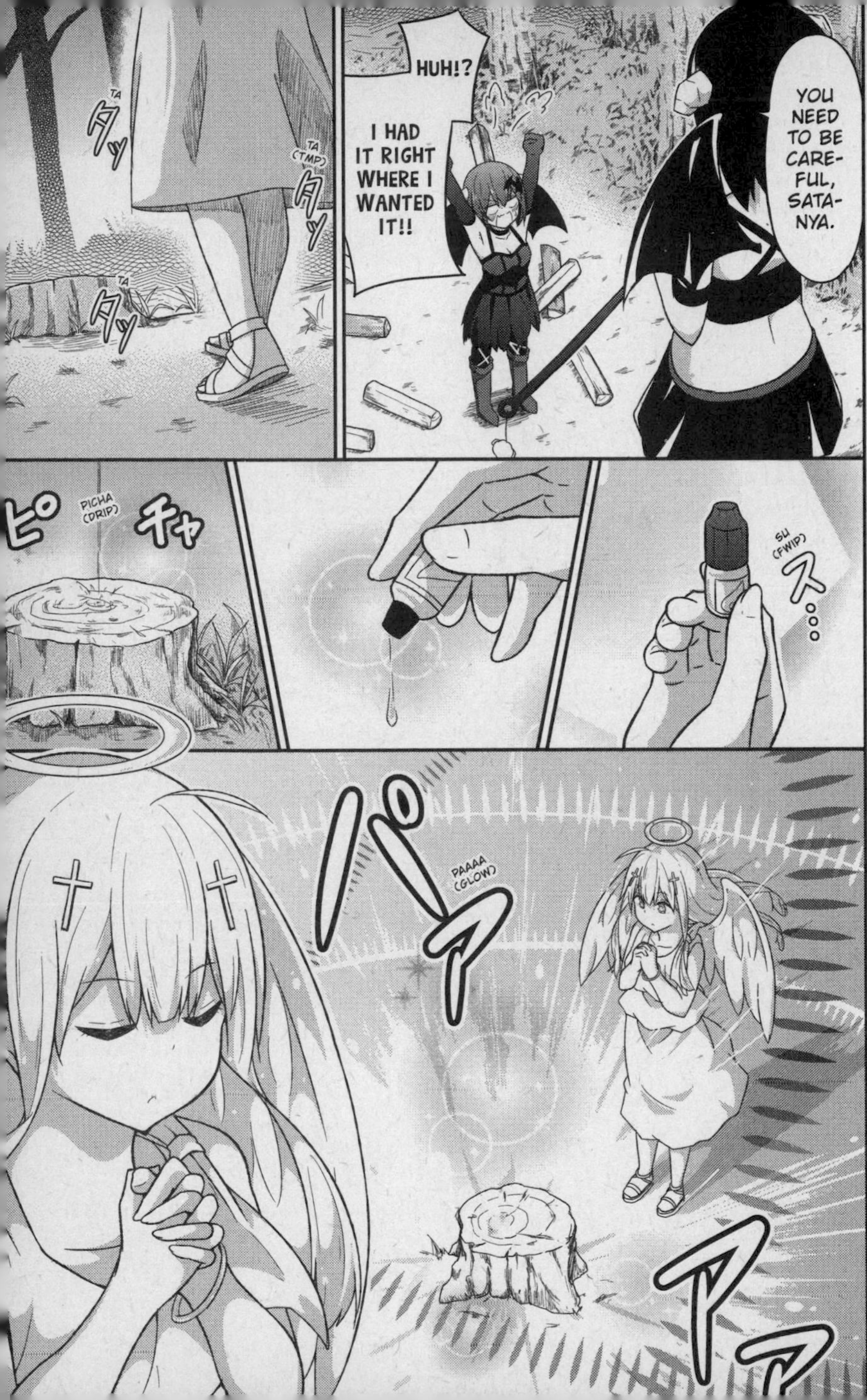
YOU NEED TO BE CAREFUL, SATANYA.
HUH!?
I HAD IT RIGHT WHERE I WANTED IT!!
TA
タッ
TA (TMP)
タッ
TA
タッ
SU (FWIP)
ス…
PICHA (DRIP)
ピチャ
PAAAA (GLOW)
パァァ

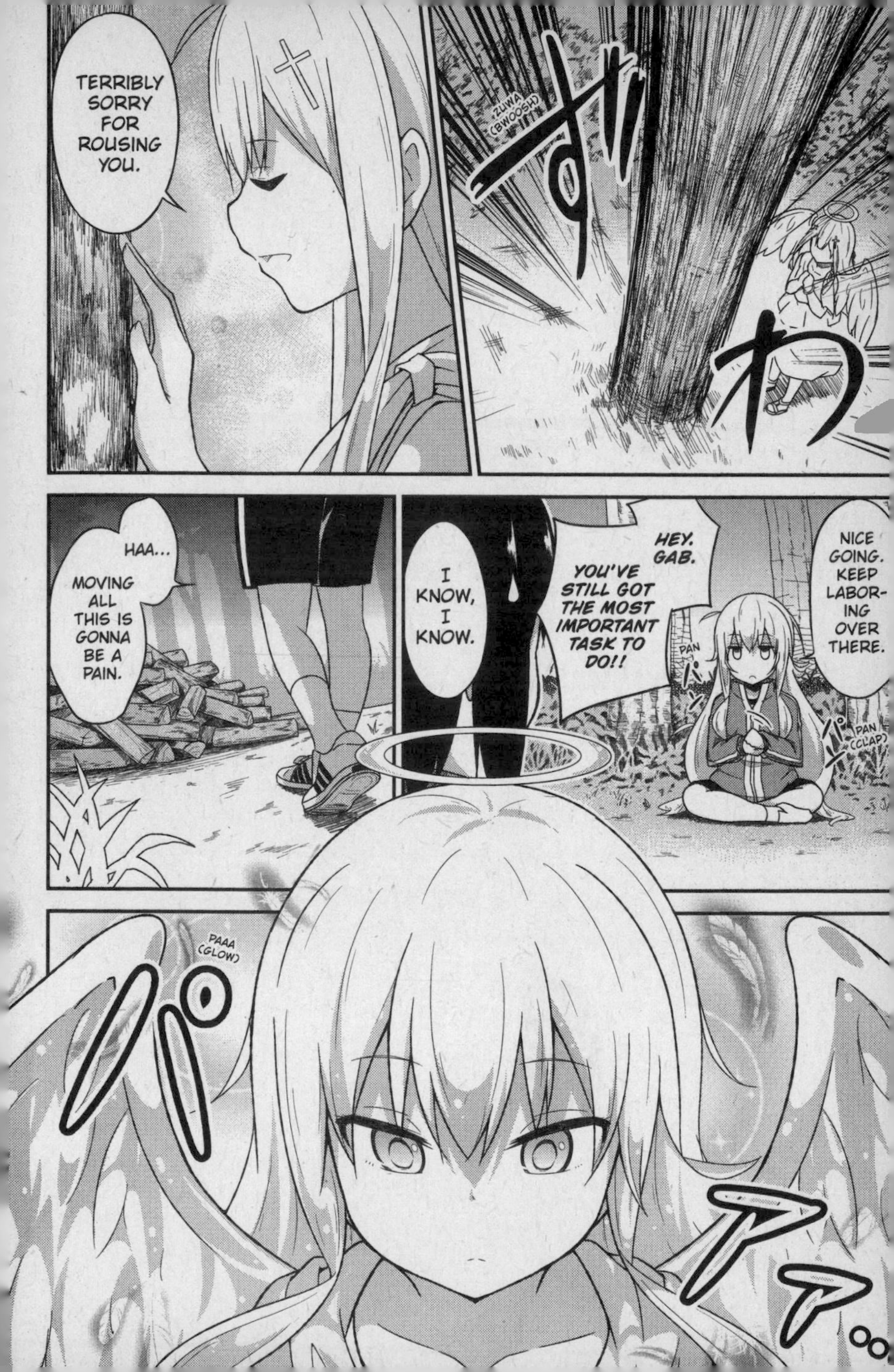
ZUWA (BWOOSH)
TERRIBLY SORRY FOR ROUSING YOU.
NICE GOING. KEEP LABOR-ING OVER THERE.
PAN (CLAP)
PAN
HEY. GAB.
YOU'VE STILL GOT THE MOST IMPORTANT TASK TO DO!!
I KNOW, I KNOW.
HAA...
MOVING ALL THIS IS GONNA BE A PAIN.
PAAA (GLOW)

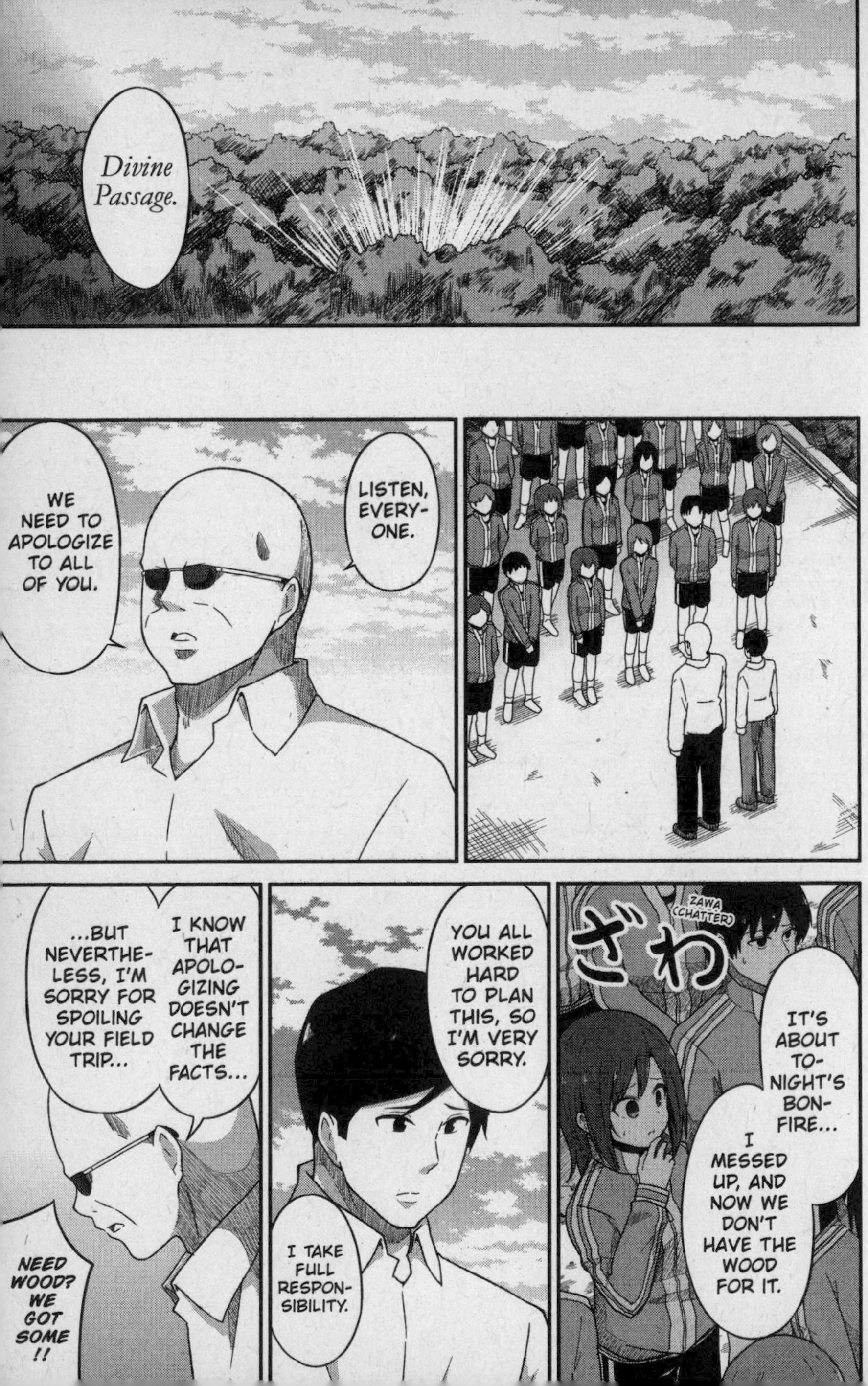
Divine Passage.
LISTEN, EVERY-ONE.
WE NEED TO APOLOGIZE TO ALL OF YOU.
ZAWA (CHATTER)
ざわ
IT'S ABOUT TO-NIGHT'S BON-FIRE...
I MESSED UP, AND NOW WE DON'T HAVE THE WOOD FOR IT.
YOU ALL WORKED HARD TO PLAN THIS, SO I'M VERY SORRY.
I TAKE FULL RESPON-SIBILITY.
I KNOW THAT APOLO-GIZING DOESN'T CHANGE THE FACTS...
...BUT NEVERTHE-LESS, I'M SORRY FOR SPOILING YOUR FIELD TRIP...
NEED WOOD? WE GOT SOME !!

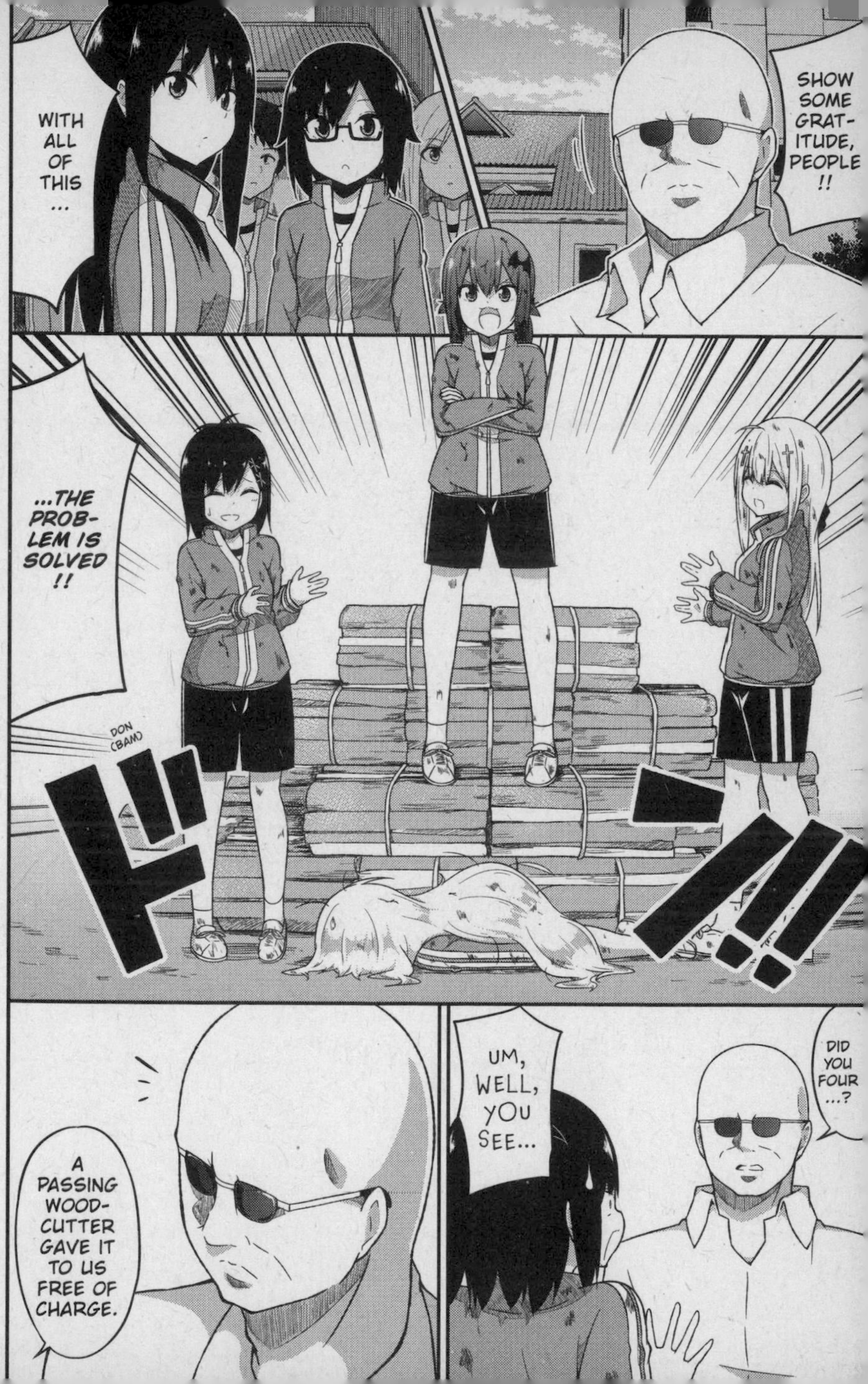
SHOW SOME GRAT-ITUDE, PEOPLE!!
WITH ALL OF THIS...
...THE PROB-LEM IS SOLVED!!
DON (BAM)
DID YOU FOUR...?
UM, WELL, YOU SEE...
A PASSING WOOD-CUTTER GAVE IT TO US FREE OF CHARGE.

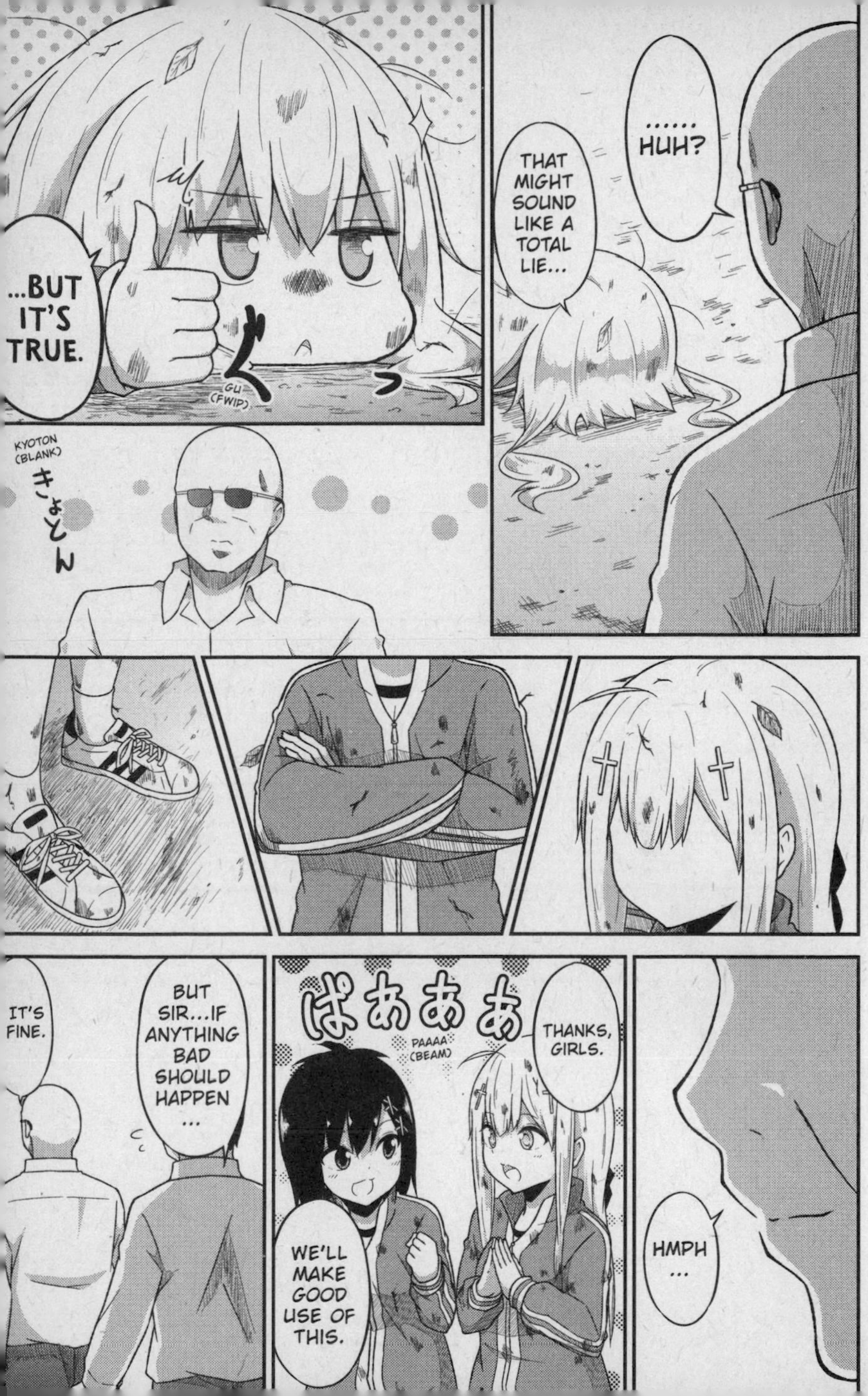
……
HUH?
THAT MIGHT SOUND LIKE A TOTAL LIE…
…BUT IT'S TRUE.
ぐっ
GU (FWIP)
きょとん
KYOTON (BLANK)
HMPH …
THANKS, GIRLS.
ぱあああ
PAAAA (BEAM)
WE'LL MAKE GOOD USE OF THIS.
BUT SIR…IF ANYTHING BAD SHOULD HAPPEN …
IT'S FINE.

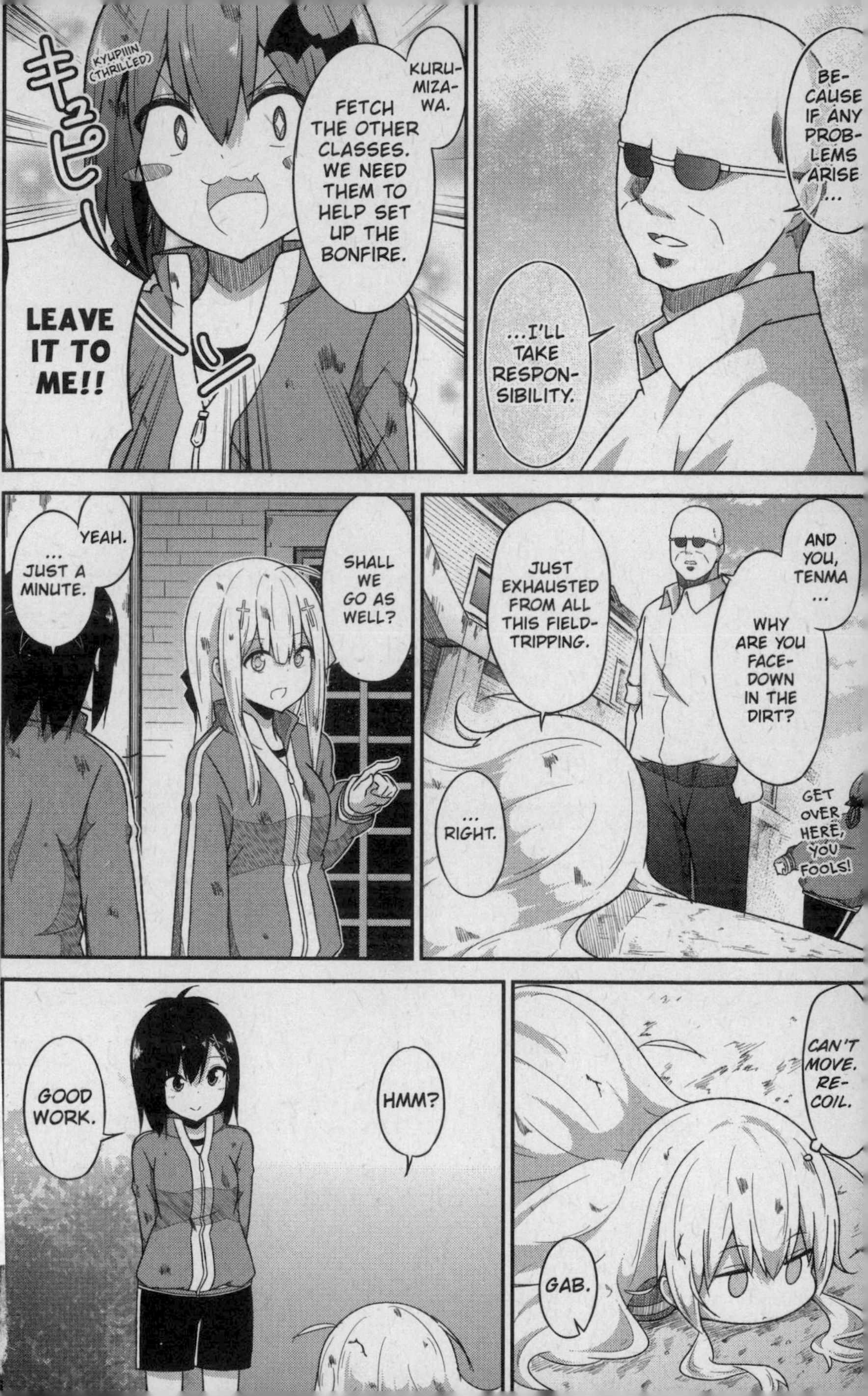
BECAUSE IF ANY PROBLEMS ARISE...
...I'LL TAKE RESPONSIBILITY.
KURUMIZAWA.
FETCH THE OTHER CLASSES. WE NEED THEM TO HELP SET UP THE BONFIRE.
KYUPIIIN (THRILLED)
LEAVE IT TO ME!!
AND YOU, TENMA...
WHY ARE YOU FACE-DOWN IN THE DIRT?
GET OVER HERE, YOU FOOLS!
JUST EXHAUSTED FROM ALL THIS FIELD-TRIPPING.
...RIGHT.
SHALL WE GO AS WELL?
YEAH.
...JUST A MINUTE.
CAN'T MOVE. RECOIL.
GAB.
HMM?
GOOD WORK.

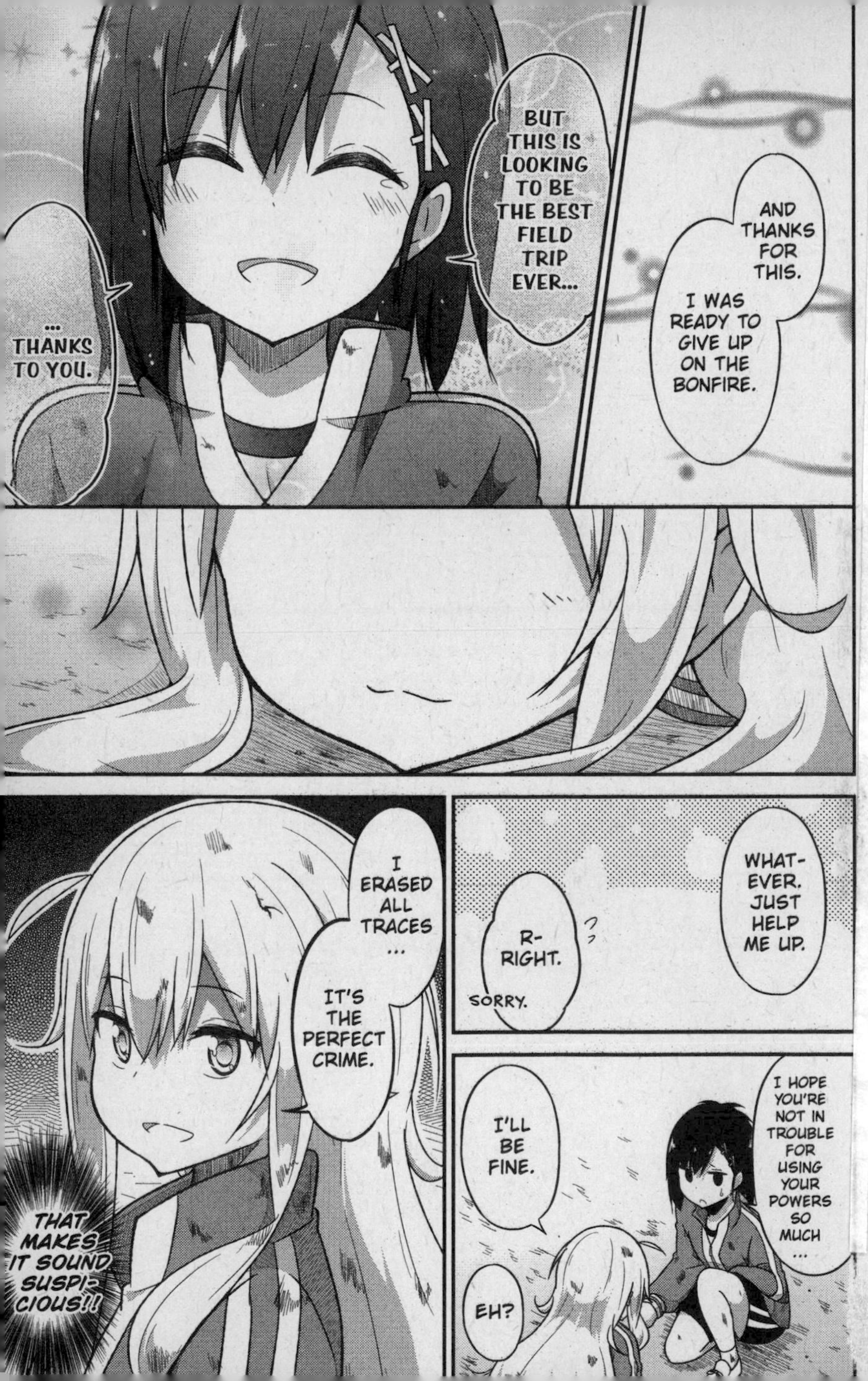
AND THANKS FOR THIS.
I WAS READY TO GIVE UP ON THE BONFIRE.
BUT THIS IS LOOKING TO BE THE BEST FIELD TRIP EVER...
...THANKS TO YOU.
WHAT-EVER. JUST HELP ME UP.
R-RIGHT.
SORRY.
I HOPE YOU'RE NOT IN TROUBLE FOR USING YOUR POWERS SO MUCH...
I'LL BE FINE.
EH?
I ERASED ALL TRACES...
IT'S THE PERFECT CRIME.
THAT MAKES IT SOUND SUSPI-CIOUS!!

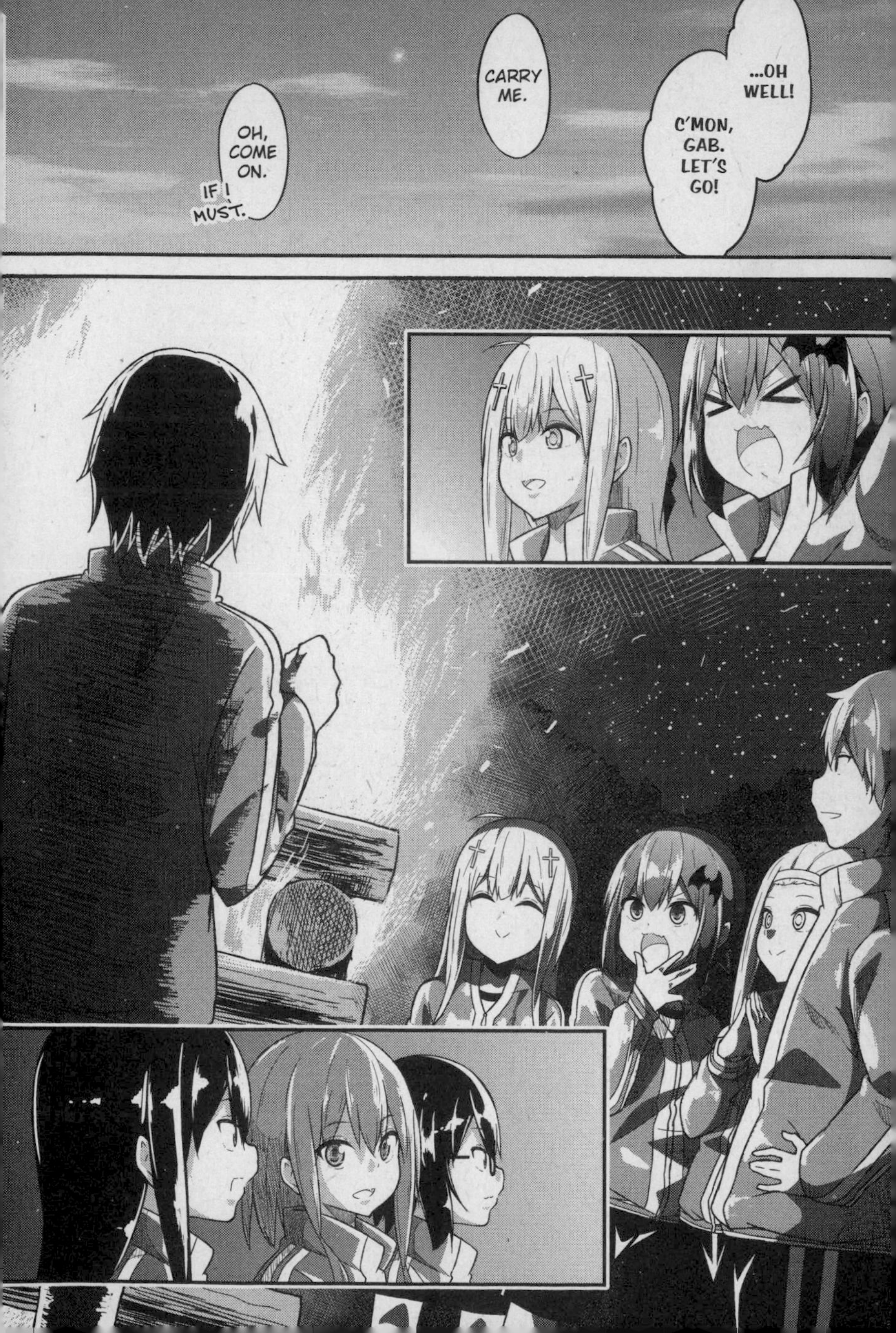
...OH WELL!
C'MON, GAB. LET'S GO!
CARRY ME.
OH, COME ON.
IF I MUST.

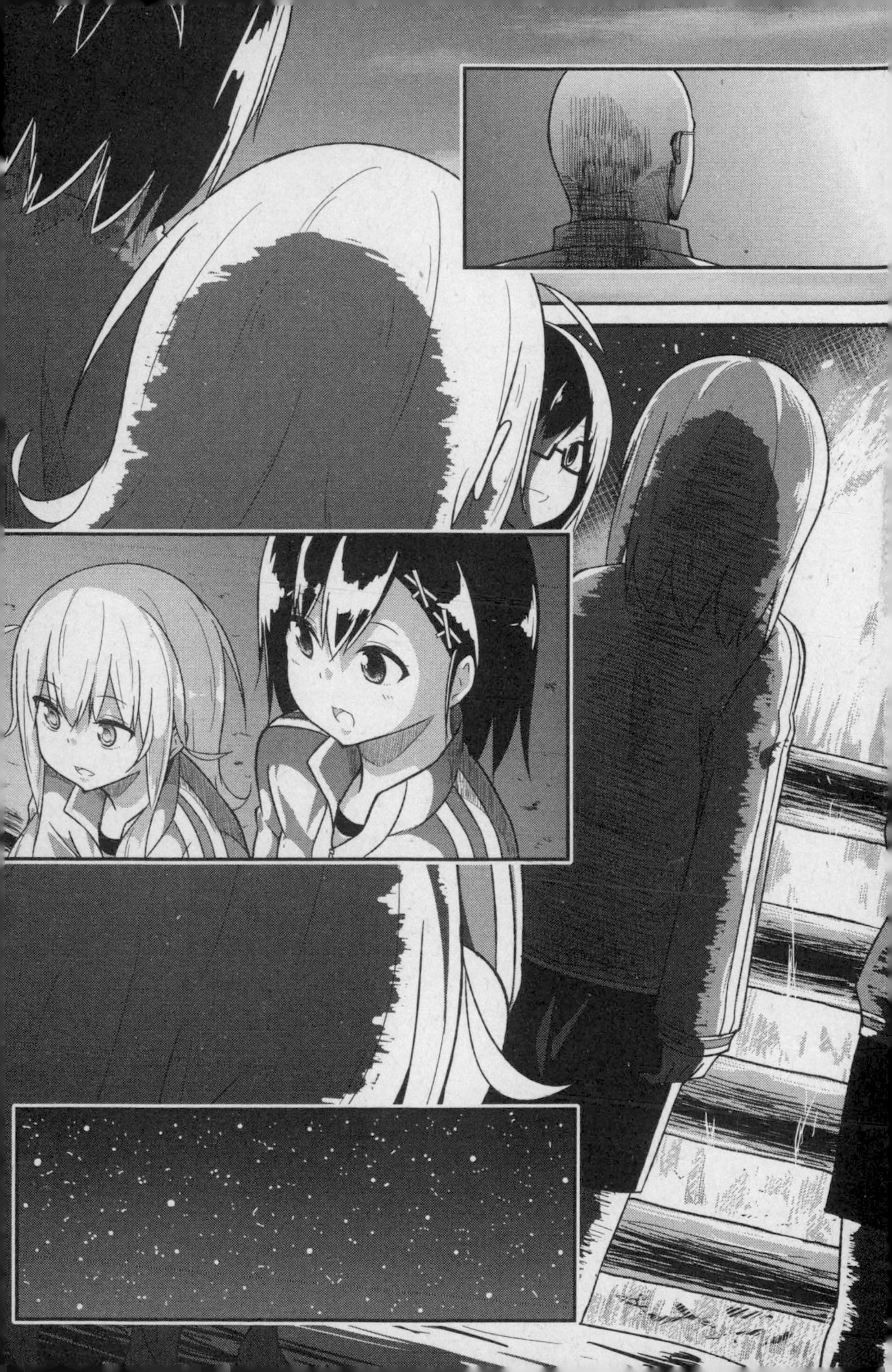

THE NEXT FEW PAGES TAKE PLACE AFTER THE BONFIRE, Y'HEAR?

DEROOON
(LOOM)
でろ～ん

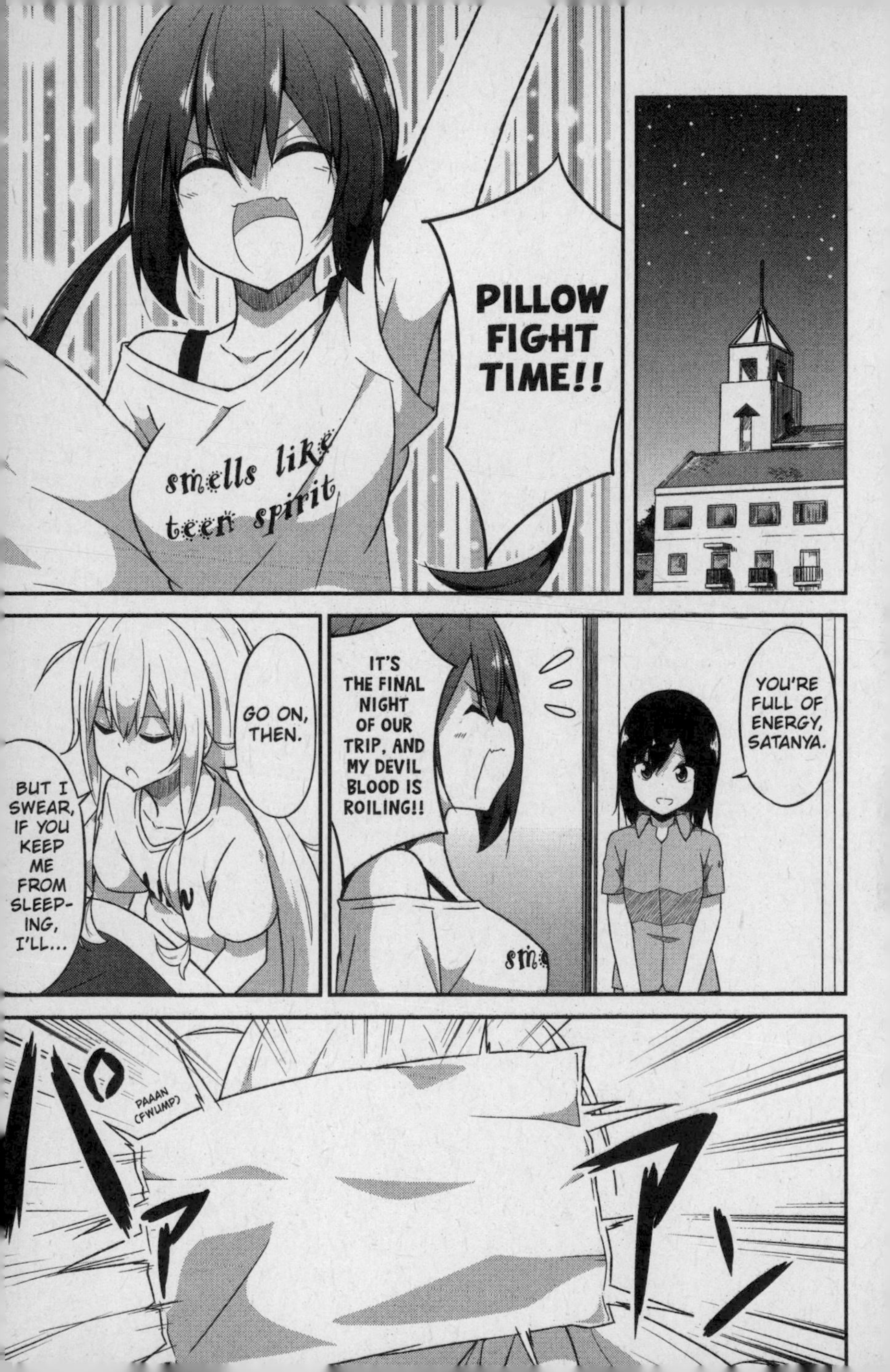
PILLOW FIGHT TIME!!
smells like teen spirit
YOU'RE FULL OF ENERGY, SATANYA.
IT'S THE FINAL NIGHT OF OUR TRIP, AND MY DEVIL BLOOD IS ROILING!!
GO ON, THEN.
BUT I SWEAR, IF YOU KEEP ME FROM SLEEP-ING, I'LL...
PAAAN (FWUMP)

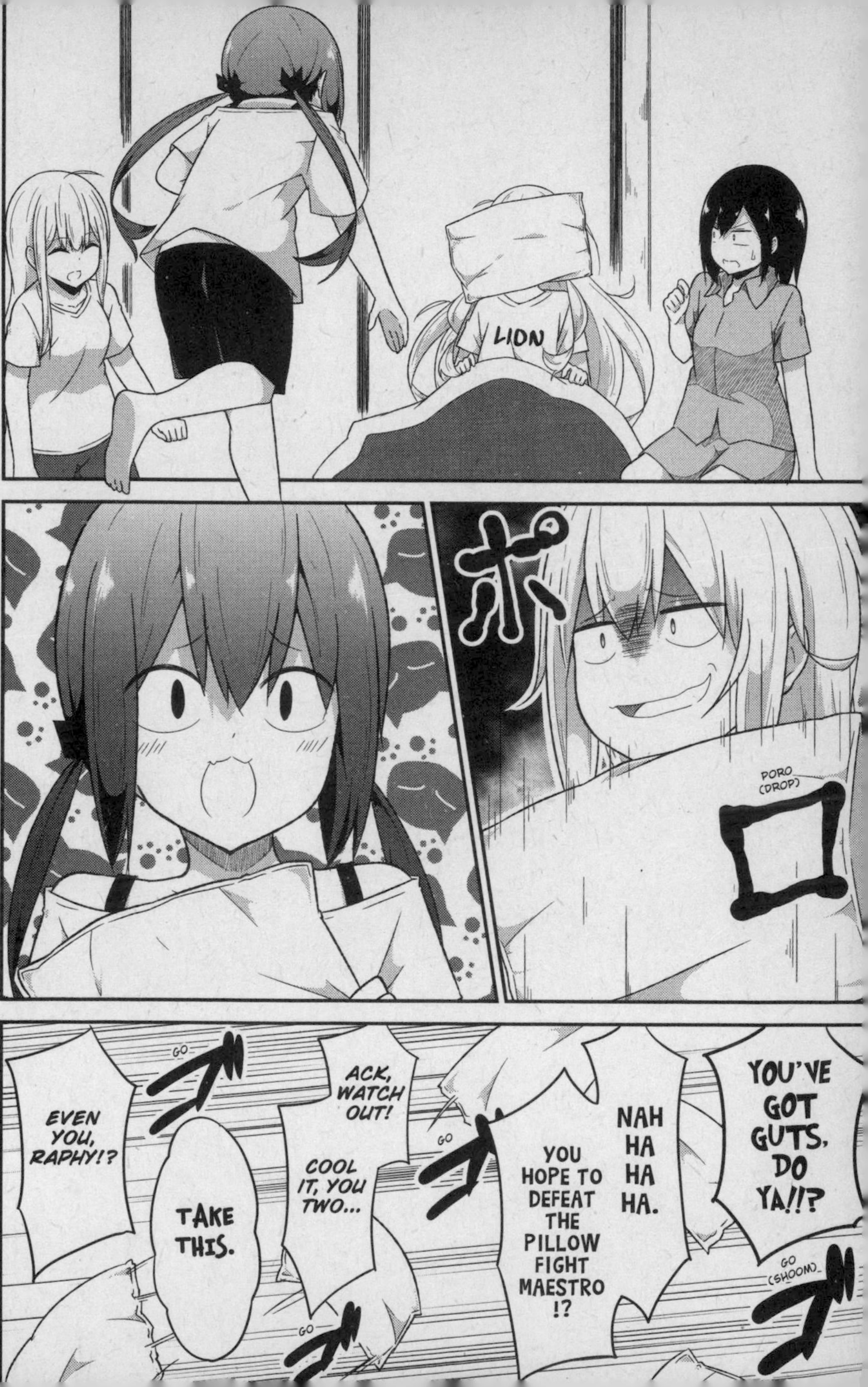
LION
ポ
PORO (DROP)
GO (SHOOM)
YOU'VE GOT GUTS, DO YA!!?
NAH HA HA HA.
YOU HOPE TO DEFEAT THE PILLOW FIGHT MAESTRO!?
GO
ACK, WATCH OUT!
COOL IT, YOU TWO...
GO
TAKE THIS.
GO
EVEN YOU, RAPHY!?

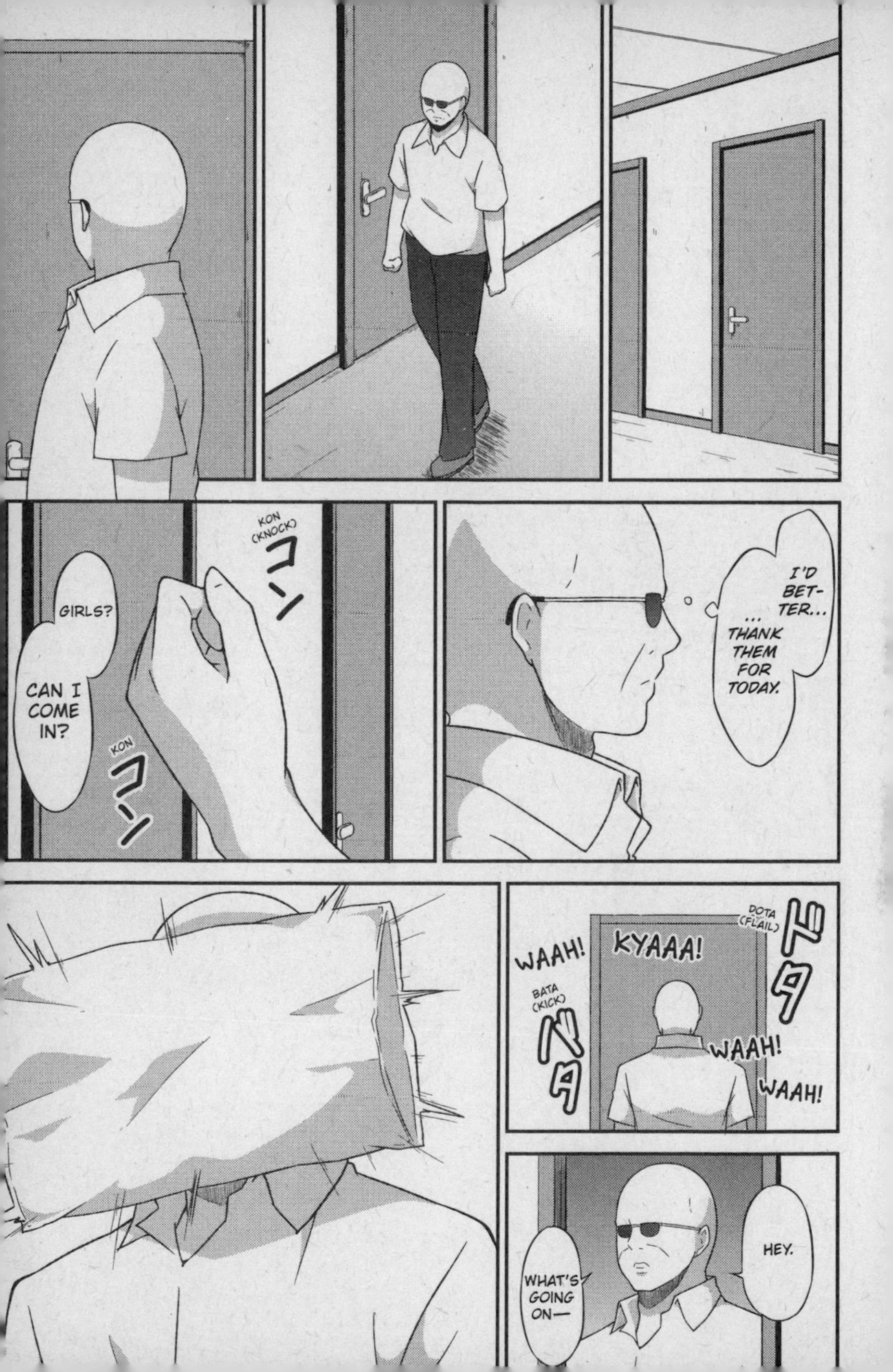
I'D BETTER...
...THANK THEM FOR TODAY.
KON (KNOCK)
コン
GIRLS?
CAN I COME IN?
KON
コン
DOTA (FLAIL)
ドタ
KYAAA!
WAAH!
BATA (KICK)
バタ
WAAH!
WAAH!
HEY.
WHAT'S GOING ON—

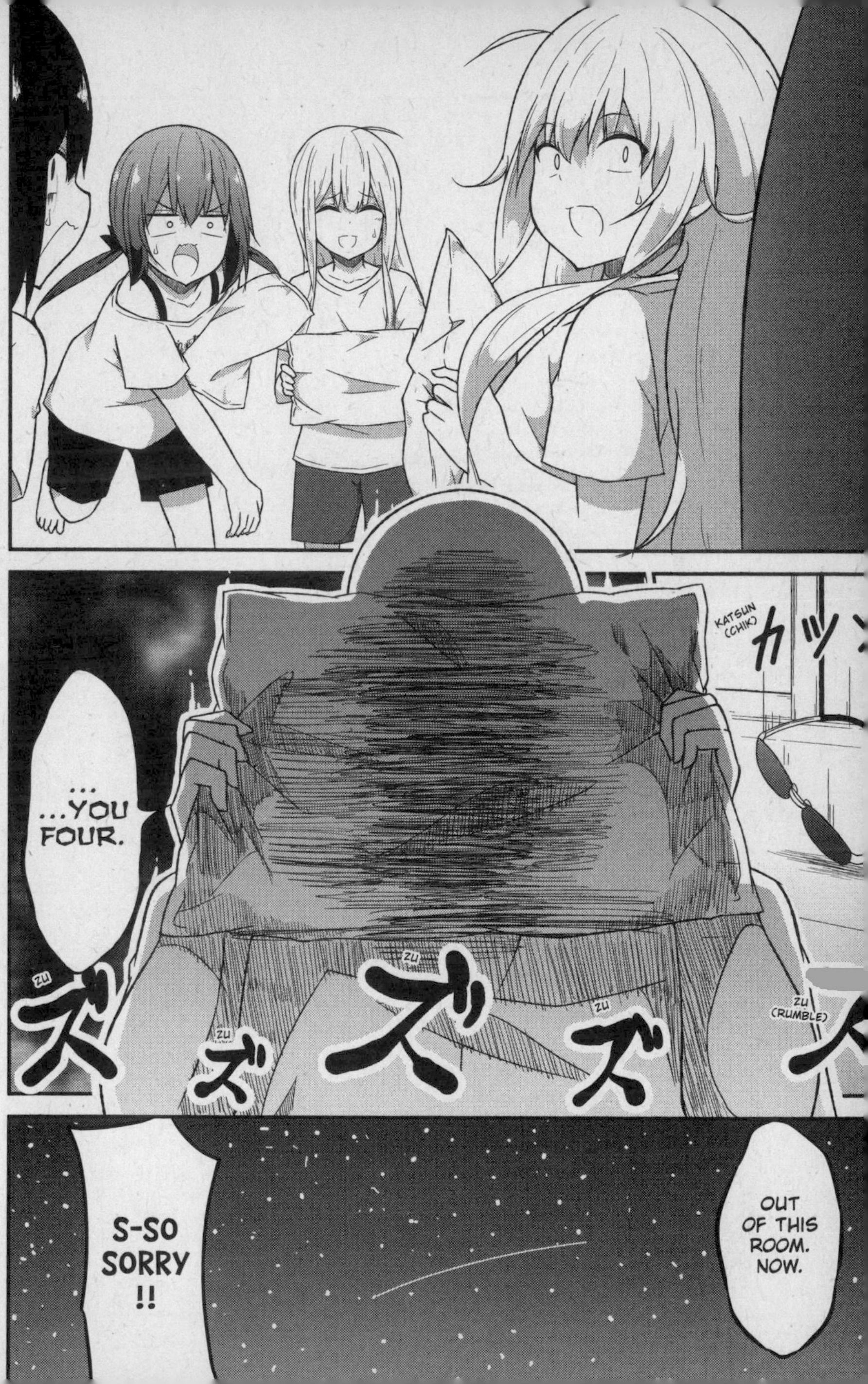
KATSUN (CHIK)
カッ
...
...YOU FOUR.
ZU (RUMBLE)
ZU
ZU
ZU
ZU
OUT OF THIS ROOM. NOW.
S-SO SORRY !!

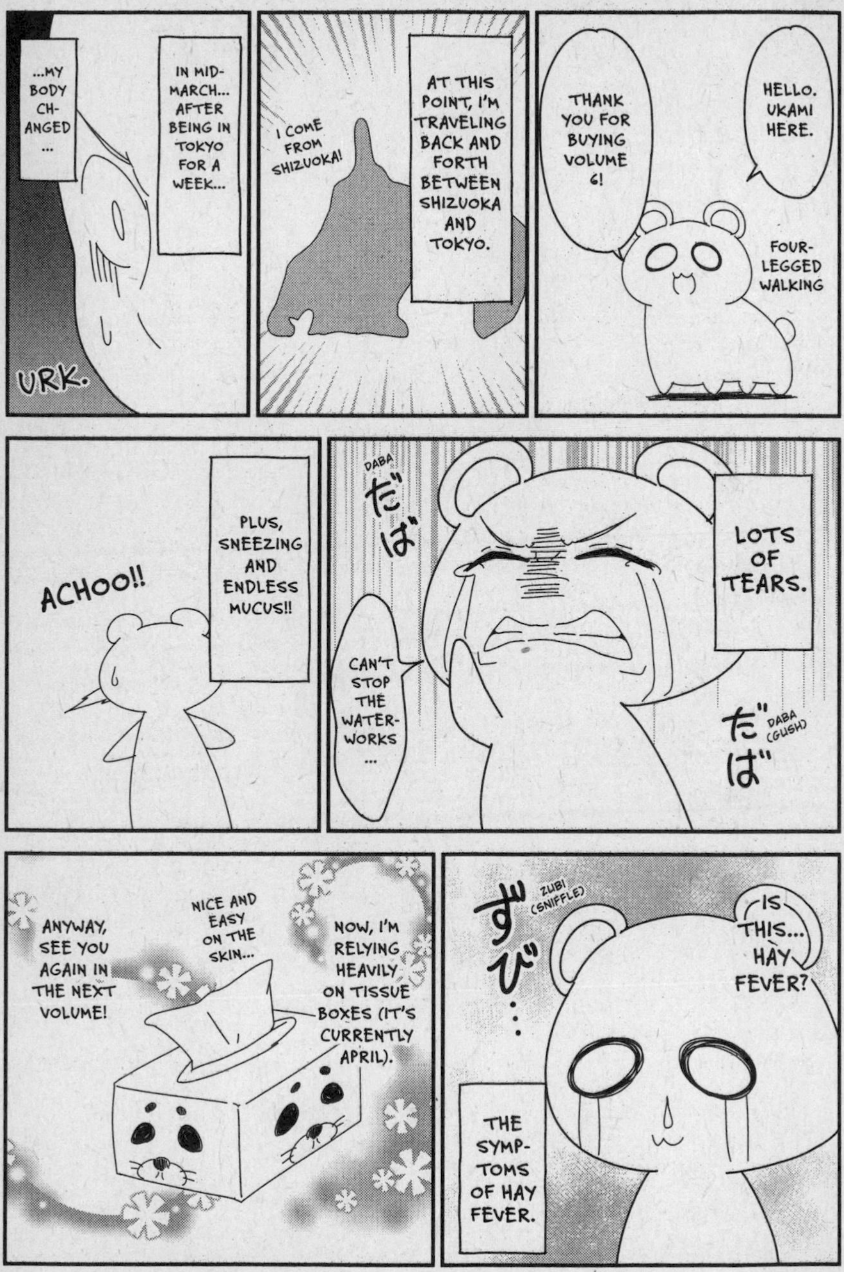
HELLO. UKAMI HERE.
THANK YOU FOR BUYING VOLUME 6!
FOUR-LEGGED WALKING
AT THIS POINT, I'M TRAVELING BACK AND FORTH BETWEEN SHIZUOKA AND TOKYO.
I COME FROM SHIZUOKA!
IN MID-MARCH... AFTER BEING IN TOKYO FOR A WEEK...
...MY BODY CH-ANGED...
URK.
LOTS OF TEARS.
DABA
だば
CAN'T STOP THE WATER-WORKS...
だば
DABA (GUSH)
PLUS, SNEEZING AND ENDLESS MUCUS!!
ACHOO!!
IS THIS... HAY FEVER?
ずび...
ZUBI (SNIFFLE)
THE SYMP-TOMS OF HAY FEVER.
NOW, I'M RELYING HEAVILY ON TISSUE BOXES (IT'S CURRENTLY APRIL).
NICE AND EASY ON THE SKIN...
ANYWAY, SEE YOU AGAIN IN THE NEXT VOLUME!

UKAMI

Translation: Caleb D. Cook ✎ **Lettering: Rochelle Gancio**

This book is a work of fiction. Names, characters, places, and incidents are the product of the author's imagination or are used fictitiously. Any resemblance to actual events, locales, or persons, living or dead, is coincidental.

Gabriel Dropout Vol. 6
©UKAMI 2018
First published in Japan in 2018 by KADOKAWA CORPORATION, Tokyo.
English translation rights arranged with KADOKAWA CORPORATION, Tokyo through TUTTLE-MORI AGENCY, INC., Tokyo.

English translation © 2019 by Yen Press, LLC

Yen Press
1290 Avenue of the Americas
New York, NY 10104

Visit us!
✎ yenpress.com
✎ facebook.com/yenpress
✎ twitter.com/yenpress
✎ yenpress.tumblr.com
✎ instagram.com/yenpress

First Yen Press Edition: February 2019

Yen Press is an imprint of Yen Press, LLC.
The Yen Press name and logo are trademarks of Yen Press, LLC.

The publisher is not responsible for websites (or their content) that are not owned by the publisher.

Library of Congress Control Number: 2017945425

ISBNs: 978-1-9753-8259-9 (paperback)
       978-1-9753-0348-8 (ebook)

10 9 8 7 6 5 4 3 2 1

WOR

Printed in the United States of America